D0629846

Schools for Ontario

Schools for Ontario

Policy-making, administration,
and finance in the 1960s

DAVID M. CAMERON

University of Toronto Press

© University of Toronto Press 1972
Toronto and Buffalo
Printed in Canada
ISBN 0-8020-5259-2
Microfiche ISBN 0-8020-0075-4
LC 70-163805

To Margaret

Contents

List of tables

List of figures

Preface

The governing and financing of public education is everywhere a complex undertaking. With its extensive and varied geography, its large and diverse population, and a history that is both lengthy and pervasive, Ontario exhibits this complexity to a degree surpassed by few political jurisdictions in North America. A book which seeks to describe and analyse even a segment of this activity must tread a narrow and often tortuous path from which it is easy either to slip and become bogged down in the very complexity of the subject matter or to be diverted into an oversimplification which avoids the complexities by avoiding the real issues involved.

Few individuals are capable of treading that path unaided, and this author is certainly not among their company. In fact, others have contributed so much to the completion of this book that single authorship borders on injustice. To those who have shared so much of their knowledge and experience I can only offer this inadequate expression of gratitude and the assurance that while they can justly claim a share of any credit the book may warrant, they have had no part in any of its shortcomings or errors.

The people who provided information and advice in sometimes lengthy interviews during the course of the research for this book were far too numerous to permit their individual mention here. But while most of them must remain anonymous, their contributions were certainly appreciated and have often proved invaluable.

Of the many officials of the Ontario Department of Education who assisted the author, special appreciation is extended to P.H. Cunningham, now retired but formerly director of financial administration, and F.S. Wilson, supervisor of the grants division. General appreciation is extended to the other members of the Legislative Grants Committee of the department.

Within the Ontario Institute for Studies in Education, where most of this study was conducted, four people are deserving of special thanks. R.W.B. Jackson, director of the institute, assisted in gaining access to essential financial data and acted as adviser during the doctoral thesis stage of preparation. E.B. Rideout not only shared his vast and intimate knowledge of school grants but patiently guided the author through an apprenticeship in this esoteric domain. W.G. Fleming offered many constructive comments on the manuscript and willingly shared his own much more comprehensive study of education in Ontario. And a very special debt of gratitude is owed Mrs Jean C. Ross for her painstaking and always accurate statistical work and even more for her warmth and integrity which did so much to make my association with OISE a pleasant one.

Appreciation is expressed also to J.E. Hodgetts, president of Victoria University in Toronto, who acted as thesis adviser, to W.J. McCordic, director and secretary-treasurer of the Metropolitan Toronto Board of Education, who offered many helpful comments on the manuscript, and to R.M. Schoeffel, R.I.K. Davidson, and Rosemary Shipton of the University of Toronto Press who good-naturedly guided the manuscript through the difficult transition from thesis to book. Publication has been made possible by grants from the Social Science Research Council of Canada (using funds provided by the Canada Council) and the Publications Fund of the University of Toronto Press.

Finally, the contributions of two people, while altogether different, were together responsible for so much of this study that I could not possibly express my appreciation adequately. J. Stefan Dupré, former thesis supervisor and current colleague, said at the outset of our association that he was more concerned with the development of a sound thesis than with a personal friendship. Others must judge the extent to which he achieved his primary objective, but that the personal was never sacrificed in pursuit of the academic is to me the true measure of his stature as a scholar. And to my wife, Margaret, while the gesture is hardly commensurate with the quality of her involvement in the enterprise, I offer the dedication of this book.

Halifax, NS
May 1970

Schools for Ontario

1
Introduction

The individual – be he politician, administrator or citizen – who confronts provincial-local relations today confronts an institutional pattern of fractionalized subordination which the political process has distinctly complicated by intensifying decentralization and weakening subordination. To coin terminology no less horrendous than it is apt, the nature of provincial-local relations can be defined as a pattern of hyper-fractionalized quasi-subordination.[1]

The above statement outlines the conceptual framework within which J.S. Dupré developed a comprenhensive overview of provincial fiscal policy as related to local governments in Ontario.

Focussing attention primarily upon the nature of provincial-local fiscal relations in education, this book constitutes a detailed case study in one of the areas mapped out by Dupré. The author recognizes, as did Dupré, that 'finance is but one facet of provincial-local relations.'[2] The study is therefore placed within a framework which is much broader than just provincial education grants. We are seeking greater insight into the nature of the intergovernmental political system in Ontario by examining the formulation, content, and impact of provincial policy in one functional area of that system.

This investigation draws upon the assets and incurs the liabilities inherent in the case-study approach. We are able to concentrate the available resources of time and space upon a comprehensive analysis of a single aspect of the area of concern rather than spread these resources over a superficial analysis of the whole. By the same token, however, we are restricted in the scope of our conclusions, for there are serious dangers in political generalizations drawn from an examination of only one functional area of the political system.

If the strengths of a case study are maximized and the weaknesses minimized, two highly desirable consequences should result. Insofar as the project is incremental to others in the same general area, and the author cognizant of the need for eventual generalization, a contribution will be made to our slowly developing fund of knowledge about inter-governmental relations. Insofar as it is thorough and accurate in its primary objective, light will be shed upon the intergovernmental decision-making process in the selected subject area. Consequently, both those concerned with intergovernmental relations in general and those concerned with provincial policy in the financing and governing of elementary and secondary education in Ontario should find something of value in this study.

There appears little need for a defence of the subject matter selected for detailed examination. Providing public education is now one of the primary, if not the primary, responsibilities of provincial governments. In Ontario, elementary and secondary education alone consumes nearly one-third of all provincial and local governmental expenditures. The provision of public education lies at the very centre of the governmental, and intergovernmental, process.

To a very large extent the dual purpose of this book dictates the organization of its presentation. We are seeking a clear and straight-forward description and analysis of the formulation, content, and impact of provincial policy upon the provision of public education by local school boards. In so doing, we hope to reveal something of the general pattern of intergovernmental relations.

The body of the book begins, as Part I, with an analysis of the provincial-local context within which the policies of the provincial government were developed. This is done in terms of five problem areas. These by no means exhaust the range of problems in contemporary education, but they do appear to define the major demands and constraints imposed upon the provincial government.

The five specific problem areas consist of: territorial units of govern-ment (their inadequacy and inequality), local fiscal resources (again their inadequacy and inequality), separate schools (the relative deficiency of resources), enrolment (the increasing demand for education and the unequal distribution of this demand), and finally, expenditure (the alloca-tion of an increasing proportion of the province's resources to education and the unequal burdens imposed by this allocation). A specific chapter is devoted to an examination of each of these problem areas. At the same time, however, each problem area is clearly a component of the larger context of challenges to provincial policy. A concluding examination of

this context, therefore, explores the intimate nature of the interrelationships among all of the problems.

The three subsequent parts of the book will deal respectively with the
three categories into which the policies developed in response to these
problems have been placed. Each of the policies or programmes was
developed and implemented during the decade of the 1960s. Taken together they represent a set of policies to some extent complete in themselves but to a greater degree a distinguishable phase in what Robin
Harris so aptly described as the 'quiet evolution' of the educational system
and policy in Ontario.[3] Each of these policies will be examined from three
perspectives: the nature of the process through which it was formulated,
its content, and its impact upon the problems previously presented.

Part II consists of two chapters dealing with that programme of grants
from the province to the school boards, the Ontario Foundation Tax
Plan – both as the plan was introduced in 1964 and as it was changed
between 1964 and 1968. In this analysis we shall encounter a grant plan
which attempted to attain the objective of educational and fiscal equalization but which was severely constrained in doing so by the problems of
local units of government. The plan was developed and changed through
a highly interesting process involving the provincial cabinet, a committee
of the Department of Education, and a group of academic consultants.

Part III comprises an analysis of two policies developed in a federal-
provincial context. The first of these, capital grants for the construction
of vocational schools, provides a unique opportunity to explore a three-
level intergovernmental relationship. The programme was the product of
the federal government's concern over inadequate manpower training and
a growing level of unemployment. Not only did it conflict with the capital
grants provided under the Ontario Foundation Tax Plan, but it produced
a worsening of the problems of enrolment and expenditure. Significantly
as well, implementation of the scheme involved a basic reorganization of
the course of studies in Ontario's secondary schools.

The second policy developed in this context was embodied in the
Ontario Education Capital Aid Corporation, a programme under which
the province used funds generated by the federal pension plan to purchase
local school debentures. This programme resulted in a significant reduction in the rate of interest borne by such debentures. However, since it
was simply superimposed upon the existing capital grant schemes it illustrated something of a lack of overall provincial policy in the financing of
education.

Part IV examines three policies affecting the structure of educational
government in Ontario. The first of these, the consolidation of rural and

small urban public school districts into township school areas in 1965, produced a modest reduction in the problems of local units of government but was more significant for the change in provincial attitude which it represented – a change from fiscal incentives to legislative coercion in the reorganization of school district boundaries.

This consolidation was followed in 1965 and 1966 by an internal reorganization of the Department of Education. While initially prompted by a concern for administrative efficiency, the policy represented a rather basic change in the role of the provincial government in education. That change could not be given full effect, however, without a complementary change in the role of local governments, a change which was constrained by the inadequate and unequal territorial units of local government. These constraints were finally removed by the consolidation of school districts in 1969 into county units in the south and designated larger areas in the north. This provincial response changed the nature of provincial-local relations in education in a number of essential respects, and therefore serves as a logical terminal point for the study.

These policies had direct and indirect effects both upon the problems in response to which they were designed and also upon each other. In knitting together the highlights of the study, Part v pays special attention to this complex but revealing interrelationship between problems, policies, and the intergovernmental political system of Ontario. Attention is focused first upon the overall impact of the interrelated policy responses upon the interrelated problems. This examination indicates the extent to which problems were resolved, ameliorated, or even exaggerated by the combined effect of the provincial and federal-provincial programmes. The focus is then shifted to the years 1969 and 1970, the period immediately following that subjected to intensive review here, with the purpose of exploring the changed nature of provincial policy emerging from within an apparently changed context of provincial-local relations. Finally, the study is concluded with a brief examination of the extent to which this and related studies can support even tentative generalizations about the intergovernmental political system in Ontario.

PART I

The problems

2
Problems of local government

In 1964 one school board in Ontario operated a school with an average daily attendance of 0.93 resident pupils. Another school board operated schools with a combined average daily attendance of 86,266.97 resident pupils.[1]

Two interrelated problems flowed from this situation, stated in its most extreme form in the above example. First, the Ontario school system contained a great many local jurisdictions which were simply too small to provide, at a reasonable or even tolerable cost, the educational services required or desired by the provincial government. Second, the provincial government has for some time expressed a determination to equalize the educational opportunities of children in different local jurisdictions, but the disparities in size made this difficult if not impossible. The territorial extent of local units of government generated problems for provincial policy, then, because certain provincial policies called upon these units to do things which because of their size many of them simply could not do.

From a provincial perspective, the resolution of these twin problems was ostensibly simple: rationalize the boundaries of school units. The problems have not been so amenable to resolution, however, because there is a perspective other than the provincial. School boards serve local as well as provincial interests. And the local interests are constituents of the provincial policy makers. The problem for provincial policy has been one of finding ways to manipulate local units – ways that would maintain the electoral support of the government – so that these units could carry out previously established provincial educational policies. The units of local government have not been problems in themselves; they have been problems because their nature was a barrier to the realization of other provincial policies.

In large measure the entrenched position of the small unit of local government was a function of its historical development. A brief recounting of the major events and periods in that background is therefore a necessary condition of a proper understanding of the recent significance of the problems.

HISTORICAL BACKGROUND

Institutions for the provision of formal elementary and secondary education in the area of the Quebec colony that is now Ontario originated as a result not of government action but of the unco-ordinated activities of local entrepreneurs, missionary-oriented clergymen, and, especially, concerned parents. When the government of the new Province of Upper Canada* did enter the field of education, in 1807,[2] it provided only a system of exclusive grammar schools, which adopted the name 'Public' from their English models.

Public elementary schools
The historical development of units of local government for public elementary schools may be conveniently divided into three periods, 1807–43, 1843–1930, 1930–64, each of which illustrates a unique phase in intergovernmental relations.

Almost immediately upon passage of the Grammar School Act of 1807 pressure was exerted upon the provincial legislature, primarily in the form of petitions, to establish a system of schools which would be of some benefit to the large numbers of yeoman and artisans who had come, and were still coming, to Upper Canada in the wake of the American Revolution. In 1816 the legislature finally succumbed to this pressure and passed the famous Common Schools Act.[3] This Act provided legislative sanction to the informal schools established by groups of parents by incorporating three-member Common School Boards of Trustees in 'any Town, Town-

---

* / By the Constitutional Act of 1791 the colony of Quebec was divided into two provinces, Upper and Lower Canada. Upper Canada, though much smaller in area, was the predecessor of the present province of Ontario, established by Confederation in 1867. The government of the colonial province consisted of a lieutenant-governor, an appointed upper house (the Legislative Council), and an elected lower house (the Legislative Assembly). The lieutenant-governor appointed an Executive Council, responsible to himself, to advise him and to carry out the administrative duties of government. Members of both the Legislative and Executive councils tended to belong to a small circle of wealthy families, thus generating the epithet 'family compact.' In the 1830s the movement to shift the Executive Council's responsibility from the governor to the Assembly aroused bitter debate and eventually, armed rebellion.

ship, Village, or place.'* These boards were elected by the local householders and freeholders and were responsible for virtually the whole range
of educational policy in the schools, although certain of their decisions
were subject to review by a board of education appointed for each district
by the lieutenant-governor. Beyond this, provincial concern extended only
to the provision of grants in proportion to attendance, with a minimum
attendance of twenty pupils required to qualify for a grant. The maximum
grant for any one school was £25, and the total of all grants was not to
exceed £6000. (In just four years the total grant was reduced to only
£2500, resulting in the closing of over half the existing common
schools.[4])

In this first legislation, two fundamental principles of this phase of the
development of the Ontario school system were established. First, the
primary responsibility of the school board was owed to the local community, not to the provincial government. Second, the territorial extent of
the units of local educational government was to be the attendance area of
a single school.

The concept of a school district containing only a one-room school has
been the subject of much concern throughout the history of Ontario education, and was contested even at the time of the legislation. Vigorous efforts
were made in the 1830s to have the township replace the local school
district as the basic unit of government.† These efforts were unsuccessful,
primarily because the dominant interests at both the provincial and local
levels did not want the province to assume a more positive role in common
school education. It was the public, or grammar, schools, designed to educate the children of the privileged, which were of prime concern to the
provincial government. Common schools were not actively discouraged,
but responsibility for their government had been delegated to local groups,

* / Local government, as known in Ontario today, was not organized until 1849.
From 1792 until 1841 the Courts of Quarter Sessions in each district handled
matters of only local concern. In 1824 the 'town' of Kingston was separated from
the District of Midland for certain purposes. In 1832 the first local self-government
was provided in legislation permitting the ratepayers of Brockville to elect a local
'Police Board.' Within five years such boards were established in Hamilton,
Cornwall, Port Hope, Prescott, Belleville, Cobourg, and Picton. Toronto became
the first incorporated municipality, with an elected council and mayor, in 1834.
Kingston followed suit in 1838. In 1841 the districts were incorporated, being
governed by an elected council and appointed warden. Finally, in 1849, the basis of
the present organization was established, with elected councils and mayors, reeves,
or wardens for cities, towns, villages, townships, and counties. See K.G. Crawford,
Canadian Municipal Government, Toronto, University of Toronto Press, 1954,
chap. 2, and R.K. Ross, *Local Government in Ontario*, Toronto, Canada Law
Book Company, 1962
† / At this time townships were not political, but merely geographic entities,
laid out to facilitate orderly settlement.

and these groups were not particularly anxious to relinquish that responsibility.

When the political system of Upper Canada was shaken by the rebellion of 1837, and the balance of power upset by the union of Upper and Lower Canada in 1840, the dominant view of common school government was not immediately given up, however. The new Parliament of the united Province of Canada set about to integrate the common school systems of the two former provinces and to mold each into a true *system* of schools. To this end it passed the General Common Schools Act of 1841.[5] This Act, which incidentally introduced the principle of separate schools, established the township as the basic unit of local school government in Upper Canada or Canada West (to correspond to the parish in Lower Canada). The Act was never effective and in 1843 was replaced by legislation[6] applying only to Upper Canada and reintroducing a system of local school districts.*

In part the 1841 Act failed because it attempted to integrate two dissimilar educational systems too quickly. But the Act also failed because it upset the local political systems which had been developing in Upper Canada during the previous half-century. In 1841 educational decisions such as the character of the teacher and the biases of textbooks were still primarily matters of values. The school board of the small district was an effective agency for the translation of the dominant values of a small community into political decisions, thence into educational policy, and the subsequent inculcation of these values into the socialization process of the children. The Act would have destroyed the identification of the community with the school and its government (in few cases could a township be considered to define a community). Since the provincial government had no intention of operating the common schools itself, there was no alternative, then, but to return to the type of organization which had already become so strongly rooted.

Attitudes towards education change slowly, but around 1843 a change becomes evident. What marks this change is a gradual shift in the locus of power from the local community, where schools were viewed as extensions of parental responsibility, to the provincial capital, where schools were coming to be seen as vehicles of provincial policy.

Although outlasting his tenure as chief superintendent of schools, the second phase in the development of public school government in Ontario (1843–1930) was very much dominated by the person and thinking of Egerton Ryerson. And although Ryerson made far-reaching changes in

* / In 1847 the term school 'district' was changed to school 'section.'

the educational system of Ontario, few of them were in the area of the government of public elementary schools (called common schools until 1871). In fact, the governments of these schools, and the interests which supported them were very effective barriers to many of the changes desired by Ryerson.

This second period is characterized by two interrelated and crucially important trends, growing professionalism and the bureaucratization of the administration and supervision of education. Both followed a shift in the balance of power away from the local school board to the provincial government generally and to the Department of Education particularly.* Neither trend proceeded with any great rapidity. Yet the whole regime of Ryerson consisted in large part in laying the groundwork upon which these twin characteristics of twentieth-century education might be built. If education were to be professionalized and bureaucratized, one condition above all others had to be met in Ontario. The units of school government had to be enlarged.

The first successful venture in this regard was the abolition of school sections in incorporated cities and police towns in 1847.[7] (After 1849 this applied to incorporated cities and towns.) These municipalities became single governmental units for common schools, with the board of trustees appointed by the municipal council. The appointment of trustees proved unsatisfactory† and in 1850 the single board became elective. Consolidation of school districts had long been regarded more favourably in urban centres than in rural areas. The provincial government recognized this fact in 1847 and made no comparable provision for rural consolidation.

Legislation in 1850[8] did permit the newly-created township councils to combine any two or more contiguous school sections into single units, later to be known as township school areas.‡ In apparent deference to local democracy, the province required that any proposed merger be approved at the next annual meeting in all the school sections concerned.

* / The Department of Education did not exist, as such, until Ryerson retired in 1876. In 1822 the first provincial office of education, the General Board of Education, was established to administer the sale of the 'School Reserves' granted by King George III in 1797. This board was abolished in 1832 and its duties transferred to the Council of King's College (the predecessor of University College in the University of Toronto). In 1846 the Advisory Board of Education was created, which was later renamed the Council of Public Instruction. This body, chaired by Ryerson, administered the provincial normal school, prescribed textbooks, and generally advised the government on educational matters. It normally reported to the government through the provincial secretary. In 1876 the executive of this council become the Department of Education.

† / See below, p. 36

‡ / If the enlarged unit contained sections from two or more municipalities, it was known as a 'union school section.'

Only one enlarged school district was ever formed under the authority of this provision.*

In a series of draft bills in 1868–70, Ryerson made a major attempt to upset the balance of power which preserved the small, rural school section. He attempted to transfer the responsibility for forming larger units from township to county councils and to remove any requirement of popular approval. His proposals were abandoned in legislative committee, however, and what emerged in the Act of 1871[9] was only a modest extension of the provisions of 1850. Township councils were authorized to create enlarged districts if supported in two-thirds of the sections concerned. No further consolidations took place under this authority.

The next step was taken in 1896[10] when newly-organized township councils in the territorial districts of northern Ontario were given the choice of dividing the township into school sections or creating a single township school area without formal reference to the local ratepayers. In 1921[11] suburban township councils were permitted to create township school areas without a referendum but after a four-fifths majority vote in council.† Here again the tendency for urban areas to favour the larger unit of government eventuated and a substantial number of such areas were established in the 1920s.

Something of a watershed in the evolution of public school government was reached in 1925–6 with G.H. Ferguson's Township School Board Bill.[12] Ferguson, minister of education, introduced his bill into the legislature in 1925 and immediately forwarded it, along with a covering letter,[13] to all the rural public school boards in the province. The bill would have merged all rural public school sections into township districts. Each township would consist of from one to ten 'areas' (depending on the number of existing sections and township areas) and the consolidated school board would be made up of trustees elected from these areas.

The fate of Ferguson's bill clearly indicates the antagonism in rural Ontario towards larger units. To a majority of parents and trustees, enlargement was inexorably associated with the consolidation of schools and the consequent transportation of pupils to central schools (which was, of course, the major purpose of larger units). Ferguson tried to counter this fear by arguing that the justification of larger units lay in a reduction of costs and that there was no necessary relationship between larger units and the centralization of schools. The bill elicited such a negative response, however, that it was thought unwise to proceed with the question and the bill effectively passed into limbo at the close of the legislative session.

* / Enniskillen Township in the county of Lambton.
† / The four-fifths requirement was dropped a year later.

For some seventy-five years now, Ryerson and his successors had been pressing for an enlargement of local government units of rural public schools. Every attempt had failed because the dominant interests in the local political systems were in opposition. Compulsion had been considered twice and abandoned because these rural interests comprised a powerful force in the provincial political system.

By 1930 the professionalization of public school teaching had been achieved, marking the third phase in the development of Ontario education. Whereas in 1875 only 22 per cent of all teachers had received professional training in a provincially controlled institution, by 1929 this proportion had risen to 95 per cent.[14]

The key factor in accounting for the changes which occurred after 1930, however, is the development of a thoroughly professionalized cadre of provincial inspectors. Prior to 1930 all public school inspectors were appointed by the county councils or, in the case of the large city school systems, by the school boards themselves.[15] They tended to be older teachers, often high school teachers, who served in the position for a few years prior to retirement. As one departmental publication referred to the county inspectors, they were often appointed '... for personal, local, and political reasons.'[16]

Beginning in 1930,[17] all inspectors, except those in the cities, were to be appointed by the Department of Education:

The new species ... represents an elaborately trained product ...
He must be a University graduate ... the holder of a Permanent First Class Certificate with adequate experience as a Public School Teacher ...
In addition he is required to pass a searching and comprehensive Inspector's examination conducted by this Department.[18]

A 'new species,' young, ambitious, usually having taught in an urban school system, and dedicated to bringing modern education to the rural areas – this was a major figure in the adoption of township school areas in rural Ontario.

Two changes in provincial policy also assisted in the development of larger units of government. The first was a 1932 legislative amendment[19] which removed all requirements for local referenda prior to the adoption of township areas, and gave full authority to the township councils. The second was the provision from 1938 of a special stimulation grant of $100 each year for each school section included in a township school area.*

* / The grant also applied to separate school organizations. The $100 was increased several times, finally becoming $500 in 1959.

16

The product of these changes was a relatively sharp transformation in the attitude of township councils and rural school boards. As Chief Inspector V.K. Greer reported in 1938:

A rapid acceleration in organization of these [larger] units took place in 1938. This was due largely to the adoption by the Department of Education of a more vigorous policy towards this problem. As a result, the local inspectors are constantly informing the ratepayers in rural areas regarding the advantages of larger units ...[20]

TABLE 1
Annual formation of township school areas, 1938–57

Year	Net no of TSA s formed	Total no of TSA s	No of school sections included
Before 1938	15	15	84
1938	15	30	154
1939	43	73	366
1940	26	99	513
1941	31	130	665
1942	35	165	862
1943	22	187	1008
1944	61	248	1421
1945	149	397	2340
1946	58	455	2841
1947	29	484	3071
1948	15	499	3224
1949	15	514	3325
1950	22	536	3465
1951	11	547	3488
1952	7	554	3547
1953	0	554	3529
1954	1	555	3527
1955	8	563	3565
1956	6	569	3577
1957	5	574	3607

SOURCE: 1938–50, Minister's Report, 1950; 1951–7,
Minister's Report for individual years

Table 1 summarizes the annual establishment of township school areas from 1938 to 1957 (the last year for which detailed information is available). The peak of activity in the formation of these units was reached in 1945, after which the number of these formations declined swiftly.

By 1957 a total of 3607 rural sections had been merged voluntarily into township school areas. As the annual number of new consolidations declined, provincial educators became more and more convinced that even the township area was too small a unit to provide the kinds of services they desired to have implemented. We shall return to this problem after reviewing the backgrounds of the governmental units for separate and secondary schools.

Separate elementary schools
Separate schools originated in a different context from common schools and were largely excluded from the concern of the provincial bureaucracy. The motivating force in separate school organization has, from the beginning, been the Catholic hierarchy. Nevertheless, separate schools are a part of the provincial school system and their supporters are constituents of provincial politicians.

The interaction of these three factors – bureaucratic detachment, clerical pressure, and political concern – produced two basic principles of provincial policy towards separate school organization. These principles are not wholly free of conflict and have only recently begun to be reconsidered. In the first place, the provisions for separate school organization must always appear to be reasonably similar to those for public schools. And second, separate schools must never be permitted to organize in ways that would enable them to challenge the public schools as a system. A brief perusal of the historical development of separate school governmental organization will indicate more clearly the nature and implications of these two principles.

Separate schools were born out of a unique combination of factors in the first years of the union of Upper and Lower Canada. There had always been strong sentiment in favour of a religious orientation of common schools in Upper Canada, but so long as these schools were products of local, and not provincial, concern, such sentiments were effectively embodied in a pluralistic school system. With the central government preparing to assume a more active role in school organization and regulation, however, great concern was aroused over just what kind of orientation a provincial system of schools might assume. Forty-two petitions were presented to Parliament when it began consideration of the new school act in 1841. Of these, thirty-nine were from Protestants seeking sanction for the full use of the Bible as a classroom text.[21] This, of course, was anathema to Catholics, and Catholics comprised an effective majority of the Assembly. The only possible solution to this basic conflict was, in the words of William Morris, chairman of the parliamentary committee, that 'the children of both religious persuasions must be educated apart.'[22]

The legislation provided, therefore, that any group of residents in a township might establish their own school when they professed a religious faith different from the majority and dissented 'from the regulations, arrangements, or proceedings, of the Common School Commissioners.'[23] When the general act of 1841 was replaced by the Upper Canada Act of 1843, separate school privileges were restricted to two groups: Catholics and Protestants. The establishment of a separate school was made conditional upon the teacher in the common school being a member of the other group, and upon the application of ten or more resident householders or freeholders.*

The principle of allowing separate schools was not much debated in these early years and very few schools were actually established. By 1853, twelve years after the original provisions, there were only twenty-five separate schools in Upper Canada; four coloured, three Protestant, and eighteen Roman Catholic.[24] Protestant and coloured separate schools have never been of much consequence in Ontario; the provisions for coloured schools were revoked in 1964,[25] by which time there were only two Protestant separate schools. The contemporary problems concerning provincial policy have been related to the Roman Catholic separate schools and it is toward these that our attention will henceforth be directed.

Organizationally, separate schools were consistently treated as dissentient schools in the first half-century of their existence: their organization was tied to that of the 'parent,' or common, school system. When the school section replaced the township as the basic geographic unit for common schools in 1843, it did so too for separate schools. One separate school would be permitted to parallel each common school. In 1847, however, school sections were abolished in incorporated cities and towns,[26] and the resultant confusion was not resolved for some sixteen years. In the 1847 legislation Ryerson had tried, in effect, to obviate the need for separate schools as such by authorizing common school boards in cities and towns to designate any of their schools as denominational. This experiment collapsed the following year when the Toronto School Board unanimously rejected applications for denominational schools from both the Church of England and the Roman Catholic church. Legislation in 1850 then left it to the common school board to 'prescribe the limits of the divisions or sections for such [separate] schools.'[27]

---

* / In 1849 separate school privileges were extended to 'coloured' persons and required application from at least twelve heads of families. In 1855 the requirement was changed to majority support (but at least ten) at a meeting called by at least five resident heads of families. The minimum of ten supporters was removed in 1865. Provisions for separate schools in unsurveyed and unincorporated areas were made in 1899 and 1903 by which ten Roman Catholic heads of families (this provision did not apply to Protestants or coloured persons) might call a meeting and the majority present establish a separate school organization.

Again this solution collapsed when the Toronto board refused an application from the Catholic bishop, the Rt Rev. Armand Francis Marie, Comte de Charbonnel, for a third separate school district in that city. The provincial government thereupon amended the 1850 Act and permitted 'a separate school in each ward, or in two or more wards united, in each city or town in Upper Canada.'[28] This compromise was still not acceptable to the Catholic bishops, who kept up a steady pressure on the government throughout the 1850s. The issue was not satisfactorily resolved until passage of the Scott Separate School Act of 1863,[29] which placed common and separate schools on the same basis in urban municipalities; that is, there would be one public and one separate school board for the whole municipality.

A slightly different, but related, problem arose in the rural areas of the province. School sections had been prescribed as units sufficient in size to support a one-room school. Only in the most rapidly growing sections could a second (separate) school be jutsified. The Catholic hierarchy pressed for authorization to draw separate school boundaries in conformity with concentrations of separate school supporters, rather than being tied to common school boundaries. This request was never granted. Rather, the Catholic interests were further antagonized when the Act of 1850[30] granted common school supporters only (through the township councils) the right to merge sections into Township School Areas and Union Sections.

It was not until 1863 that an acceptable compromise was worked out to remove this latter inequity. The Scott Act of that year permitted separate schools in neighbouring sections (and not necessarily in the same municipality) to merge into single organizations, designated as union separate schools. At the same time, however, a further and long-standing restriction was placed upon the territorial extent of individual separate school organizations. The nineteenth section of the Act prescribed that within any public school section, 'no person shall be deemed a supporter of any separate school unless he resides within three miles (in a direct line) of the site of the School House.'*

By the Act of 1863, then, urban municipalities were to have one separate school organization for the whole municipality. Rural municipalities were to have separate school organizations with jurisdiction over areas radiating three miles about the school site, with the possibility of two or more of these merging into one organization. These 'minimum rights'

* / In 1963 this area of three miles about the school site was designated a separate school 'zone.' The designation of a union of zones was changed from a union section to a 'combined separate school zone' (11 & 12 Eliz. II, c. 132, so).

were entrenched in the British North America Act of 1867. With but two exceptions prior to 1968, the provincial government showed itself completely unwilling, or unable, to alter or extend these provisions.

The first exception occurred in legislation of 1899 and 1903. The Act of 1899[31] permitted Catholic schools to be established in territory not yet surveyed into townships if such establishment were approved at a meeting called by ten heads of families. The Act of 1903[32] extended the same provisions to areas which, while surveyed, had not been incorporated as municipalities. These are 'separate' schools in name only (being governed by the provisions of the Separate Schools Act) for they are not necessarily separate from any other school in the area. In the municipally-organized portions of the province, the first school established in an area is the public school, regardless of whether its board, supporters, and pupils are Catholic, Protestant or both. The dissenting school is then the separate school. In the unorganized areas, however, Catholic schools (separate) and Protestant schools (public) may be established as such from the outset.

The second exception to the inviolability of the provisions of the 1863 Act was the creation, by a special Act,[33] of the Toronto and Suburban Separate School Board in 1941. This board was given jurisdiction, not only over the City of Toronto, but also over a substantial portion of the suburban area. It represented an attempt to bend the basic principles of provincial policy to meet the pressing and unique problems of separate schools in the greater Toronto area. With the creation of the federated Municipality of Metropolitan Toronto in 1953, the board was transformed, again by special Act,[34] into the Metropolitan Toronto Separate School Board. This board gained jurisdiction over almost the whole of Metropolitan Toronto (at that time the city and twelve suburban municipalities). The town of Mimico and two districts in the township of Etobicoke remained distinct.*

* / Eight of the thirteen municipalities were urban in status (Toronto, Weston, Leaside, Mimico, New Toronto, Longbranch, Forest Hill, and Swansea). The other five were 'rural,' being designated townships (Etobicoke, Scarborough, York, North York, and East York). Each of the urban municipalities would have been one unit for separate schools while the townships consisted of distinct three-mile zones or unions thereof. Thus the Metropolitan Separate School Board was given jurisdiction over the whole of the 'urban' area (excepting Forest Hill which had no separate schools, and Mimico which chose to remain distinct) but only over those parts of the 'rural' area which were included in existing separate school organizations (excepting the one union school in Etobicoke which also chose to remain distinct). The separate school organization was unaffected by the reorganization of Metropolitan Toronto in 1967 (into one city and five 'boroughs') except that what had been an 'urban' separate school board in Mimico became a 'rural' zone within Etobicoke (the municipality of Mimico was dissolved into the enlarged municipality

In the period just reviewed, there had been no transformation of provincial policy towards the organization of units of government of separate schools comparable to that with respect to public schools. The motive force for the latter transformation had come from the group of professional educators and civil servants working in or out of the provincial Department of Education. This group wanted public school governments reorganized because such was considered a necessary step before public schools could offer the kinds of programmes and services the group desired. No reorganization of separate school governments had been sponsored, largely because this group had not been able to overcome its opposition to the very ethos of separate, denominational schools. Separate schools were viewed by many as barriers to the optimum development of the public schools. Clearly, this concept of separate schools has now been rejected to a large extent, and we shall have cause to return to it in a later context.

The provincial policy of promoting larger units of public school government was carried out in the main by a professionalized cadre of inspectors. Separate school inspectors were recruited, trained, and supervised under the same terms as their public school counterparts. Yet they were a group apart, operating in an atmosphere approaching that of paranoia on the part of many of their client governments and of noninterference on the part of their parent government. As a result they seldom acted as catalysts in the consolidation of small separate schools. Furthermore, separate school reorganization was a wholly voluntary act on the part of the school boards. There was no external body comparable to the township council to impose a more extensive interest (with the possible exception of the church, when it became involved). Separate school units were left susceptible to the full force of the naturally parochial interests of the school boards themselves.

Table 2 shows the annual formation of union separate schools from 1939 to 1957. It will be noticed that whereas the formation of township school areas reached its peak in 1945 and thereafter declined rapidly, the formation of union separate schools had not reached a peak even by 1957:

Secondary schools
The local government organization of Ontario's secondary schools has not presented problems for provincial policy to nearly the same extent as

of Etobicoke). The change in name from township to borough did not change the 'rural' nature of Etobicoke for separate school purposes. It was not until 1968 that the two isolated zones in Etobicoke were dissolved into the Metropolitan Toronto Board (taking effect on 1 January 1969).

TABLE 2
Annual formation of union separate schools, 1939–57

Year	Net no of unions formed	Total no of unions	No of former schools included
1939	3	3	9
1940	1	4	11
1941	0	4	11
1942	2	6	15
1943	0	6	15
1944	3	9	23
1945	8	17	44
1946	2	19	49
1947	0	19	50
1948	5	24	67
1949	6	30	83
1950	6	36	104
1951	10	46	133
1952	5	51	146
1953	1	52	150
1954	6	58	166
1955	7	65	189
1956	7	72	208
1957	10	82	233

SOURCES: 1939–51, Minister's Report, 1951; 1952–7,
Minister's Report for individual years

have the public and separate elementary schools. The reason for this is to be found in four historical factors.

Firstly, modern secondary schools evolved out of the original exclusive grammar schools. These were never widespread or popular, and were all located in urban centres. As a result, the province has not been faced with the problem of a province-wide network of local units of government. Furthermore, the boards of trustees of the grammar schools were appointed, not elected,* and this practice was continued when the grammar schools were officially changed to public secondary schools in 1871.[35] With appointed boards, the province had to deal with a much smaller group of participants in advocating the enlargement of units of government. But perhaps most important of all in this regard, the grammar schools had been county schools, and the involvement of the county councils provided an excellent mechanism for imposing a wider-than-local interest in the drawing of boundaries.

Secondly, high school inspectors had been appointed by the provincial

* / Between 1807 and 1853 the grammar school boards were appointed by the lieutenant-governor or governor of the province. Between 1853 and 1865 appointments were made by the county councils. After 1865 appointments in cities were made by the city councils, and in counties by the county, town, and village councils.

government ever since 1855. This factor contributed considerably to the exercise of greater provincial control over the secondary school system. Thirdly, the demand of a large number of groups, parents included, for greater emphasis on vocationally-oriented education provided a compelling reason for the enlargement of units of government which was lacking in the case of elementary schools. Finally, the obvious inequity of the system of financing secondary education when large areas of the province were not included in high school districts reached such proportions in the 1930s and early 1940s that some form of reorganization became virtually unavoidable.

Compared with the two elementary systems, then, the process of creating larger units of secondary school government has been easy. Two factors, however, have resulted in a considerable number of small high school units.

The first again stems from the territorial organization of grammar schools. The grammar schools were urban schools, and the jurisdictional boundaries were normally coterminous with those of an urban municipality (city, town, or village). This situation remained in the 1871 change from grammar schools to public secondary schools. The result was that many secondary school governments served only very small towns and villages.

The second factor is the legacy of the continuation school. Because grammar and high schools tended to be relatively inaccessible to rural children, the practice developed in the latter years of the nineteenth century of offering limited secondary programmes in the public and separate elementary schools. These programmes came to be known as 'fifth' or 'continuation' classes. In 1909, however, the province enacted the Continuation Schools Act[36] and provided for such schools to be established either by elementary school boards (in which case the elementary and continuation school districts were coterminous) or by county councils (in which case the councils were free to draw the boundaries as they saw fit). In 1913[37] the county continuation schools were declared to be high schools, and thus a significant number of very small high school districts was sanctioned in the rural areas of the province.

The earliest impetus for the formation of larger high school districts came not from the Department of Education, as was the case with public school districts, but from the school boards and especially the county councils. A 1946 publication of the department made the following observations:

During the past twenty years some larger high school districts have been established in the Province. In some cases these were established to avoid county rates,* with no thought of improving secondary education in the rural area. In other cases, financial support for a local high school would have been lacking without the formation of a larger district ...

The Ontario Department of Education is pleased that the conception of larger county high school districts has come from the school boards, the municipal councillors and the rate-payers themselves. It is evident that public-spirited citizens are anxious to give rural children the opportunity of securing a secondary school programme that will meet their needs. In response to this desire, the Department is pleased to assist any county or part of a county to establish large high school districts.[38]

The first truly larger high school district (that is, one not created by appending a small portion of technically 'rural' land to an urban district) was established in Essex County in 1944.[39] The great movement toward larger units came after the Second World War. Legislation of 1937[40] had provided the necessary machinery. County councils were authorized to establish consultative committees, composed of three members appointed by the council, one appointed by the Department of Education, plus, interestingly, the public school inspector as secretary. It was not until the movement was well advanced that the department actively intervened. When it did, it used the same technique as with public school reorganization, relying upon the inspector as a persuader and means of access to the local systems.

By 1951 the bulk of the area of southern Ontario (the area organized into counties) had been included in larger units. Most of the remainder was incorporated in the subsequent decade, and in 1964 the province instructed county councils to complete the reorganization.† That this was accomplished prior to any legislative coercion must be considered a remarkable achievement, and one in marked contrast to the two elementary school systems.

There remains the problem, however, that since the county was used as the 'lever' for reorganization, the whole northern portion of the province, not organized into counties, was omitted. Reorganization there was dependent upon action by the local municipal councils, where such existed, and by the lieutenant-governor in council (the cabinet). The cabinet was

---

* / The 'county rate' refers to the property tax levied on all property in a county which was not situated within a high school district. The local cost of educating pupils resident in a district was borne by the municipalities comprising the district. The local cost of educating non-resident, or 'county' pupils was borne by the remainder of the county.

† / Legislation of that year required that all parts of every county be included in a high school district (12 & 13 Eliz. II, c. 106, so).

reluctant to force change and local councils could not be expected to pursue wider-than-local interests. The fact that the province bore virtually the full cost of educating pupils not resident within high school districts effectively prevented any local pressure for inclusion. As a result, only a fraction of this vast area of the province was ever included in high school districts.

Boards of Education

One relevant subject which does not fit the separate treatment given the three systems above is that of the integrated governments of both public elementary and secondary schools. This has traditionally been the form of government favoured by the professional educators and provincial civil servants.

Two types of integrated governments have been developed in Ontario. The first, authorized in 1853[41] and known as a union board of education, consisted of delegates of distinct common and grammar (later high) school boards who met as a united board for the purpose of operating one or more union schools. This organizational device was designed to encourage the development of grammar schools into public secondary schools and to encourage municipal support for such schools. Authority to form such boards was withdrawn in 1954.[42]

The second, known as a municipal board of education, or more often simply as a board of education, is characterized by a single, elected school board responsible for the governing of all public elementary and secondary schools in the district. Ryerson attempted to make such boards mandatory in all urban municipalities in his draft legislation of 1868. Blocked in legislative committee, his attempt remained until 1968 the only one aimed at forcing the integration of the public elementary and secondary systems.

In 1903[43] provision was made for Toronto to combine its public, secondary, and technical schools into a single organization governed by an elected board of education.* In the following year the same permission was granted to all cities, towns, and villages which were not situated in county high school districts.[44] In 1909[45] any urban municipality was authorized to adopt a board of education type of school government so long as its municipal and school district boundaries were coterminous (in 1943 this criterion was applied to rural municipalities as well).[46] In 1911[47] legislation required the approval of a majority of the ratepayers before a board of education might be established. Then in 1948[48] county

---

* / The legislation actually applied to any city with a population of over 100,000. Toronto was the only such city.

councils were authorized to establish a board of education in any high school district, upon the request of the municipal councils involved but without reference to the ratepayers. Finally, in the following year[49] the requirement of ratepayer approval was removed as a condition in all cases.

The great postwar movement towards large high school districts, supported by the Department of Education, resulted in a corresponding decline in the number of boards of education. In large part this reflected the basic division of both the department and the educational professions into elementary and secondary areas of concern. Teachers were normally trained in different institutions, the inspectors were recruited from the different teaching ranks, and the supervisory role of the department (with personnel largely recruited from the inspectoral staff) was, until 1965, divided into elementary and secondary branches. Furthermore, high school district boundaries were drawn by the county councils in the interests of secondary education. Public school boundaries were drawn by the township councils in the interests of elementary education. With no one speaking for an integrated form of government and no overriding authority prescribing the boundaries, it became very difficult to establish coterminous public and high school districts.

As a result, boards of education tended to remain only in the larger cities (where the high school district consisted only of the city)* and in those rural areas in which single townships were established as high school districts.

Table 3 shows the postwar decline and recent stabilization in the number of boards of education.

RECENT DIMENSIONS

This chapter began with the statement that problems had arisen from the territorial extent of units of local government of schools because this extent did not permit the schools to provide those services desired of them by the provincial government and an increasingly professionalized group of educators.

A brief perusal of a recent general legislative grants regulation[50] will indicate some of the special services and programmes which the department has been promoting. Among others, these include the services of

---

*/ The exception to this pattern is in cities with large proportions of separate school supporters. Since a board of education tends to isolate (in appearance at least) the separate school system, councils in such cities are not likely to favour the adoption of such a board. Thus, the cities of Ottawa, Sudbury, North Bay, and Cornwall never instituted integrated systems.

TABLE 3
Number of boards of education in
Ontario, 1940–63

Year	Number	Year	Number
1940	112	1952	59
1941	111	1953	59
1942	111	1954	60
1943	116	1955	56
1944	117	1956	55
1945	122	1957	53
1946	125	1958	53
1947	87	1959	53
1948	87	1960	52
1949	87	1961	52
1950	85	1962	54
1951	65	1963	53

SOURCE: Minister's Reports

psychologists; the conducting of classes for the blind, emotionally disturbed, and neurologically impaired; the provision of opportunity classes; and the employment of speech-correction teachers. The department is also developing sophisticated facilities and programmes for educational television and electronic data processing.

Few if any of these programmes or facilities can be utilized by a school board with but one classroom of twenty or thirty pupils. Yet, of the 2846 elementary school boards (including boards of education) which operated schools in the province in 1964, 810 or 28 per cent had total average daily attendances of fewer than thirty pupils.[51]

The basic framework of school government was developed at a time when thirty pupils was quite sufficient to operate a school. Problems arose because the school units of government were not altered to match the changes in minimum or optimum size. But the problems have been deeper than merely the mechanical ones involved in changing the units of government, and nothing illustrates this more clearly than a comparison of the three provincial systems of schools; public, separate, and secondary. The depth of the problems varied with each of the three systems, and it varied with the degree to which authority was delegated by the provincial government.

In the secondary school system, the delegation of authority was never complete, for the province appointed the original grammar school boards of trustees. When this power was relinquished it was delegated, not to self-contained local communities, but to confederations of communities, namely the counties. The early identification of grammar schools with urban society had bequeathed a number of small high schools in the towns and villages. The traditional involvement of the county councils, however, had enabled a regional influence to be exerted on the reorganization of the units of government. In turn, of course, the lack of county government in the northern portion of the province had prevented reorganization (or in many cases organization) from penetrating that region to any substantial degree.

The case of the public schools was quite different. In the original legislation of 1816, the district, with an appointed board of education, was established as an intermediate tier of government between the small school section and the province. In 1850, however, the bulk of this role was transferred to the township council, a much less extensive, and a directly elected, body.

In the preceding pages we have traced the steps by which the province attempted to effect a restructuring of the units of public school government. It was effective in stimulating change only when it succeeded in gaining direct access, through the inspector, to the political systems of the townships. The provincial government was not willing to employ force and it therefore had to rely on a persuasion of the local systems to change themselves.

Reliance on local action (or reaction) did not provide a satisfactory resolution of the problem of inadequate units of government, and by 1957 the momentum had gone out of the movement toward township school areas. To go further, the province had to break the hold of the local political systems upon the public schools (or, to state the same thing in different terms, to reclaim for itself control over the size of units of public school government).

Ryerson tried to break this hold in 1868 but his attempt was not even accepted by the government. Ferguson tried in 1925 but he was defeated by local opposition. Success did not come until a number of problems, to be discussed in subsequent chapters, had combined to force local politicans and their constituents to accept much greater provincial involvement. The working out of that situation, however, we shall leave to a later point.

The territorial organization of separate school government was even more difficult to change than that of public school government. Primarily, this was due to the attitude of the provincial government itself, an attitude provincial politicians apparently believed to be shared by a majority of the electorate. The ostensible barrier to change in the separate school system was section 93 (1) of the British North America Act:

93 In and for each Province the Legislature may exclusively make laws
relating to Education, subject and according to the following Provisions:

   i) Nothing in any such Law shall prejudicially affect any Right or Privilege with respect to Denominational Schools which any Class of Persons have
by Law in the Province at the Union.[52]

The relevant right of Roman Catholic separate school supporters (who
constitute the 'class of persons' in this context) was that of establishing a
school upon the favourable vote of a majority of those present at a meeting called by at least five heads of families. When established, the school
board would exercise jurisdiction over an area radiating three miles about
the site of the school (or over two or more such areas if the schools were
united).

   Because of its concern that separate schools not be allowed to flourish,
the provincial government tied its own hands in the matter of changing the
units of government. The BNA Act states only that the rights and privileges
of Roman Catholic separate school supporters may not be *prejudicially*
affected (this was an essential guarantee in the Confederation bargain, for
there was a strongly held, and probably well founded, belief that without
it separate schools would be abandoned once the union of Upper and
Lower Canada was dissolved). But as Chief Justice Meredith of the
Supreme Court of Ontario noted with respect to one of the famous
Ottawa separate school cases of 1915:

   The narrow view that the imperial enactment [the BNA Act] made all the
provisions of the Separate Schools Act, in force at the time of the passing of
the Imperial Act, unalterable, is without any kind of substantial support ...

   It was never meant that the separate schools, or any other schools, should
be left forever in the educational wilderness of the enactments in force in 1867.
Educational methods and machinery may and must change, but separation,
and equal rights regarding public schools, must remain as long as provincial
public schools last, unless the federal or Imperial Parliament, whichever may
have the power, decrees otherwise.[53]

The same approach was adopted by the Privy Council in upsetting the
particular decision reached in the above case: 'It is quite possible that an
interference with a legal right or privilege may not in all cases imply that
such right or privilege has been prejudicially affected.'[54]

   The provincial government made one important change in the separate
school legislation in 1963.[55] The centre of the three-mile radial zone was

changed from the school site to a point designated by the separate school board. This meant that separate school organizations could be established without the condition that a school be erected. It was still not possible to create an enlarged separate school district except through the dissolution of existing districts. The combination of these two provisions led to a rather ludicrous situation.

In order to establish a large unit, the separate school supporters in the area concerned, in a township, for example, had first to establish a series of single units (each established at a meeting called by five heads of families and having jurisdiction over three-mile radial zones) and the governments of these units had then to vote to dissolve their units into a larger one. These individual organizations came to be known as 'dummy' zones when the sole reason for their creation was to serve as a means of circumventing the statutory prohibition of larger units established *de novo*. With considerable ingenuity, a combined zone could be organized which encompassed the bulk of the potential separate school supporters in the area, but the process of formation was surely an irrational one.

Furthermore, even if a township were all but covered with 'dummy' separate school areas, a Roman Catholic not living within any one of the prescribed zones could not opt to support the separate school system. This point may be illustrated in simplified form in Figure 1. In this example, school zones A and B were dissolved into a combined zone and a single school located at the centre of B. Any Roman Catholic living in either of the shaded areas A or B could support this school, and any one

FIGURE 1
Effect of union of two separate school organizations

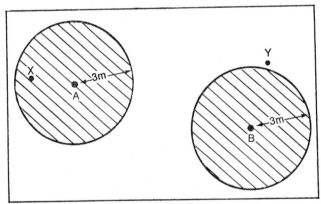

SOURCE: Based on a similar illustration in J.R. Durrah, *Roman Catholic Separate School Support*, The Municipal World, 1963

not within these areas could not. A Roman Catholic living at point X, fifteen miles from the school could be a supporter, but a Roman Catholic living at point Y, three and one-half miles from the school, could not. The only way for a person at point Y to become a separate school supporter would have been to persuade four other heads of families to call a meeting, establish a 'dummy' zone, and then dissolve the zone into the combined zone.

The problem of separate school governmental units was thus more deep-rooted than even that of the public schools. Not only did the province delegate the authority for establishing and changing these units to local political systems and their spokesmen, but it placed, or allowed to be placed, a rigid control upon the extent to which the structures of these units could be altered. Any resolution of the problem would need to involve one or both of two changes – a clarification of the atmosphere within which the separate school professionals (primarily the inspectors) worked, or the imposition of a reorganization from the provincial level. Both would involve the abandonment of the century-old attitude of the

TABLE 4

Types of school boards in Ontario in classes
of average daily attendance, 1964

		Average daily attendance				
Type of board	Total no	30 or less	31 to 100	101 to 500	501 to 1000	Over 1000
Separate school boards rural	278	70	114	86	6	2
urban	157	1	26	73	20	37
Combined separate school boards	183	2	46	122	4	9
Public school section boards rural	1313	700	514	96	3	
urban	245	3	41	124	28	49
Township school area boards	622	31	145	389	33	24
Continuation school boards	11	3	6	2		
High school boards	55		5	37	6	7
District high school boards	172		3	71	65	33
Boards of education	54			6	7	41
Boards not operating schools	382	311	70	1		
ALL BOARDS	3472	1121	970	1007	172	202

SOURCE: Ontario, Department of Education, *Schools and Teachers in the Province of Ontario*, 1964

provincial government towards separate school organization. The first change, however, would in effect free the separate schools to develop according to their response to the pressures of the professionals. The second would require the government, and especially the bureaucracy, to make, or share in, this response.

In all three systems of schools, the problems arising from the units of local government, problems of inadequate and unequal size, were inherited from previous provincial policy decisions. In the public and separate systems their resolution required the reassertion of a provincial involvement in the structuring of local governments. In the secondary system the resolution required an extension of provincial involvement which was never fully abdicated.

To indicate more clearly the extent of inadequacy and inequality in the size of local units, Table 4 shows the distribution of the various types of school boards by size (as measured by the average daily attendance of pupils).

3
Problems of local fiscal resources

There is a generic relationship between the problems which arose from the organization of units of local government and from the local tax base supporting education. Whereas in the former case the problems were basically ones of inadequate and unequal size, in the latter they were problems of inadequate and unequal fiscal resources. The relationship is strengthened by the fact that the smaller governmental units tended also to have the smaller taxing capacities. One can glimpse the nature of the problems to be dealt with in this chapter by noting that in 1964 two school boards had tax bases of $2500 and $5,025,000 respectively, measured in terms of equalized taxable property assessment per class-room.[1]

The provincial government has for some time committed itself to a policy of equalizing the educational opportunities of all children in the province. This implies that all school boards, regardless of fiscal capacity, will be enabled to support, at reasonably similar costs, an educational programme which meets provincial standards. The province has also committed itself, however, to maintaining the political and fiscal autonomy of school boards so that modified and experimental programmes may be instituted at the local level. This has required that local districts have sufficient resources to permit a certain degree of inequality in the programmes offered. The central problem, then, has been one of equalizing the fiscal resources of local governments without at the same time excessively restricting the innovation and experimentation which comes from inequality.

As was the case with the size of units of government, it is necessary to trace the development of the system of financing education before the problems this system has posed for contemporary policy makers can be fully comprehended. This will be done by examining, first, the development of local taxation and, second, the evolution of provincial policy in response to the peculiarities and inadequacies of such taxation.

Development of local taxation
The contemporary fiscal base of local school boards can be compared to a fabric, woven from a number of threads over a period of one hundred and fifty years. The contemporary pattern is meaningful only if one appreciates the contributions of the various threads. The main threads, what we might call the warp of the fabric, were woven with regard to the common schools. The basic pattern was formed from five such threads: the adoption of the property tax as one means of raising local revenue; the free school movement which led to the use of the property tax as the sole source of local revenue; the battle over the power of school boards to requisition funds from the municipalities; the right of school boards to borrow for capital purposes; and the periodic expansion and then contraction of the property tax base itself. Interwoven with these five threads are two significant cross, or woof, threads: the support of secondary schools from the proceeds of property taxation, and the gradual removal of barriers to the use of the property tax for the support of separate schools.

The taxation of individuals on the basis of their wealth in real and personal property is one of the oldest forms of taxation in Ontario, dating almost from the earliest white settlements. It was some time, however, before its use for the support of education became acceptable. So long as schools were considered essentially as extensions of parental responsibility, it seemed only reasonable that the cost of such schools should be borne by the parents of those children who benefitted from them. Thus the ratebill on parents* constituted the major source of revenue in the early common (elementary) schools of the province.

By about 1840 it was becoming clear that this notion of public education was being replaced by one which viewed schools as public institutions promoting government policy. With that change in attitude, a change in the system of fiscal support became essential. Beginning in 1841,[2] the new municipal councils of the province's districts were re-

---

*/The ratebill differed from a general tax in that it was really a device for eliciting payment for services rendered to individuals, as parents. It is interesting to note that this device was not used by the grammar schools. In the latter case revenue was raised by tuition fees, charged against the pupil and not his parents. Although the final incidence of the two charges would likely be the same (the parents), the difference in method of application of the charge reflected a difference in attitude towards the roles of the two types of schools.

quired to distribute among the common schools of the district an amount equal to the district's share of the provincial school grant. This money was to be raised by the general tax on property.

The second success for those who wished to use common schools to provincial advantage followed in 1843,[3] when the councils of incorporated cities and police towns were permitted to raise the full amount of the local share of the cost of common schools from a general property tax. As of this date urban common schools might be 'free,' being totally financed by general taxation.* This right was extended to the rural areas of the province in 1847.[4] In the latter case, the decision to abolish rate-bills and rely entirely upon taxation was to be made by the district council, the decision applying to the whole district, to one or more townships only, or to one or more school sections only, at the discretion of the council.

A significant change was made in 1850[5] which presaged the controversy over school board requisitions of funds. The authority to choose taxation over ratebills was removed from the municipalities and placed in the school boards in urban centres and in the annual meetings of taxpayers in rural school sections.

By the time of Confederation and the creation of the Province of Ontario in 1867, a substantial majority of the common schools were 'free.' In 1868 Ryerson moved to force all common schools into the established pattern. In the resultant legislation of 1871[6] his move was sanctioned and the tax on property became virtually the sole source of local revenue for the province's newly renamed public schools.

When the property tax was introduced in 1841 as one ingredient of the revenue 'mix' of Ontario's schools, the tax was in no way distinct from that levied for other local governmental services. The district councils, the few towns, and one city were the only units of local municipal government and the property tax was their peculiar source of revenue. The significance of the 1841 legislation lay in its requirement of support for common schools by the municipal corporations. Given that requirement, the use of the property tax was unavoidable. At that time, municipal support of schools was limited to a fixed and known amount, an amount equal to a municipality's share of the provincial school grant.

The real controversy did not begin until 1843 when municipalities were authorized to support common schools beyond this fixed limit. Originally, the onus of responsibility for determining the amount of tax

* / The word 'free' here is technically a misnomer. The schools were, of course, not free at all, but this was the term normally applied to schools which did not levy a specific fee for admission but were paid for by the whole community.

support was placed on the municipal council. The school board was left to rely on its own ingenuity to make up any balance between its net revenue needs and the tax support provided by the municipality.

Obviously, if the current operations of schools were to be financed completely by tax revenue, this was an unsatisfactory situation. Either municipalities would need to be forced to satisfy all the revenue needs of the school boards or else school boards would need to be given the power to levy their own taxes. In fact both alternatives were adopted at first, and only after the experience of sixteen years was the second abandoned.

The School Act of 1847[7] established all cities and towns as single districts for common schools, prescribed that boards of trustees were to be appointed by the municipal councils and, apparently, that these boards could requisition funds from the councils. At least this was the interpretation given by the Attorney-General, for the Act made no provision for raising revenue by any other means.[8] In 1848 the city council of Toronto refused to comply with the requisition and consequently allowed the city's schools to close. The situation was not rectified until 1850[9] when trustees were once again to be elected and authorization was given to raise revenue through ratebills.

Beginning in 1850, taxpayers in rural school sections were given the responsibility, at their annual meetings, of approving the method of supplying the current revenue needs of the common school. They could vote to place sole reliance upon the general property tax. The school board could then request that the tax be levied and collected by the newly-organized township council. If the request were refused, the school board had the authority to levy its own taxes. This applied to current revenues only. As we shall note shortly, taxation for capital needs could be levied only by the township council.

Municipal councils evidenced some reluctance to serve as tax collectors for school boards. In response, the province granted all school boards complete authority to levy and collect their own taxes in 1853.[10] This appeared to be a somewhat inefficient scheme and the legislation was changed in 1869[11] giving school boards power to requisition their current revenue needs. Power to levy taxes was not removed from the common school boards until 1885,[12] but by that time it had become virtually meaningless through disuse.[13] This was to be a long-lasting measure. Requisitioning funds from the municipality has remained the method of obtaining property tax revenue for common (now public) schools ever since 1859.

The question of borrowing funds to finance the acquisition of capital assets (land, buildings, furnishings, and various items of equipment) did not arise in the early schools of Upper Canada. Such assets tended to involve only modest expenditures and were financed either by ratebills on parents, by general subscriptions, or, most commonly, by a combination of the two.

The District Municipal Act of 1841[14] required the district councils to levy a tax on property, not exceeding fifty pounds, in every school district not having a schoolhouse and to use the proceeds of the levy to acquire such a building.

In 1846[15] the district councils were authorized to levy taxes both for the current operations of school boards and the erection and furnishing of school buildings. As the Hope Report notes, however, this provision was largely nullified by a second provision which limited the total district levy, for all purposes, to a rate of twopence in the pound.[16] The latter provision was removed in legislation of the following year,[17] the effect of which was to permit district councils to provide the full revenue needs of the common schools, both current and capital, from the proceeds of current property tax revenues.

As was noted above,* the Common Schools Act of 1850[18] allowed both rural and urban common school boards to request the municipal council to levy taxes for both the current and capital requirements of the board. The council's compliance was discretionary in the case of current funds but essential in the case of capital funds (boards could not levy taxes for capital revenue). But the 1850 Act also provided, for the first time, for the borrowing of funds to meet capital requirements. The borrowing could be undertaken by the council or authority to borrow could be delegated by the council to the school board. In either case, the raising of funds by taxation to repay the debt could be undertaken only by the council. Any such debt could extend for a period of no more than ten years.

In 1879[19] all public school boards were required to channel all borrowing through the respective municipal corporations. Such borrowing was to be approved at an annual or special meeting of ratepayers in the rural sections, but was subject to ratepayer approval only as a means of arbitration in the case of rejection by the municipal council in urban centres.

The situation assumed essentially its contemporary proportions in 1932[20] with the creation of the Ontario Municipal Board[21] and the requirement that all municipal borrowing be approved by that body. The Municipal Board is normally concerned with two factors, the legal and

* / See above, p. 36

financial integrity of the borrowing documents and instruments, and the ability of the municipality to support its proposed debt level. In the latter regard, the board determines debt-assessment ratio ceilings which municipalities are not permitted to exceed.

We have spent some time now discussing the gradual adoption of the property tax as the sole source of local revenue for common schools. It is fitting at this time to consider the evolution of the base of that tax, especially since changes in the definition of 'property' have contributed greatly to the contemporary problems arising from its use.

When common schools first gained access to the revenue produced by property taxation, in 1841, both the definition and valuation of property were statutory functions of the provincial legislature. The nature of the system is well illustrated in the following excerpt from the Report of the Ontario Committee on Taxation (the Smith Report):

> Arbitrary values were placed by statute upon various items of real and personal property. If the property was not named in the statute, it was not taxable ...
> Arable land was to be assessed at £1 an acre ... merchant's shop at £200, regardless of size.[22]

The basis of property taxation was substantially changed in 1850, however. The legislation[23] spelled out what was taxable (land, buildings, and a short list of items of personal property) and delegated to the local assessors the function of affixing to each item its full value.

A significant change was made in the property tax base in 1853[24] when the definition of personal property was considerably extended. It now included 'all goods, chattels, shares in incorporated companies, money, notes, accounts and debts at their full value.'[25] If adequately administered, this extension would have made the property tax a comprehensive tax of both income and wealth. The taxation of personal income and property was never adequately administered, however, and the effective tax base became real property supplemented by some measure of the stock-in-trade of business enterprises.

The first provincial recognition of the inability or unwillingness of municipalities to administer a tax on personal property came in 1890 when the option was provided of substituting a special business tax based on the value of the business premises, for the taxation of the personal property of businesses.[26] Not a single municipality made use of this option, but in 1904 the business tax was made compulsory.[27] This was a part of a larger reform by which all personal property, except income, was removed from the tax base. The compulsory business tax was changed in principle from its optional predecessor of 1890, becoming a percentage of the real property assessment which varied with the nature of the business conducted in the premises. A distillery, for example, was subject to a supplementary tax calculated by applying the local mill rate to 150 per cent of the real property assessment. For breweries the percentage rate was 75; for manufacturing plants it was 60.

The special business tax was a device enabling municipalities to raise revenue from sources other than the real property tax. As such it was a rather crude substitute for the taxation of personal property, the latter having proved incapable of administration. Yet the complete abandonment of the personal property tax was the first step in the abandonment of a local base comprising a comprehensive measurement of income and wealth. Two further steps completed the movement.

In 1936[28] the province assumed responsibility for the taxation of personal income and as a consequence removed this item from the local base.* Then in 1942[29] corporate income was also removed. The Smith Report notes that at no time did Ontario municipalities make proper use of their ability to tax income or personal property. However, the report also states:

... in spite of the failure of municipal government to use these taxing powers fully or well, they did represent a key source of potential revenue capable of yielding large amounts of money, broadening greatly the base for local taxation and materially improving its over-all equity.[30]

By the Second World War, then, the property tax base consisted only of real property and the supplemental business assessment. This was the smallest base local governments had enjoyed for nearly one hundred years, and it came as the prelude to the period of the greatest demands ever placed on the revenue-producing capacity of local taxation.

The major features in the pattern of financing schools from property taxation were worked out with respect to the common schools. Once the decision was made to bring grammar schools into this pattern, the only remaining questions were the extent of reliance on general taxation and the mechanism for levying the tax.

Municipalities were permitted to grant funds to grammar schools in 1853.[31] At the same time an incentive for such grants was created in the

*/Municipalities were guaranteed provincial grants equal to the yield of the income tax in 1935, and such other amounts as the lieutenant-governor in council determined.

provision for the combination of grammar and common schools into a single or 'union' school under a board of education. It was not until 1871,[32] however, when grammar schools were officially transformed from essentially private institutions receiving public support to truly public secondary schools,* that municipal support became compulsory.† And because the secondary school district boundaries often differed from municipal boundaries, an informal scheme developed whereby support was shared by local and county municipalities.

While high schools were given the power to requisition funds from municipalities, many of them continued to make use of tuition fees as one source of revenue.[33] It was not until 1921[34] that high schools became completely free as public schools had been since 1871. Secondary schools were included in the provisions of 1879[35] governing the power to borrow for capital purposes. Like public school boards, they could borrow only through the municipal council. Where the council did not comply with a request for capital borrowing, recourse could be had to a vote of the ratepayers or, later, to the Ontario Municipal Board.

For the first nine years of their existence, separate schools were considered to be merely special, or separate, common schools. As such they received the same proportion of all public monies as they had of the pupils attending common schools. This applied to both the provincial grant and the compulsory district property tax levy. Theoretically, separate schools were also included in the provisions of 1843[36] and 1847[37] whereby all of the current revenue requirements of common school boards might be furnished by the municipal council.

Ryerson and the provincial government were determined that separate schools not be encouraged and were convinced that if sufficient barriers were placed in the way of their development they would soon pass entirely from the Upper Canadian educational scene. Thus Ryerson's education bill of 1850,[38] which passed through Parliament with only a few changes, prohibited municipal support of separate schools beyond the compulsory amount matching the provincial grant.‡

* / Secondary schools were known as either high schools or collegiate institutes. The designation of a school as a collegiate institute required at least four masters and sixty boys studying Latin.

† / The appointed secondary school boards were never accorded the right to levy their own taxes.

‡ / Some of the provisions which were enacted by the Canadian Parliament in these years can only be credited to the assumption that education generally, and separate schools particularly, were of very minor concern. In 1849, for example, the minister of public works, Malcolm Cameron, introduced a school bill which removed all mention of separate schools and 'contrived pretty completely to upset the system in process of evolution' (C.B. Sissons, *Church and State in Canadian Education* (Toronto 1959), p. 24). The bill had become law before its implications were realized and the government had to pass an embarrassing order-in-council

In 1852 both Belleville and Chatham instituted 'free' common schools.[39] This marked the real opening of the nineteenth-century conflict over separate schools, for it forced the question of whether or not separate schools were to be financed wholly by taxation. The original practice in Belleville and Chatham was for all local property taxation to support only the non-sectarian common schools. This meant that separate school supporters were supporting the non-sectarian schools by taxation *and* separate schools by ratebills and subscriptions. This inequity was removed under heavy pressure from the Catholic bishops in 1853. In an amendment of that year,[40] separate school supporters were freed from paying common school property taxes if they had contributed to the separate school an amount at least equal to that for which they would have been liable as common school supporters. At the same time the separate school boards were authorized to levy their own property taxes upon those who declared their desire to support a separate school for that year. In 1855 the Taché Act[41] removed both the requirement of support equal to the common school taxes and that support of a separate school be declared annually.

Unless separate school boards were to duplicate the whole assessment function of the municipalities, they needed access to the municipal rolls in order to levy their own taxes. It was not until the Scott Act of 1863[42] that this right of access was granted unequivocally. There is some doubt as to just when separate schools acquired the right to use the municipality as a tax-collection agency. The power of the non-sectarian common schools was clarified in 1869[43] but the Hope Commission commented that 'we could find no record as to whether this power of public school trustees was extended to separate school trustees at that time.'[44] It was not until 1877[45] that the question was finally settled in favour of the separate schools.

By the latter date, the financial situation of separate schools had very nearly assumed its contemporary proportions. The local tax base consisted of the assessed property of those Roman Catholics, residing within three miles of the school, who had declared their support of the separate school organization.* A property tax might then be levied against this property by the school board directly or by the municipal council at the

---

setting it aside. It was not until after 1850 that the Catholic hierarchy developed an effective lobby in Parliament. This example also illustrates the weakness of having no minister of education in the government.

* / In many cases, no formal declaration is ever made. If the assessor knows a person to be a Roman Catholic this is *prima facie* evidence of his support of the separate school and he may be assessed accordingly. If the person so assessed wishes to support the public school he must protest the assessor's decision.

request of the school board (separate school boards have never lost the right to levy their own taxes).

In the mechanics of raising current revenue, then, separate schools were treated not unlike their public elementary counterparts. In the case of capital funds, however, this was not to be the case. Prior to 1879, capital borrowing for public schools was usually undertaken by the municipal council. After 1879 this was always the case. The resultant indebtedness, however, was an obligation of the municipal corporation (not the school board) and was supported by the taxable property assessment of the municipality. The notion of the municipality supporting debt incurred on behalf of the minority separate school system was not to be entertained. Consequently, the separate schools were excluded from the provisions of 1879[46] whereby all borrowing for public and high schools was to be undertaken by the municipality. To this day, separate school boards have had to undertake their own capital borrowing. Furthermore, it was not until 1966 that separate school boards were in any way made subject to the oversight of the Ontario Municipal Board.[47]

The situation wherein only the property of declared supporters may be taxed for separate school purposes has created one of the most enduring problems of public policy in Ontario. How ought the property of a public corporation be taxed when an unknown and unknowable proportion of its shareholders are Roman Catholics and separate school supporters? Because this problem is so central to the financial situation of separate schools and is so distinct from the general problems of school boards, we shall deal with it separately in the following chapter. Suffice it to say at this point that the major attempt at solving the problem, in 1936,* proved to be quite inadequate, whereas the most successful attempt at tackling the problem, in 1964,† achieved its success by attacking the consequences and not the causes of the problem.

The pattern of the local financing of schools was settled relatively early in Ontario. As the Hope Commission commented: 'The pattern of local financial support for schools had assumed its main outlines by 1874 in relation to public and separate schools and to high schools. Only a few changes have taken place since that date.'[48] Had education been totally dependent on revenue raised from property taxation it would long since have been starved to a state of serious illness. For, as we have seen, the development of more widespread, sophisticated, and expensive educational programmes has been paralleled by a narrowing of the local tax base. The provincial government's unwillingness or inability to enlarge

* / See below, p. 61
† / See below, pp. 119–22

the local tax base or improve its administration has been complemented by a boldness in devising and revising conditional and unconditional grant schemes to compensate for, and supplement, the unequal and inadequate revenues produced by property taxation. Some knowledge of the evolving pattern of these schemes is essential for a proper appreciation of the contemporary problems of local fiscal resources.

Provincial responses

The provincial government was involved in the financing of Ontario's schools almost from their very beginning. It was expending the proceeds of general taxation on formal education some thirty-four years before local governments became involved. This early provincial involvement was designed to stimulate the establishment of schools, to provide existing schools with at least a guaranteed minimum stable source of revenue, and to maintain an element of provincial control over the schools.

With the introduction of local property taxation for education, the emphasis of provincial policy began to shift. In 1850, for example, the basis upon which the provincial grant to common schools was distributed within the counties was changed from population to the actual average daily attendance in the several schools.[49] In 1859 a condition was placed on the same grant stipulating that it be applied only to expenditures on teachers' salaries.[50] Both of these measures were designed to use provincial resources to stimulate local governments to adopt certain policies or practices – the first a greater concern for attendance (it was not yet compulsory) and the second the employment of more highly qualified teachers.

The principle of stimulation or reward for effort reached its height in the 'payments by results' fiasco of the 1875 high school grant plan.[51] Ryerson had tried to implement such a scheme as early as 1865. It had not been feasible then because no reliable gauge for measuring 'effort' or 'results' had been found. But the introduction of the Intermediate Examination[52] provided this gauge, or so Ryerson and his colleagues believed. A part of the high school grant would be distributed in direct proportion to the results obtained by the pupils of each school in this formal examination.[53]

The Hope Commission commented as follows on the accomplishments of the scheme:

The direct consequences ... was an increase of pressure and 'cram' in the schools. Teachers' journals were filled with examination questions and answers; English literature books were published with two pages of notes for every page of text; pedagogical skill tended to consist only in drilling into the student whatever could be made use of in a test. The scheme was discontinued in 1882, but it was probably influential in raising the written examination to a position of dominance which it was to retain long after 1882.[54]

With the failure of the direct-payment-by-results scheme, financial stimulation came to be accepted as the normal method of encouraging specific projects or programmes. The first such stimulation grant was for special high school accommodation units (libraries, gymnasiums, laboratories) begun in 1885.[55] This type of grant was destined to proliferate in Ontario, and by 1936 there were no fewer than ten separate grant formulae covering such services as kindergartens, night schools, and medical inspections.[56]

By the turn of the century, a new principle had begun to gain pre-eminence in educational circles – equalization of educational opportunities and fiscal burdens. A policy of equalization demanded the establishment of objective criteria for determining educational need and fiscal capacity, and the use of provincial resources to bridge the gaps between the two. The basic problem was that there were no acceptable measures of the two crucial factors – need and capacity. Similar educational services varied in cost from locality to locality depending on such factors as pupil-teacher ratios, teacher qualifications, density of population, geographical terrain, and the relative cost of goods and services. Fiscal capacity could not be equated with the assessed value of taxable property because there were no standard criteria for assessing the value of property.

The solution to the problem developed in Ontario was the classification of school boards into groups which were deemed to be reasonably similarly situated in terms of needs and capacities. The boards in each group could then be treated similarly and the assumed differences between groups reflected in differences in treatment.

This approach was first adopted in the grant plan for rural elementary schools in 1907,[57] was extended to urban elementary schools in 1908,[58] and was finally broadened to include high schools in 1936.[59] The approach dominated provincial thinking throughout the first half of the twentieth century and was not superceded until the introduction of the foundation tax plan in 1964. The ingenuity of provincial policy makers was greatly taxed over the years in devising ever more sophisticated schedules for the grouping of schools and localities. In the original elementary school grants of 1907–10 there were but four groupings: rural schools in counties, urban schools in counties, rural schools in territorial districts, and urban schools in territorial districts.

The approach reached its climax in the revised grant plan of 1958.[60] Under that plan, which lasted until 1963 with modest annual revisions, school boards were grouped into fifteen basic categories.[61] Within each category fiscal need was measured on three dimensions: average daily attendance of pupils (weighted for those receiving special instruction), approved expenditure, and what was termed 'recognized extraordinary expenditure per class-room.' Fiscal capacity was measured as equalized taxable assessment per classroom for elementary schools or per capita for secondary schools. Of the three measures of need, the first two require little comment. The first entailed grants on a per-pupil basis and the second as a percentage of approved expenditure. The third dimension represented one of the two major innovations of the 1958 plan and was an attempt to measure what was termed the 'growth need' of a school board.[62] It included the approved portions of debt charges, capital expenditures from current funds, and expenditures on transportation.

As a result of the postwar formation of larger secondary school districts* – a process encouraged by the provincial government – a new dimension was added to the problems of financing capital and transportation expenditures. Larger school districts were desirable precisely because they extended the services of centrally-located school buildings to pupils residing beyond reasonable walking distances from such buildings. The very formation of an enlarged district, then, generated a need for extraordinary expenditures (on new and enlarged buildings with supporting equipment and furnishings, and on transportation). Furthermore, the relative magnitude of these expenditures varied widely between school districts. Where a small rural area was attached to what had been an urban district, the marginal expenditure relative to the student population and revenue-raising capacity of the whole district would be small. Where an entirely new district was created for a rural area, requiring a new building project to house the entire student population and a transportation system to carry virtually all of the students, the relative marginal expenditure could be very large.

The effect of this situation was the generation of the greatest fiscal burdens in precisely those areas in which the programme of school district enlargement had been most effective. The concept of 'growth need' was introduced to take account of this dimension. Need was measured as recognized extraordinary expenditure per classroom, and provincial grants increased as this need increased.

The use of equalized assessments in the measurement of fiscal capacity represented the second major innovation of the 1958 plan. Local

* / See above, pp. 23–4

assessments were equalized by the Department of Municipal Affairs under a scheme which involved the application of factors designed to relate local assessments to the equivalent of full value in the base year of 1940. The factors were developed from a series of spot checks in each municipality.

The manner in which the grant plan in effect from 1958 to 1963 attempted to use provincial grants to bridge the gaps between need and capacity can be seen in Table 5 which reproduces one of the grant schedules used in 1963. The total grant was a combination of a dollar amount per pupil and a percentage of approved (or 'recognized') costs. The first two measures of need were thereby incorporated. As well, however, these grants increased as the recognized extraordinary expenditure per classroom increased, thus incorporating the third measure of need. Finally, the total grant increased as equalized assessment per classroom decreased, thus taking account of the measure of fiscal capacity.

A clearly discernible watershed was reached in 1943 in the slowly evolving pattern of provincial policy towards the financing of education. The Liberal government of Mitchell Hepburn, elected in 1934 and returned to office in 1937, had begun to disintegrate by the early 1940s. And as it did so the Conservatives, under George Drew, and the Co-operative Commonwealth Federation, under E.B. Jolliffe, launched a vigorous electoral battle in preparation for the impending election. Certainly one of the turning points in the election campaign was reached when Drew made this famous remark:

There will be a sweeping revision of our whole system of real estate taxation so that the owning and improving of homes and farm lands, which are the very foundation of our society, will not be discouraged by excessive taxation. As an initial step in that direction, the Provincial Government will assume 50 per cent of the school tax now charged against real estate.[63]

The statement was generally interpreted literally, meaning that the property tax supporting education would be halved. The *Globe and Mail* quoted the wistful comment of Harry C. Nixon, former premier and leader of the Liberal party, in the ensuing Throne Speech debate:

'It was the boldest and most attractive bid for support in any general election in this Province,' said Mr. Nixon. With the prospect of his own tax bill of $194 being cut in two, he declared, 'I almost voted Conservative myself.'[64]

In the years that followed, the provincial government consistently failed

TABLE 5

Reproduction of 1963 grant schedule for elementary schools in urban municipalities with populations of 110,000 or more

| Assessment per classroom | Recognized extraordinary expenditure per classroom | | | | | | | | | |
| | Under $500 | | $500–700 | | $700–900 | | $900–1100 | | $1100 or more | |
	% of recognized cost	Grant per pupil	% of recognized cost	Grant per pupil	% of recognized cost	Grant per pupil	% of recognized cost	Grant per pupil	% of recognized cost	Grant per pupil
$600,000 or more	34	$53	35	$54	36	$55	37	$56	38	$57
500,000–600,000	35	54	36	55	37	56	38	57	39	58
400,000–500,000	36	55	37	56	38	57	39	58	40	59
300,000–400,000	38	57	39	58	40	59	41	60	42	61
250,000–300,000	40	60	41	61	42	62	43	63	44	64
225,000–250,000	42	63	43	64	44	65	45	66	46	67
200,000–225,000	44	68	45	69	46	70	47	71	48	72
175,000–200,000	47	73	48	74	49	75	50	76	51	77
150,000–175,000	50	78	51	79	52	80	53	81	54	82
125,000–150,000	52	83	53	84	54	85	55	86	56	87
Under $125,000	54	87	55	88	56	89	57	90	58	91

SOURCE: O. Reg. 32/63, Part 1, section 10

or refused to redeem that promise. Even the more limited objective of supporting one-half the total cost of education, which the government generally argued had been the intent of the commitment, eluded the province's grasp, and as recently as 1967 – twenty-four years after the promise was made – the Conservative prime minister, John P. Robarts, was still forced to defend his government's position.[65]

The election promise of 1943 did usher in a new phase of provincial policy. This phase has been characterized by a growing concern for the burden imposed upon the owners and users of real property by the rapidly increasing cost of education, and by a vague notion or policy objective that some arbitrary proportion (such as the 50 per cent) of the total cost ought to be the responsibility of the provincial treasury. The two characteristics of this phase in policy are, of course, intimately related, but their realizations have often been sought in separate programmes.

The revised grant scheme of 1945[66] was designed to realize the promise of meeting 50 per cent of the cost of education from provincial funds. In this it came very close to success. Only one year later, however, the following statement appeared in the departmental circular containing the grant regulations:

> Boards of Trustees are reminded ... that the total of all General Legislative Grants to be paid in 1947 will be limited to the total paid by the Province for all such grants in 1946 ...
>
> This limitation of the 1947 grants will be effected in the following manner: The grant for each individual Board will be calculated in accordance with the Regulations, after which it will be reduced by a certain percentage. The amount of this percentage will be announced early in 1947 ...[67]

The government thus underlined that it would not remain committed to this arbitrary level of support.

A number of schemes were introduced in pursuit of the goal of property tax relief (or, more accurately, partial satisfaction of the demands of certain vocal groups of property owners). As a part of the election campaign of 1955 a special grant plan was announced: 'These payments were made out of treasury funds in response to particularly urgent submissions from school boards for additional revenue and will not be found in either the general or the special regulations.'[68] The grants amounted to $4 per pupil in 1955, and were raised to $6 in 1956. Then in 1957 the grant was raised to $11, $20, $25, and $30 per pupil in elementary, continuation, academic high, and vocational high schools respectively. They were discontinued in 1958 upon the introduction of a new and more generous grant plan.

Within little over a year the cry for tax relief was again being raised. This time the government responded with the Residential and Farm School Tax Assistance Grant, first paid in 1961.[69] Under this special scheme, the province paid a grant of $5 per pupil. In turn, the municipal councils were required to levy a dual tax rate, one rate applying to residential and farm property and the other to commercial and industrial property. The proceeds of the grant were then used to lower the former tax. The cleverness of this grant, as opposed to the 1955-7 special grants, lay in its visible effectiveness. A simple comparison of residential and commercial tax rates would indicate to a local resident the extent to which his taxes had actually been reduced. In 1962 the grant was augmented to $15 per elementary pupil but remained at $5 per secondary pupil. It was increased again in 1963, this time to $20 per elementary and continuation pupil, $30 per academic secondary pupil, and $40 per vocational secondary pupil.

When the grants were discontinued in 1964 – upon the introduction of the new general grant plan – the tax rate differential was continued. In raising the current revenues required by school boards, municipal councils were required to establish a 10 per cent differential between the tax rates applied to residential and farm assessment and to commercial and industrial assessment.[70]

There was an obvious pattern to these special tax-relief grants. In both cases the grants were designed as supplements to the regular grant plans, were increased in value, and were then eliminated in a general revision of the grant programme. Since the revision of 1964 is to be the subject of intensive analysis in Part II, we shall return at this point to an examination of the problems flowing from the local tax base.

The basic problems of the local tax base, its inadequacy and inequality, can be illustrated fairly simply. Elementary and secondary education entailed an expenditure of some $758 millions in 1965.[71] Had this amount been raised by a uniform levy on all taxable real property in the province, valued at approximately $41 billions if assessed at current value,[72] the necessary rate of taxation would have been 18.5 mills in the dollar or 1.85 per cent. To this would need to be added the tax rate required to support the programme of the general municipal governments[73] which, if uniform across the province, would be another 26.6 mills or 2.66 per cent. The total tax rate would thus have been 45.1 mills or 4.51 per cent on property assessed at full sale value.

Whether or not this is an excessive burden on the owners and users of real property is a question which ultimately depends on the attitudes and values of the political community. It should be noted, however, that the rate of 18.5 mills for education would be over three and one-half times the rate the province considered satisfactory to support an average elementary and secondary school programme under its foundation grant scheme in 1965.[74] Even with the provincial grants supporting a much lower rate, great pressure has been exerted on the province to reduce the 'burden' of property taxation. It seems reasonable to assume, therefore, that from a political, if not an economic, point of view, real property is inadequate as the sole tax base for the support of education.

If complete reliance on property taxation would be inadequate, it would be even more obviously inequitable. The tax rate of 18.5 mills on the dollar of assessment would have enabled each school district to provide the average level of educational service if each district had had the same amount of assessment supporting each pupil. Because real estate is very unequally distributed throughout the province, this situation simply did not prevail. In fact, the average elementary school expenditure could have been provided with a tax rate of only 0.58 mills in the district with the greatest fiscal capacity, but would have required a rate of 116.04 mills (two hundred times the former) in the district with the smallest capacity.[75]

The relative magnitude of the inequalities in the distribution of the property tax base is illustrated in Figures 2 and 3. The figures are based on 1964 data. That year was chosen so as not to reflect the impact of the 1965 consolidation of rural public school districts. At the same time, however, it necessitated the use of assessment data which was equalized to the equivalent of 1940 value rather than current value (the change to the latter base was not made until 1966). Use of a different assessment base does not change the relative distribution of assessments but does change the absolute value. The 1964 value was approximately 3.5 times the equalized value evidenced in these figures.

The inequalities shown here are somewhat reduced by the inclusion of 'allocated corporation assessment' in the tax bases of separate school boards.* The allocated assessment represented a means of providing separate school boards with the equivalent of tax revenue to which they were denied access as a result of the limitations placed on separate school supporters.† The boards could not actually tax this assessment, however. Thus, separate school boards appear to have a slightly greater taxing capacity than was actually the case. Even so, the distribution is rather startling.

From Figure 2 it can be seen that for elementary school boards the

* / The data was taken from that used in the grant calculation, in which allocated assessment is treated as assessment supporting the board.

† / For a detailed account of this provision, see below, pp. 119–22.

FIGURE 2
Distribution of elementary school boards in Ontario by equalized assessment per classroom, 1964

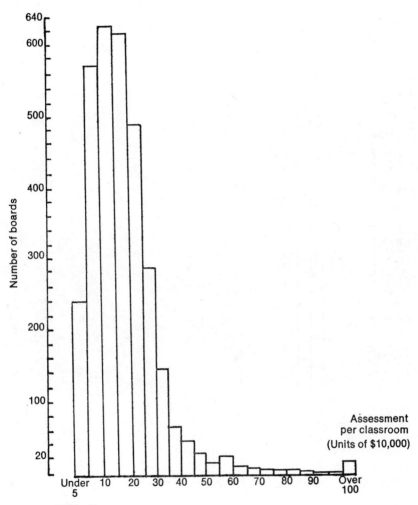

distribution is considerably skewed to the left. Of all the elementary boards in 1964, 7.5 per cent had tax bases of less than $50,000 per classroom, 25.2 per cent of less than $100,000, and 64.0 per cent of less than $200,000. In contrast, 0.5 per cent had tax bases of $1,000,000 or more. The secondary school boards exhibit a much more 'normal' distribution,

FIGURE 3
Distribution of secondary school boards in Ontario by equalized
assessment per classroom, 1964

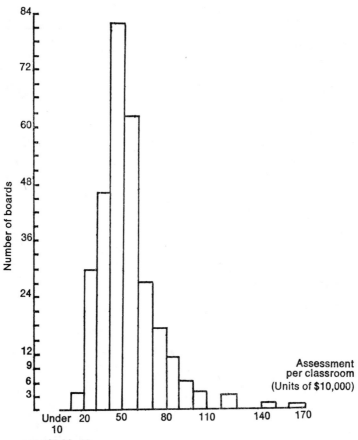

SOURCE: Table 42

although the ablest class had five times the relative taxing capacity of the
least able class.

One of the continuing problems of local taxation was the varying
standards by which property was assessed for taxation. As has been
indicated, the Department of Municipal Affairs did take a major step
toward resolving this problem in 1958 by establishing factors which would
equalize local assessments to a standard base. Both this provision and
the 1966 revision, which changed the base from 1940 to the current year,
contained two weaknesses. First, the equalizing factors were generated

on a municipal-wide basis and thus had no effect upon dissimilar assessment practices within municipalities. Second, the factor for each municipality was really an aggregate figure based on four types of real property: residential, farm, commercial, and industrial. Using only one factor created an inequity when, as was usually the case, the public and separate school boards were supported by quite different proportions of each category of assessment. Both of these weaknesses could have been overcome most effectively by actually reassessing individual properties in accordance with standard criteria. To accomplish that would have required a much greater provincial involvement in the assessment function, one of the oldest, and traditionally one of the most jealously guarded, local responsibilities.

Three developments have been responsible for an intensification of the problems of local fiscal resources since the Second World War. In the first place, the revenue required from property taxation by all local governments increased at an astonishing rate; an increase of 532 per cent between 1945 and 1963.

TABLE 6	
Revenue from property taxation in Ontario	
1945	$117,954,000
1963	745,895,000
SOURCE: Smith Report	

TABLE 7	
Revenue from property taxation for education in Ontario	
1945	$ 34,485,000
1963	341,611,000
SOURCE: Smith Report	

Secondly, the property tax revenue required for education increased even more rapidly than that for general municipal purposes. There was thus an increase of 891 per cent in property taxation for education. The effect of this disproportionate increase was that education consumed a substantially greater proportion of the total property tax. This is indicated in Table 8 and, graphically, in Figure 4. The third factor was a much more rapid increase in the revenue derived from property taxation than in the tax base of assessed property.

The rather obvious consequence of this third factor was a constantly increasing rate of taxation. One cannot estimate the real increase in tax rates from the above figures since only locally established, and therefore unequalized, assessment data have been used (equalized figures have been available only since 1958). Nevertheless, the relative magnitude of the increase is quite apparent.

One important product of the postwar pressure on the property tax has been an increased reliance on deferred taxation – that is, borrowing.

TABLE 8	
Proportion of total property taxation devoted to education in Ontario	
1945	29.2 per cent
1963	45.8 per cent

TABLE 9	
Increases in property assessment and property tax revenue in Ontario, 1945–63	
Property assessment	3.63x
Property tax revenue	6.32x
Property tax revenue for education	9.91x

SOURCE: *Annual Report of Municipal Statistics*

FIGURE 4
Proportion of total property taxation devoted to education in Ontario, 1945–63

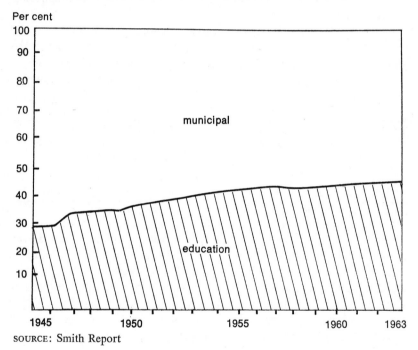

SOURCE: Smith Report

Under conditions of extreme need, such as the depression of the 1930s, municipalities have been permitted to borrow on a long-term basis (more than one year) for current operating expenses. Normally, however, and the Ontario Municipal Board is insistent, borrowing may be undertaken only for the purchase of a capital asset.* Since such assets have a

* / Separate school boards, not borrowing through the municipalities and not necessarily subject to the Ontario Municipal Board, are free from this restraint. It

long-term life and are therefore purchased irregularly, revenue raised through borrowing has obvious benefits and can be justified easily on the grounds of stabilizing the annual tax rates or of requiring those who will benefit from the asset in the future to contribute towards its cost.

Large-scale capital borrowing, however, imposes a prior claim on tax revenues for the full term of the indebtedness. As each new debt is incurred, the annual rate of taxation necessary to raise the current revenues of the local government is increased for the subsequent twenty to thirty years, depending on the term of the debt.

Municipal debt has increased markedly since the war. The total debt, excluding that for self-sustaining enterprises and for separate schools (which is not a municipal liability and for which accurate data are not available) is shown in Table 10. The debt thus increased 8.7 times. As was the case with current tax revenue, the proportion of the total debt incurred for schools increased substantially (again, separate school debt is excluded here).

TABLE 10
Gross municipal debt outstanding in Ontario

| 1945 | $ 166,996,000 |
| 1963 | 1,457,813,000 |

SOURCE: *Annual Report of Municipal Statistics*

The above proportion had actually reached 46.6 per cent in 1957, declining very gradually thereafter as the general municipal debt increased at a slightly faster rate.

The essential pattern of problems of local fiscal resources may be summarized as follows. The tax base developed through an evolutionary historical process from a comprehensive measure of income and wealth (and consumption as well if the purchase of shelter is considered as such) to a limited measure of the ownership and use of real property, supplemented by an arbitrary measure of the value of business conducted on or in real property. This tax base, being distributed very unevenly throughout the province, produced an inequitable tax-rate structure. Furthermore, the taxation of property was called upon to provide an amount of revenue which increased considerably more rapidly than the tax base. Taxation for educational purposes increased more rapidly than taxation for other local functions. The result was both a persistent and

---

is not altogether uncommon for separate school boards to sell debentures in order to raise revenue for some abnormal current requirement.

TABLE 11
Proportion of municipal debt incurred for
schools in Ontario

| 1945 | 25.8 per cent |
| 1963 | 43.2 per cent |

SOURCE: *Annual Report of Municipal Statistics*

general increase in the rates of taxation and an increase in reliance on borrowing. All of this led to increased provincial involvement in the financing of education and to a growing conviction that even that involvement was insufficient.

4

The special fiscal problem
of separate schools

Roman Catholic separate schools have shared the problems discussed in the two preceding chapters. There is, however, one problem which warrants special treatment: the disparity in the taxable capacities of the public and separate systems. While this disparity is related to the local tax base, it arises from the historically inherited and constitutionally sanctioned principles of separate school government.

Not all separate schools have fewer resources than all public schools; separate schools in prosperous areas of the province often have greater resources than public schools in depressed or undeveloped areas. Similarly, a number of socio-economic factors may result in a smaller relative tax base for separate schools. The basic problem remains, however, that in virtually every local community with a dual elementary system, the separate school has had a significantly smaller fiscal capacity than the public school. This situation has created a problem for provincial policy for two reasons: first, because it generated pressure from separate school supporters for provincial action to rectify the situation and, second, because separate schools are 'public' schools in the normal usage of that word and their relative incapacity has stood as an indictment of the provincial government's failure to fulfil its promise of equalizing educational opportunities. The fact that separate and public schools often exist side by side in a local community has served to highlight the inequality of fiscal resources.

In its impact upon provincial politics, this problem may be analysed in terms of two aspects which, though they contribute to the same end result, are distinct in origin and impact and whose resolution is normally conceived to lie in separate policy responses.

The first aspect of this problem arose basically from two factors: the imposition of the three-mile radial separate school zone in rural areas, and the placing of the choice of supporting a separate school upon the individual Catholic property owner or tenant. The first factor, by which only Roman Catholics residing within three miles of the school site (or a designated point after 1963) could opt to direct their property assessment to the support of the separate school, obviously resulted in a situation in which many Catholics were prevented from supporting such a school (even should their property have extended to within an inch of the three-mile boundary of the zone). The legislative amendment of 1963 and considerable ingenuity on the part of separate school supporters made it possible to create 'dummy' zones* which, when merged into combined zones, might contain the bulk of the potential support at a given time. Property ownership and tenancy are fluid factors, however, and an organization which at one time contained most of the Catholic separate school supporters in an area could shortly find itself in dire financial straits should a number of parcels of property pass into the hands of Protestants or non-separate-school supporting Catholics.

At this point one is perhaps justified in asking whether the solution to this problem does not lie simply in expecting separate school supporters to carry a somewhat higher burden of taxation. Certainly this has been the traditional attitude among non-Catholic taxpayers and educators in Ontario, as this statement from the Orange Association of Ontario in 1963 typifies:

It is argued that separate schools are financially embarrassed. In the common parlance, the answer should be 'so what?' *If supporters of separate schools are unable to operate and properly maintain religious schools of their choice by the revenue that is legally theirs, why should it be expected that those who are not supporters of separate schools should bail them out?* [italics theirs][1]

It is here, however, that the second factor becomes relevant, namely, that each Catholic property owner or tenant must choose to support the separate school. Separate school boards are unique in that the service they provide is subject to the price mechanism of the market. A non-Catholic has no choice but to pay, through taxation, the price of public elementary education, even though the price might be lower in a non-public institution. A Catholic, however, has this choice. Whenever the tax rate for separate schools (the price of this service) is greater than that for public schools, the economic interest of Catholics lies in supporting

* / See above, pp. 30–1

the public system. This is not meant to suggest that some Catholics will not be willing to pay this higher price, believing that it is purchasing a service of superior quality. Many Catholics, however, have only a secondary interest in the relative qualities of the two systems. Experience tends to suggest that the optimum price (tax rate) of separate school education is one that does not depart significantly from that established for the public schools.[2] Separate school revenue is maximized then, when the tax rate is equal to the public school rate, or virtually so. But because of its smaller tax base, this rate produces less revenue per pupil than it does in the public school system in the same community.* The result is a chronic relative revenue deficiency for the separate schools.

The second aspect of the problem also arises directly from the principle of granting to individuals the choice of supporting either the public or separate school system. The problem may be stated most simply as follows. How are public corporations, whose ownership is not tightly held and controlled, and public utilities, whose ownership is vested in the crown or a subordinate level of government, to be encompassed by this principle? The answer is, of course, that in most cases they are not encompassed. As a result, separate schools are denied access to a lucrative source of tax revenues and public schools gain whatever revenue is not allotted to the separate schools.

The historical factors contributing to the first aspect of the special problem of separate schools have already been outlined in the two preceding chapters. Further treatment here would simply be repetitive. Suffice it to say that both the three-mile limit and the right of tax-payer choice in the allocation of support were measures designed to appease the Roman Catholic interests in ways that would not challenge the effectiveness of the non-sectarian public school system. In the first case the Catholics demanded freedom to define the jurisdictions of their own schools and were given jurisdiction over three-mile radial zones. In the second case the demand was for the exclusive right of separate school boards to tax Roman Catholics and the response was permission to tax declared supporters of separate schools. Both issues were settled in the Scott Act of 1863.[3]

The historical background of the second aspect of the problem requires further amplification, however. The question of taxing property held in the name of corporate entities had not arisen as a political issue before

* / This situation is somewhat analogous to the hypothetical use of a municipal retail sales tax. A higher rate of taxation in one municipality could result in reduced revenue if it induced residents to shop outside that municipality.

Confederation and no reference was made to it in the early legislation. By the Act of 1863 only individual property owners had the option of directing their property taxes to the support of separate schools.

In 1886[4] legislative amendments were passed which, it was believed, were of a nature to remove two newly emerged inequities in the financial position of separate schools. Tenants were given the right to direct the tax on the property they used to the support of separate schools. Furthermore, public corporations were permitted to direct a municipality to tax their property as separate school supporters. The corporate property, however, had to be divided between the public and separate schools in the same proportions as Catholic and non-Catholic owners or shareholders. This last provision produced little revenue for separate schools because, in effect, only tightly held corporations were able to determine the precise ratio of Catholics to other owners or shareholders.

In 1913[5] the provisions were liberalized, requiring only that the proportion of property allocated to the support of separate schools must not be greater than the proportion of Catholic owners or shareholders. This change meant that a corporation no longer needed to know the precise ratio of Catholics to total shareholders. If it knew definitely that at least a certain proportion (say 10 per cent) of the shares were owned by Catholics, then it could allocate this same proportion of its property to the support of separate schools. While this amendment did enable corporate entities which were desirous of supporting separate schools to do so, it did nothing either to compel such support or to extend the provisions to cover public utilities.

When the financial situation of separate schools became acute, if not desperate, in the depression of the 1930s, it is not surprising that the issue of unequal access to corporate property taxation should have been seized upon as the major issue of separate school political action. The argument of separate school supporters was based on the contention that since most, if not all, of the property taxes levied against business enterprises and public utilities were shifted in the form of higher prices or lower wages, and not lower profits, revenue from these taxes should be apportioned to the two school systems on the basis of school enrolment and not capital ownership. The reference to the Quebec 'panel system' of taxation,[6] though seldom made explicit, was never far from the minds of the advocates of this reform.

The campaign for tax reform was undertaken by a newly formed pressure group, the Catholic Taxpayers' Association, supported by the bishops and led by a layman, Martin J. Quinn. In January of 1933 the association presented its brief to the Conservative government of George S. Henry.

Henry effectively rejected the brief, announcing his intention to refer the whole matter to the courts through a series of legal questions. The association thereupon threw its efforts behind the electoral campaign of the Liberal leader, Mitchell F. Hepburn. When Hepburn won a sweeping victory in the election of 1934, the tax reform leaders expected their support to be rewarded by prompt action. Hepburn's reaction was not immediate. Conscious of the opposition of many Protestant leaders and groups, and especially of the Loyal Orange Lodge, he shelved the issue for nearly two years. In the interim, he announced the establishment of a committee of enquiry into the costs of education, to be chaired by the deputy minister of education, Duncan MacArthur.

When Hepburn did act, he did so with surprising haste. On 3 April 1936, five days before the end of the legislative session, he introduced his amendment to the Assessment Act. The Hepburn bill did not embody the principle advocated by the Catholic Taxpayers' Association. It divided corporations into two categories: those which were able to determine the proportion of Catholic shareholders, and those which were not. In corporations of the first type, shareholders were to notify the directors of their wish to have their shares designated for the support of separate schools. Having determined the proportion of shares held by separate school supporters, the directors of the corporation were then required, no longer just permitted, to ensure that the same proportion of the corporation's property be taxed for the support of separate schools. A corporation which notified the municipality that it was unable to determine the ratio of separate school supporting shareholders was placed in the second category. The property assessment was to be divided in the same ratio as the value of individually owned property of public and separate school supporters in the municipality. Again, no mention was made of public utilities.

The debate on the measure was lively, to say the least. Every move of the Catholic Taxpayers' Association was countered by the Loyal Orange Lodge and other Protestant protective associations. The immediate outcome is summed up by Walker:

Voting took place just before dawn on April 9th. Sixty-five of the 71 Liberals voted for the bill, while three Liberals joined 17 Conservatives to vote against it, and three Liberals and one member of the C.C.F. party were absent. Immediately the prominent Conservative W.H. Price pledged himself to the repeal of the legislation 'at the earliest opportunity.'[7]

Not only did the Act[8] elicit the concerted opposition of many Protestant leaders, but its hasty construction rendered it quite unworkable. One source cites the necessity of the Toronto Separate School Board planning some four thousand appeals against corporations apparently not abiding by the intent of the law.[9] The Assessment Act amendment had a short life, being repealed on 24 March 1937 by a vote of eighty to nothing.[10] The position of business corporations vis-à-vis separate school support thus reverted to that established in 1913, a position which has not been changed to this day.

The repeal of the Assessment Act amendment was followed in 1941 by the famous decision of the Privy Council in the Ford Motor case.[11] The Ford Motor Company had, in 1937, directed that 18 per cent of its taxable property assessment be taxed for the support of the Windsor Separate School Board. The Windsor Board of Education successfully appealed this action before the Windsor court of revision. This decision was thence appealed to the county court of Essex, wherein the appeal was dismissed. Appealed once more to the Court of Appeal of Ontario, the decision was unanimous in favour of the Ford Company's action. This decision was upheld by a majority of the Supreme Court of Canada. Finally, the case was allowed to cross the Atlantic to be heard by the Judicial Committee of the Privy Council, which granted the appeal, thus striking down the decisions of the two highest courts in Canada.

The grounds upon which the Privy Council ruled against Ford were, essentially, that since the legislation required that the allocation of support to separate schools be not greater than the proportion of Roman Catholic shareholders, the onus was on the company to establish that at least 18 per cent of its outstanding shares were held by Roman Catholics. The company had argued that this was an impossible responsibility; there were some 20,000 different shareholders in 34 countries, holding 1,658,960 shares of common stock, 665,874 of which shares had been transferred in 1937 alone.[12] No matter, countered the Privy Council, the law was clear: the company could direct to the support of separate schools only a proportion of its shares which could be shown, with reasonable certainty, to be held by Roman Catholics.

The decision went even further, however. The Privy Council held that no court could assume the responsibility of altering the allocation of support. This meant that should a company allocate, say, 10 per cent of its assessment to separate school support, and should it be able to establish, when challenged, that only 9.9 per cent of its shares were held by Catholics, then the whole of that company's property would be taxed for the support of public schools. Not until the following year could the company direct any support to the separate schools.

Traditionally in Ontario, the relatively smaller fiscal capacities of separate schools have been counter-balanced by relatively smaller fiscal needs. Outlining the constraints on complete fiscal equalization by the province, Maxwell Cameron described the situation in 1936 as follows:

The general rule ... is for separate schools to have about half as large an assessment per teacher or per pupil as the public schools, and to spend about half as much.

... it must be recognized that to a large extent expenditures in these [separate] schools are low because of the small salaries paid for teachers who are members of religious orders ...[13]

But while that situation still prevailed in 1936, the reliance on religious teachers declined rapidly after the war. Table 6 shows the dramatic decline in the proportion of religious teachers between 1949 and 1965. By 1965 the proportion had fallen to just over 15 per cent.* Between 1963 and 1965 both the proportion and the absolute number of these teachers declined.

TABLE 12
Number and proportion of separate school teachers
members of religious orders: selected years, 1949–65

Year	Total no of teachers	No of religious teachers	Per cent of religious teachers
1949	3760	1728	46.0
1956	6350	2003	31.6
1963	11,278	2147	19.0
1965	13,532	2085	15.4

SOURCE: Ontario, *Schools and Teachers in the Province of Ontario*, 1949–50, 1956–7, 1963–4, and 1965–6

As a result, the separate school system entered the contemporary period with a fiscal capacity much smaller than the public system but with a fiscal need very nearly equal to that of the public system.

The lower relative tax base of the separate school system can be shown simply and clearly. Table 13 sets out the numbers and proportions of both public and separate school boards in classes of equalized assessment per classroom. Figure 4 illustrates graphically the nature of the imbalance in fiscal capacity.† As in Chapter 3, the assessments shown here contain

* / The proportion was as low as 8.7 per cent in Metropolitan Toronto.

† / As in the preceding chapter, assessments for 1964 are equalized on the basis of full value as of 1940.

TABLE 13

Distribution of public and separate elementary school
boards in Ontario by number and proportion of boards
in classes of equalized assessment per classroom, 1964

Assessment	Public		Separate	
	No	Per cent	No	Per cent
Under 50,000	79	3.2	162	21.0
50,000–99,999	280	11.5	289	37.4
100,000–149,999	460	18.9	168	21.7
150,000–199,999	534	21.9	81	10.5
200,000–249,999	459	18.8	28	3.6
250,000–299,999	265	10.9	21	2.7
300,000–349,999	137	5.6	12	1.6
350,000–399,999	65	2.7	4	.5
400,000–449,999	47	1.9	1	.1
450,000–499,999	25	1.0	4	.5
Over 499,999	86	3.5	3	.4

SOURCE: Table 41

TABLE 14

Comparison of gross revenue per pupil for public and
separate school boards in selected municipalities, 1965

Municipality	Per-pupil revenue for public schools	Per-pupil revenue for separate schools	Excess of public school revenue over separate school revenue
Brantford	$314.00	$278.25	$ 35.75
Burlington	389.40	301.43	87.97
Cornwall	463.59	316.62	146.97
Hamilton	398.56	284.08	114.48
London	397.94	317.97	79.97
Niagara Falls	394.91	331.58	63.33
Ottawa	488.63	305.36	183.27
Port Arthur	356.96	297.32	59.64
St Catharines	363.12	329.01	34.11
Sarnia	359.12	285.62	73.50
Sault Ste Marie	395.94	313.01	82.93
Sudbury	430.83	328.58	102.25
Toronto	546.39	350.03	196.36

SOURCE: Ontario Separate School Trustees' Association and
L'Association des Commissions des Ecoles Bilingues
d'Ontario, *Brief Presented to the Prime Minister and
the Minister of Education of the Province of Ontario*
(October 1966), p. 12. (Corrections were
made to overcome a slight error in calculation.)

FIGURE 5
Distribution of public and separate elementary school boards in Ontario by
proportion of boards in classes of equalized assessment per classroom, 1964

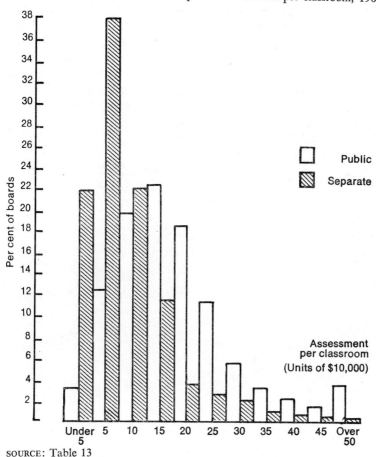

SOURCE: Table 13

the portion allocated under the terms of the corporation tax adjustment
grant. The *taxable* assessment supporting separate schools is thus even
less than is shown here. However, the nature of the discrepancy in fiscal
capacities is quite clear.

Of all the public school boards in the province in 1964, 55.5 per cent
had equalized assessments per classroom of less than $200,000. Of all
the separate school boards in the same year, 90.6 per cent had assessments below that level. Similarly, the proportion of public school boards

with assessments per classroom of $400,000 or more was over six times that in the separate schools.

Even though provincial policy attempted to equalize local fiscal resources from as early as 1907, the disparities between public and separate schools persisted. Table 14 illustrates the net result of these disparities, comparing the per-pupil revenues from local taxes and provincial grants of thirteen pairs of urban public and separate school boards in 1965. In every case the tax rates of the two systems were identical or virtually so; the resulting revenue differential thus reflects the lower taxing capacity of the separate school systems and the failure of provincial grants to compensate fully for this.

5
Problems of enrolment

The postwar increase in total enrolment in Ontario's elementary and secondary schools has been dramatic to say the least. Figures shown in Table 15 represent an overall increase of 140 per cent.

TABLE 15
Total enrolment in elementary and secondary
chools in Ontario, 1945/6 and 1963

1945/6	666,284
1963	1,597,374

SOURCE: Minister's Report (given for school years until 1953–4 and for calendar years thereafter)

An increase in enrolment is essentially an increase in the demand for educational services. An increase in demand may elicit either or both of only two responses. The price may be increased, thus rationing the available supply, or the supply may be increased, thus satisfying the demand. An earlier chapter,* however, has outlined the evolution of government policy which, by placing full reliance on taxation for the support of education, rendered the price inelastic. Schools had to be accessible to all (with limitations applied only on the bases of age, ability, and desire), not just to those who could afford to pay the price.†

Without an elastic price, then, the supply of educational services had to be increased to satisfy this increased demand. The supply of accom-

* / See above, pp. 34–5
† / The contrast between this situation and that which to a considerable extent still characterizes most phases of post-secondary education is fairly obvious. In the latter case the price of admission is still used to ration the available supply of facilities and personnel.

modation, personnel, equipment, instructional aids and supplies, and all the other components of an educational programme had all to be increased in proportion to the increased enrolment. These items cannot be provided immediately. A school building must be designed, approved, financed, and constructed. Teachers must not only be trained but must be induced to enter the profession in the first place (since greater numbers of teachers are required, the traditional channels of recruitment would invariably prove to be inadequate). Increasing the supply of educational services thus generated an increased demand for the components of such services, and here the price is not inelastic. The problems arising from that situation are to be discussed in the following chapter, however.

It is true that to a considerable extent enrolment increases can be anticipated. An increased birth-rate in one year is bound to produce an increased school enrolment five or six years hence. But even if future enrolments were known with reasonable certainty, which is very seldom the case (a 1945 Department of Education projection of elementary enrolment was some 100,000 pupils under the actual figure in 1952),[1] a government would have some difficulty accounting for a policy of increasing the supply of teachers for whom there were no immediate positions, or constructing school buildings which were to stand empty for some time. The problems arising from an increasing enrolment could not, therefore, be avoided completely by early action.

The problems generated by rapidly increasing enrolment were not experienced uniformly throughout the province-wide educational system. In fact, enrolment increased much faster in some areas than in others. When the more rapid increases occurred in areas of the system already experiencing organizational or fiscal problems, the pressure of enrolment simply compounded those problems. The remainder of this chapter will attempt to reveal those areas of the school system in which the enrolment increased most rapidly.

There were four characteristics of the overall rise in enrolment which concentrated the problems in particular areas. These may be summarized as the relative shift from public to separate elementary schools, the population shift to urban and urbanizing areas, the increased holding-power of secondary schools, and the relative shift from academic to vocational secondary school programmes. We shall deal with each of these in turn.

Without doubt, one of the most important changes to have occurred in the public educational system of Ontario since World War II was the emergence of the Roman Catholic separate schools into a position of

FIGURE 6
Comparison of indexes of enrolment in public and separate elementary schools
of Ontario, 1945/6–63 (Index: 1945/6 = 100.0)

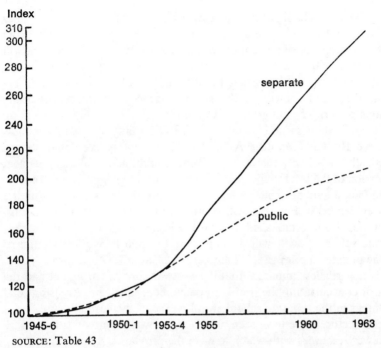

SOURCE: Table 43

educational and political maturity. Mention was made earlier* of the
declining reliance on religious teachers in these schools. We shall subsequently examine the extent to which a shift in provincial policy succeeded
in reducing to a large extent the fiscal disparity traditionally suffered by
separate schools.

During the 1950s and early 1960s, however, the separate schools were
caught in the midst of mounting pressures. Lacking the fiscal strength of
even the public elementary schools and without an adequate supply of
low-salaried religious teachers, they yet bore the brunt of the enrolment
increase at the elementary level. Figure 6 shows the comparative rates of
growth of the public and separate systems from 1945/6 to 1963. The two
systems increased at an almost uniform rate from 1945/6 to 1952/3.
Thereafter, however, the separate school enrolment increased at a faster
and steady rate while the public school enrolment increased at a slower

* / See above, p. 63

and declining rate. The impact of this may be gauged from the fact that the proportion of all elementary school pupils in separate schools increased from 20.0 per cent in 1952/3 to 26.9 per cent in 1963.

The separate school enrolment growth must be considered in its proper context. The data in Figure 6 should not be interpreted as indicating the eventual emergence of a situation in which separate school enrolment will surpass that of the public schools. Enrolment in separate schools is not only discretionary but is restricted to Roman Catholics. To a considerable extent, the rapid growth in the separate school system reflected the religious pattern of immigration to the province (with a high proportion of Roman Catholics) and also the greater availability of separate schools to native Roman Catholics. Although this cannot yet be demonstrated statistically, it is likely that separate school enrolment will increase as a proportion of the total to the point at which virtually all potential students are, in fact, attending separate schools. It is not likely, therefore, that the trend evidenced in Figure 6 will continue unabated. Once a new equilibrium has been established between enrolment in the two systems, separate school growth will depend entirely upon immigration patterns and the maintenance of support amongst the Catholic community.

It is nevertheless apparent that the postwar shift in enrolment had the effect of concentrating the problems encumbent upon an increasing total enrolment in the separate school sector of the elementary system. And it was this sector, as we have seen, which had a weaker organizational base and fewer resources with which to meet the problems.

That the population of Canada generally and Ontario particularly is becoming ever more urban is a well known phenomenon.* Such a shift has a direct and obvious effect upon school enrolment, concentrating the overall growth in the urban and suburban areas of the province.

There are difficulties in illustrating the precise effect of this trend toward urban living. It is simply not possible to obtain enrolment figures for meaningful geographic entities which can be held constant over a significant period of time. Elementary and secondary school jurisdictions seldom coincided, municipal annexations and amalgamations upset the sample of areas, and as a *coup de grace*, the available data on enrolment are categorized by criteria which vary over the years. We can, however, provide some indication of where the greatest stress has fallen. Figures 7 and 8 show the relative rates of increase in enrolment in public and separate

---

* / In 1871 Ontario's population was 22 per cent urban. By 1931 this proportion had reached 61 per cent and by 1961 it stood at 77 per cent.

FIGURE 7
Indexes of enrolment in public elementary schools of Ontario by the type of
municipality, 1955–63 (Index: 1955 = 100.0)

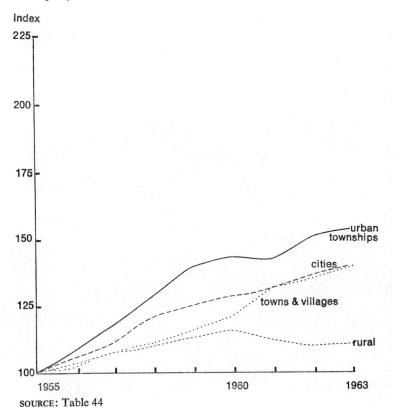

SOURCE: Table 44

schools categorized by the status* of the municipality in which the school
is located. These categories have been used consistently since 1955 and
therefore the comparison can begin only with that year.

The previously noted stress in the separate school system as compared
with the public school system is again apparent here. What is especially
significant, however, is the evident concentration of enrolment increases
in what are termed 'urban townships' and what might be better under-
stood as suburban areas.† This is true in both the public and separate

* / Municipal status designates the corporation as a city, town, village, or township. Changes within the categories prevent placing too much confidence in these
data and they should therefore be interpreted with caution.

† / 'Urban Township' is defined by the Department of Municipal Affairs as a
township contiguous to a large city.

FIGURE 8
Indexes of enrolment in separate elementary schools of Ontario by the type of
municipality, 1955–63 (Index: 1955 = 100.0)

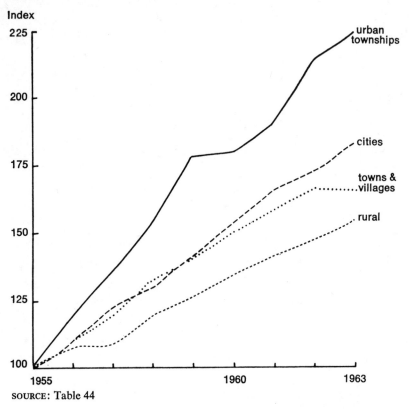

SOURCE: Table 44

systems but especially in the latter. Over the eight-year period there was
an increase of only 10.6 per cent in the enrolment in rural public schools,
compared with one of 53.2 per cent in suburban public schools. This,
however, compares with an increase of 122.9 per cent in the suburban
separate schools.

Thus, not only was the overall increase in enrolment concentrated in
the separate, as compared with the public, schools, but was even further
concentrated in the suburban municipalities of the province. The latter
characteristic can be assumed to have applied also to the secondary
schools, although the nature of secondary school jurisdictional boundaries makes illustration virtually impossible.

Enrolment increased faster in the secondary than in the elementary schools. Not only were increased elementary enrolments passed on to the secondary schools (and students from both public and separate elementary schools virtually all proceed to the public secondary schools), but an increasing proportion of all elementary pupils proceeded to secondary school and stayed longer. This was a product both of the market conditions of an increasingly technological economy, which places a premium on those workers with relatively advanced education or training, and of explicit government policies designed to augment the market effect.

Table 16 shows the rather marked increase in the proportion of the population between the ages of 15 and 19 attending secondary schools. Between 1945 and 1963 this proportion more than doubled from 35.1 to 73.5 per cent.

TABLE 16
Ontario population aged 15 to 19 and secondary
school enrolment, selected years, 1945–63

Year	Population aged 15–19	Secondary school enrolment	Enrolment as per cent of population
1945*	329,800	115,900	35.1
1950*	320,100	130,500	40.8
1955	341,400	174,600	51.1
1960	420,200	262,800	62.5
1963	495,700	364,200	73.5

*/Calendar-year enrolments estimated from school-year data.
SOURCE: Dominion Bureau of Statistics and Minister's Reports

This factor was, of course, contained in the figures of total enrolment shown in Table 15. The significance of isolating it lies in the fact that it points to the greater stress placed on the supply of secondary school facilities and all that that entails. Almost every component of a secondary school programme is more costly per unit of enrolment than is the case in an elementary school. The relatively more rapid increase in secondary enrolment, therefore, intensified the problems and concentrated them where the enrolment increased most rapidly – in the suburban areas.

One final characteristic of the pattern of postwar enrolment can be identified as leading to intensified problems in particular areas. This is the tremendous shift in secondary enrolment from the academic to the vocational streams or programmes. Figure 9, showing the relative rates of growth in the two streams, provides rather conclusive evidence of the

74

FIGURE 9
Comparison of indexes of enrolment in academic and vocational programmes
in Ontario secondary schools, 1945/6–63 (Index: 1945/6 = 100.0)

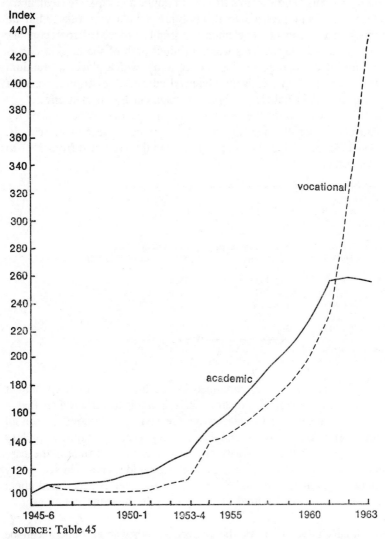

SOURCE: Table 45

extent of the shift. From 1946/7 to 1961 enrolment in the academic
stream increased more rapidly than in the vocational stream. In 1962 and
1963, however, the vocational enrolment almost literally sky-rocketted
while the academic enrolment remained constant and then even declined.

There are two rather obvious factors which can explain this sudden shift, both of which were part of a provincial policy response and will be referred to in some detail later. The first was Ontario's acceptance of the Federal-Provincial Technical and Vocational Training Agreement. The second was the introduction of the so-called 'Robarts Plan.'*

The major effect of this enrolment shift was again fairly obvious. Placing relatively greater emphasis on vocational programmes automatically increased the unit cost of secondary education, for these programmes are inherently more expensive to operate. The effect, then, was to channel the normal increment of enrolment each year into the more expensive of the two basic secondary programmes. This necessarily led to the placing of even greater demands on those areas which were experiencing the greatest annual enrolment increases.

We have seen that the enrolment in Ontario's schools increased consistently and rapidly after the Second World War. We have suggested the kinds of problems such an increase created for the governments of education, both local and provincial, in Ontario. More than this, however, we have seen that the increased enrolment was not spread evenly throughout the school system. Specifically, it was concentrated in the separate schools as compared with the public schools, in the secondary schools as compared with the elementary schools, since 1962 in the vocational branches of secondary schools as compared with the academic branches, and finally, in the suburban municipalities as compared with other, and especially rural, municipalities.

This increase in enrolment, an increase in demand for educational services, aggravated many of the problems in the supply of such services. Specifically, it strained the capacity of small units of government to organize and administer these services, and it strained the capacity of the local fiscal base to support the resultant expenditures. The strain was greatest where the increased demand was concentrated in areas with the least adequate political organizations and fiscal resources. After examining the postwar patterns of expenditure on education, we shall return to a consideration of the interrelations between all of these factors.

*/John Robarts, former prime minister of Ontario, was minister of education when the new programme was introduced.

6

Problems of expenditure

In Chapter 5 the increasing enrolment in Ontario's schools was discussed in terms of a growing demand for educational services. It was
suggested then that this rising demand for education in turn created a
rising demand for the components of the educational service package,
and that the elastic price structure of these components increased the unit
cost of education. This chapter will pursue the problems associated with
that, and related, factors.

Expenditures on elementary and secondary education increased considerably in the postwar period, specifically, 9.4 times between 1945 and
1963.

TABLE 17

Total expenditures on elementary and secondary
education in Ontario

1945	$ 62,154,000
1963	583,161,000

SOURCE: Minister's Report

Increasing the expenditure on a public service does not necessarily create
problems for the political system. The consequences of such an increase
may give rise to serious problems, however. Insofar as the expenditure
increases outstrip public resources, decisions are required affecting the
allocation of resources between the public and private sectors. Insofar as
the increases strain the legislative and administrative capacity of the
governments concerned, changes in governmental organization may be
required. Insofar as the subject of the increased expenditures affects other
public and private activities, consequent increases in expenditure may be

required in those areas as well, thus multiplying any resultant problems. Finally, the problems arising from increases in expenditure will be a function of the level of government which bears the responsibility for the particular service in question. Thus, in order to analyse the nature of such problems it is necessary to be more precise about the extent of the increasing expenditures, to appreciate their causes, and to determine their relationship to specific governmental units.

Before proceeding, however, one further preliminary remark should be made. The terms 'cost' and 'expenditure' will be used throughout this chapter, and a definitional distinction may be useful at the outset. 'Cost' will be used to denote the money price of a given good or service or of a package of goods or services. Thus, an increase in cost will indicate a rise in the price of the same, or comparable, good or service. 'Expenditure,' however, denotes the amount of money paid out by a spending agency in the provision of programmes or services. The terms 'unit cost' or 'unit expenditure' simply denote a cost or expenditure expressed in dollars per standard unit – dollars per pupil, per classroom, or per capita. Expenditure and cost are related, but not in any necessary way. An increase in costs does not necessarily result in an increase in expenditure, for lower cost goods and services may be substituted. Similarly, an increase in expenditure is not necessarily the result of increased costs, for the quality or quantity of goods and services may have been increased.

The following four sections will examine the postwar expenditure patterns in education in relation to the patterns of overall government expenditures, the resources of the province, the level and type of spending unit, and the goods and services provided. Following that, an attempt will be made to explore the causes and implications of these patterns. In most cases, data will reflect the situation up to the year 1963. This was done so as to present the problems as they existed when the major provincial response – the foundation tax plan – was implemented.

Pattern of overall expenditures
In Chapter 3 the fact was illustrated that property taxation for education had increased much more rapidly than for general municipal purposes. This is emphatically true for the expenditure side as well. Table 18 shows the total expenditures of the provincial and local governments and their expenditures for education.[1] The significance of these figures is indicated more clearly in Figure 10. Here, the percentage of total expenditure devoted to education is given for the local and provincial levels as well as for the two combined. Three points seem warranted with respect to this graph.

First, there has been a gradual, but persistent, increase in the propor-

TABLE 18
Total and educational expenditures of provincial
and local governments in Ontario

Year	Total (millions)	Education (millions)
1945	$ 256.6	$ 60.2
1963	2,293.0	728.9

SOURCES: Smith Report and *Public Accounts of Ontario*

FIGURE 10
Percentage of total, provincial, and local government expenditures devoted to education in Ontario, 1945–63

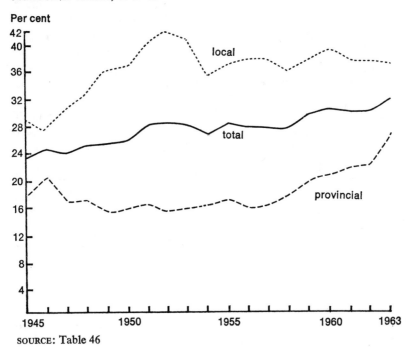

SOURCE: Table 46

tions of government expenditures devoted to education. For the two levels of government combined, this proportion rose from 23.5 per cent in 1945 to 34.8 per cent in 1963. This represented a rather major shift in the pattern of government spending in a period of less than twenty years.

Second, until 1958 the overall shift in spending priority in favour of education was wholly made up of a shift at the local level. Between 1945 and 1957 the proportion of local expenditures devoted to education increased from 28.4 per cent to 37.5 per cent (it reached 41.8 per cent in 1952). Over the same period, the provincial proportion fell from 17.8 per cent to 16.0 per cent (the highest proportion was just 21.0 reached in 1946). From the low point of 1957, however, the provincial proportion climbed rapidly, reaching 26.8 per cent in 1963.

Third, there is a clear relationship between the proportions of total expenditures devoted to education at the two levels. Between 1946 and 1952, for example, the local proportion climbed steadily, while the provincial proportion declined. This pattern was reversed and repeated several times so that both proportions took on a cyclical pattern with an overall upward movement. It can be seen quite clearly that the local proportion remained relatively constant after 1954, but this entailed the major shift in provincial priorities already noted.

Expenditures and resources
Expenditures on education have increased much more rapidly than the resources of the province. The rate of increase was nearly triple that of the selected measures of resources illustrated in Table 19.

TABLE 19
Increases in educational expenditures and provincial
resources in Ontario, 1945–63

Educational expenditures	9.4x
Provincial population	1.7x
Personal income	3.6x
Provincial domestic product	3.6x
Local property assessment	3.6x

SOURCES: Minister's Reports, *Annual Report of Municipal Statistics*, DBS *National Accounts*, Smith Report

The obvious effect of this rapid increase was the allocation of an increasing *proportion* of resources to education. This is demonstrated clearly in Table 20 in relation to personal income.

TABLE 20
Educational expenditures as a proportion of
personal income in Ontario

1945	1.7 per cent
1963	4.5 per cent

SOURCES: Minister's Reports, Smith Report

Expenditures on education, then, have not only increased more rapidly than total government expenditures, but have also risen more rapidly than the resources of the province. Every incremental dollar of expenditure on education is a dollar diverted from some other public or private expenditure. Government spending is in competition with private spending, and, at the provincial level at least,[2] each programme of the government is in competition with every other programme in the decisions of how much is to be spent and where it is to be spent. Thus, the increasing expenditure on education has involved the assignment of an ever increasing priority to education over other objects of government and private expenditure. In the early postwar years this increasing priority was essentially a local phenomenon. Since the mid 1950s, however, the increase has been shifted to the provincial level.

Units of spending authority

Table 21 shows the increases in unit expenditure in each of the three components of the provincial school system. The differentials in unit expenditure increased in absolute terms over this period. This is particularly significant with respect to the public and separate systems, although the increasingly expensive secondary programmes played a large role in increasing the total expenditure on education. The differential between the two elementary systems, however, had rather obvious political consequences.

TABLE 21

Per-pupil expenditures of public, separate, and secondary school boards in Ontario

Year	Public	Separate	Secondary
1945	$ 84.78	$ 53.21	$169.00
1963	315.08	232.52	609.45

SOURCE: Minister's Report

This increased differential occurred in spite of the fact that separate school expenditures increased more rapidly, in relative terms. The ex-

TABLE 22

Differential in per-pupil expenditures of public and separate school boards in Ontario

1945	$31.57
1963	$82.56

TABLE 23
Increases in per-pupil expenditures of public,
separate, and secondary school boards in
Ontario, 1945–63

Public	3.7x
Separate	4.4x
Secondary	3.6x

planation, of course, lies in the fact that separate school increases were relative to a much smaller base amount.

It would have been desirable to examine the expenditure patterns in the two areas in which enrolment was analysed in Chapter 5, the academic and vocational programmes of secondary schools and the rural-urban status of the local communities. Unfortunately, however, the data available are not sufficiently reliable to permit either of these analyses. In the case of secondary schools, financial data are recorded separately for the two programmes but the assignment of expenditures to either one is often accomplished by arbitrary and 'rule of thumb' devices. The result is that very often expenditures on services to both programmes, such as administration and transportation, are assigned wholly to one or are pro-rated on some basis such as the number of pupils in each of the two programmes.

Financial data are also available for schools in municipalities categorized by rural-urban status. The problem here is that the categories are not used uniformly when reporting enrolment and expenditure. The calculation of unit expenditures produced some strange results, such as a total per-pupil expenditure in suburban separate schools of $77 in 1963 as compared with $258 in the city schools. Rather than confuse the picture by using unreliable data, it seems wiser simply to pass over this area of analysis.

Items of expenditure
Table 24 shows the relative increases in expenditure on the five major items in each of the public, separate, and secondary systems. These data are available only from 1947. Some caution is required in drawing inferences from these data. School boards do not always report expenditures in completely comparable ways, so that what is considered instructional salaries by one board might be reported in part as administrative expenditures by another (especially if a single employee performed both kinds of activities). However, there is no reason why such discrepancies should

TABLE 24
Increases in expenditure on five items in Ontario
public schools, 1947–63

Item	Public	Separate	Secondary
Instructional salaries	2.8x	3.4x	2.9x
Administration, maintenance, and supplies	3.0x	2.9x	3.1x
Transportation	3.6x	16.2x	5.2x
Debt charges	4.6x	5.8x	3.1x
Capital from current revenue	3.8x	4.8x	3.7x

SOURCE: Tables 47, 48, and 49

have varied in any significant degree over this period. As a result, the
relative increases in the several categories should be reasonably valid.

The greatest relative increases in unit expenditure took place in the two
capital items and in transportation, the last being in many ways a substitute
for capital expenditures (pupils are transported to one school in place of
several schools being constructed nearer their respective residences). The
rather incredible growth in the index of unit expenditure on transportation in the separate school system reflects the tremendous growth of that
system in the suburban areas especially and the consequent emphasis
upon centrally-located schools. Similarly, the rising transportation index
in the secondary schools is a function of the postwar establishment of the
large rural high school districts with their central schools. The relatively
small increase in expenditures on debt charges by secondary school
boards undoubtedly reflects the impact of the federal-provincial capital
grants for vocational school construction, a subject to which we will subsequently turn.

Table 25 illustrates the proportion of total expenditures devoted to
each of the five items for the three systems combined.

TABLE 25
Proportion of total educational expenditure
devoted to five major items in Ontario

Item	1947	1963
Instructional salaries	61.0%	56.4%
Administration, maintenance, and supplies	24.9	24.4
Transportation	2.1	3.3
Debt charges	8.5	11.6
Capital from current revenue	3.4	4.4

SOURCE: Table 50

These shifts in expenditure over the full period are shown graphically in Figure 11.

It is apparent that there was no major change in the relative importance of the five items. Both instructional salaries and the category of administration, maintenance, and supplies declined slightly in importance, consuming a total of 85.9 per cent of the total in 1947 and 80.8 per cent in 1963. A rather interesting dependancy between these two categories is clearly visible in Figure 11. Each time there was a significant change

FIGURE 11
Per cent of total current account expenditure on education devoted to five items, 1947–63

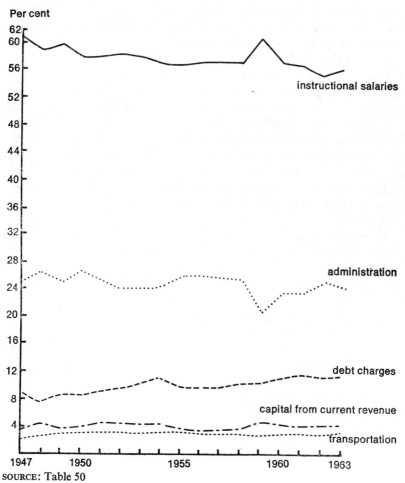

SOURCE: Table 50

in the proportion of resources devoted to one category, there was a contrasting change in the other. This may indicate a general tendency to compensate for abnormal increases in instructional salaries by reducing expenditures, for that year, on administration, maintenance, or most likely, supplies. Over the long run there is a clear tendency for the two items to regain their relative balance. The very gradual increase in expenditures on capital items, debt charges, and transportation is shown clearly here.

Causes and implications

Increases in the level of expenditure on education may occur because of increases in the cost, quality, or quantity of the goods and services used in the educational service package. The actual increases in Ontario have resulted from a combination of all three causes.

We have already (in Chapter 5) spent some time examining the extent to which the quantity of education was increased after the war. The increase in expenditure directly attributable to increases in enrolment, however, accounted for only some 17 per cent of the total increase in expenditure.* The remaining 83 per cent, then, must have been due to the combination of increased costs and increased quality. A breakdown of the contributions of the two factors, while interesting, would be beyond the scope of this study. We are concerned primarily with the political problems emerging from this increase in expenditure, rather than with the economic roots of the increase itself.

One element in the increased costs requires special consideration, however, because of its importance to an understanding of one aspect of the overall provincial response to the problem areas. This factor is the rising rate of interest on local debentures which has, along with the increased indebtedness, accounted for a rising expenditure on debt charges. Figure 12 shows the average rate of interest borne by samples of Canadian provincial and municipal securities from 1948 to 1968. While these rates reflect the national average, they give a reasonable impression of the general rise in the cost of borrowing. The average rate of interest on municipal securities rose from 3.2 per cent in January 1948 to 7.71 per cent in July 1968. The comparison of municipal and provincial rates is interesting as well, in that the rate on provincial securities has maintained an advantage ranging from 0.12 to 0.61 percentage points. This, of course, carries the implication that debt incurred at the local level is more costly

* / Multiplying the per-pupil expenditure of 1945 by the additional pupils in 1963 produces an increase in expenditure of $88,493,000. This is 17 per cent of the $520,622,000 increase which actually took place.

FIGURE 12
Average yields of samples of Canadian provincial and municipal bonds: January and July 1948–68

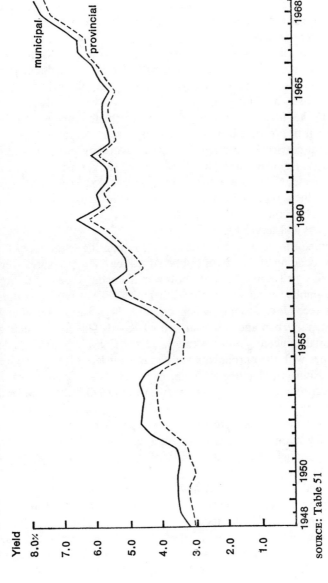

SOURCE: Table 51

to service than debt incurred at the provincial level. The Ontario practice of requiring school boards and municipalities to carry the full debt created for elementary and secondary education has thus, in itself, led to a relative increase in the expenditure on education.

The increased expenditure on education in Ontario, then, can be attributed to three factors: increases in the quantity, cost, and quality of educational services provided. Quantity increased in direct response to increases in the number of eligible children enrolling in the schools. Costs increased because of shortages in the supply of goods and services relative to the increased quantity demanded. Quality increased primarily as the result of pressure from three sources: from the public (desiring an educational service in keeping with contemporary economic and social conditions), from the professional educators (anxious to implement the latest educational experiments and innovations, and perhaps desirous of extending their own influence), and from the provincial bureaucracy (increasingly dedicated to the implementation and expansion of certain programmes and services).

All three of these pressures were exerted upon the school board as the ultimate spending authority in public education. The pressures were not felt equally by all types of boards, however. Secondary boards felt pressure from the public perhaps more than others. This is not unreasonable since it is the secondary schools which prepare the students for immediate employment. Urban and suburban school boards felt the pressure of the professional educators most strongly, because such boards tended to be the ones with the enrolments and fiscal resources sufficient to employ the professionals and to undertake the experiments and innovations. Rural boards were the centres of pressure from the provincial bureaucrats – a pressure exerted through the office of the provincial inspector. The separate school boards were pressured as much by the example of the larger and wealthier public school boards as by any of the primary factors directly, although this pressure was often exerted through the public (parents).

Costs and pupils increased and various segments of the population demanded an increased quality of education. The territorial organization and fiscal resources of the local governments providing the educational services were unable to respond adequately or uniformly to the resultant pressures. This led to the necessity of increased provincial involvement in the basic structure of the governing and financing of education.

Before examining the nature of that increased involvement, however, further attention will be devoted to the rather complex interrelations which exist between the five problem areas we have just explored.

7

The matrix of problems

In order to comprehend fully the implications of the five problem areas described in the preceding chapters, one must appreciate their interrelationships as well as their individual proportions. This is so both because the problems are causally related and because they can be resolved only by policies which attack more than one area at a time.

The problems of increased enrolment, for example, led to increased expenditures and thereby heightened the problems of local fiscal resources. Many of the problems of local fiscal resources, however, could not be resolved without a prior or simultaneous resolution of the problems of local units of government (because the many small units were incapable of sustaining a more sophisticated revenue structure).

It is not difficult to perceive the mutual dependence of the problems of local units of government and of local fiscal resources. In fact, one of the two basic problems of local fiscal resources, the unequal distribution of the tax base, arose in large measure from the size of the local units of government. The real property tax rests upon a base which is relatively fixed geographically. Therefore, the smaller the taxing units are, the greater the imbalances in the individual tax bases are likely to be. A small, rural taxing unit may contain only a few relatively unproductive farm properties, while a unit covering the same amount of area in an urban centre may contain a balanced complement of industrial, commercial, and residential properties. It is only with taxing units large enough to encompass a balanced cross-section of the economic base that the tax base of each unit can be made relatively equal.

It is clear, then, that the enlargement of the units of government was a necessary preliminary step in any reduction of the inequalities in local fiscal resources. This would not, however, remove those inequalities altogether. Nothing short of the creation of a single taxing unit for the province could accomplish that. Neither would such a step, of itself, remove the second of the problems of local fiscal resources – their inadequacy in supporting the total expenditures on education. Either large provincial transfers, the delegation of new taxing powers to the enlarged units, or both, would be necessary to continue the present levels of expenditure on education.

References were made within the context of Chapter 4 to the causal relationship between the special problems of separate schools and both the organization of local units of government and the nature of the local fiscal bases. The artificiality of separate school zones (especially 'dummy' zones) and the discretionary nature of the tax base (with the encumbent inaccessibility of important components of the potential base) are directly responsible for a significant part of the contemporary problems of the separate school system.

Reference has also previously been made to the effect of the increasing enrolment upon the increasing expenditures on education. The increasing enrolment represented an increasing demand for educational services which led directly to an increase in expenditure, because of the increase in the quantity of goods and services provided and because of the increase in prices resulting from a limited supply. The second major cause of increasing expenditures was the pressure of demand, both directly from citizens upon the school boards and indirectly through the Department of Education, for increases in both quantity *and* quality of educational services.

The increasing expenditures resulting from these demands, in turn, greatly exaggerated the problems of local fiscal resources. The value of the local tax base has grown in the postwar period – it more than tripled between 1945 and 1963. Had expenditures increased at a similar or slower rate, the problems of local resources would not have been increased in any way. Expenditures, however, have increased at a rate which far exceeded the rate of growth in the tax base, and thereby the problems were indeed increased.

Augmented costs have thus had an indirect effect upon the problems of local units of government (since we have already established the relationship between local resources and local units of government, an effect upon the former must have an indirect effect upon the latter). They also have had a direct effect. A considerable proportion of the increasing expenditures have been occasioned by the extension of educational programmes to previously excluded groups, by the provision of special programmes for previously undifferentiated groups, and by the inclusion in educational programmes of new, and expensive, technological equipment. In all three areas, economy of scale demanded larger territorial units of local government.

Special classes for the emotionally disturbed, retarded, or perceptually handicapped cannot be provided in a school district containing only one or two children in each such group. Similarly, the initial investment in equipment for vocational programmes or for programmes involving the use of electronic data processing equipment requires a relatively large student body before the unit cost becomes acceptable. Economy of scale has become an inescapable ingredient in the provision of education in Ontario. Here again, the pressure has been greatest in the separate school sector where the units of government have not only been the smallest, but have virtually been held so by constitutional interpretation.

The five problem areas may be divided into two categories: problems of organization and problems of pressure. In the first category would be included the problems of local government, local fiscal resources, and the special problems of separate schools. These three areas reflect the fundamental principles upon which the provision of public education has been organized in the province. They became problem areas precisely because the organization was incapable of responding adequately to the unique pressures of the postwar period.

These unique pressures thus comprise the second category of problems. They consist above all of the pressure of increasing enrolment and increasing expenditure. Enrolment and expenditure, however, have become problems only because they have placed such heavy strains on the organizational components of the educational system. We thus have a dichotomous situation in which the organization of educational institutions became a problem because of its inability to respond adequately to the postwar demands for education, and the demands for education became problems because they placed such heavy pressure on the capacity of the organization to satisfy them.

This leads inexorably to the conclusion that none of the problems could be resolved apart from a resolution of the others. To a certain extent, this conclusion appears to have been accepted by the provincial government and its bureaucracy. But this acceptance followed many years of growing political pressure. Consistently, for example, the province attempted to respond to the problems of local fiscal resources while largely ignoring the problems of local units of government. The result, at best, was to delay the time when the intimate interdependence of these two problem areas would have to be recognized.

The specific provincial responses to the five problem areas discussed in the preceding pages are to be the subjects of discussion and analysis in the following three parts of the study. In that context we shall examine a number of attempts at the independent resolution of specific problems which developed into a response which appears likely to lead to a basic alteration in the pattern of intergovernmental relations in education. In concluding the study, we shall return to a consideration of the five problem areas, attempting to assess the impact of the matrix of responses upon the matrix of problems.

PART II

Provincial fiscal responses

8
The Ontario Foundation Tax Plan, 1964:
background and overview

In addition to the problems just outlined, three sets of factors appear essential to a description of the background or context of the provincial grant plan of 1964, the Ontario Foundation Tax Plan. These are the nature of the decision-making process, the policy orientations or preferences of the participants in this process, and the pressures or demands emanating from individuals or groups not actively involved in developing the grant programme.

THE DECISION-MAKING PROCESS

The 1964 grant programme was the product of a decision-making process involving three basic units or groups. The three units consisted of an educational grants committee of the provincial cabinet, a similar committee of the provincial Department of Education, and two academic consultants. The membership of the cabinet committee consisted of the premier, the provincial treasurer, and the minister of education, although the minister of education from 1951 to 1959, W.J. Dunlop, apparently had taken a rather unconcerned attitude towards meetings of this committee and sometimes failed to attend.[1] This membership was sometimes supplemented by other ministers, depending upon the topic under consideration and the minister's areas of interest and responsibility. The minister of municipal affairs, for example, would sometimes participate in the committee deliberations. The departmental committee consisted of the superintendent of business administration, the chief of the grants office, and one member from each of the elementary and secondary supervision sections. The two academic consultants were Dr R.W.B. Jackson, director of the

Department of Educational Research in the University of Toronto,* and
Professor E.B. Rideout, a member of the same department.

These three units participated in a highly interesting triangular relationship. The general division of responsibilities between the cabinet and
departmental committee was that between policy and administration.
Specifically, the departmental committee was charged with responsibility
for the translation of cabinet decisions into departmental regulations, for
the oversight of the collection of information necessary to calculate the
grants, and for the oversight of the actual calculation and payment of the
grants. The cabinet committee assumed responsibility for the basic decisions concerning the magnitude of provincial grants and the method to
be used in their distribution.

As in most government activities, policy and its administration are
overlapping areas of responsibility. In giving effect to policy decisions a
certain amount of interpretation is virtually inescapable – and an interpre-
tive decision is often, in its effect, a part of the policy decision itself.
Similarly, in order for the intent of a policy decision to be stated clearly,
it may be necessary for the policy to be written in great detail, including
a statement of how it is to be administered. Thus, it is not possible to
describe the respective roles of the two committees in terms of mutually
exclusive categories. The practice appeared to be, however, that when
the departmental committee recognized an issue as involving policy implications and for which no clear direction was apparent, that issue would
be referred to the cabinet for decision. Furthermore, the fact that the
minister of education was both a member of the cabinet committee and
the head of the bureaucratic hierarchy within which the departmental
committee functioned provided an effective means of communication
between the two bodies.

The two academic consultants were, of course, outside the formal governmental organization. Nevertheless, they participated directly in the
deliberations of the two committees. This rather unusual involvement of
outside experts in the development and implementation of government
policy had developed some years earlier as a result of a rather unique
set of circumstances. In 1944 V.K. Greer† had been appointed superintendent of elementary education and financial adviser to the minister
of education. In the latter capacity Greer had been the chief adviser to
the cabinet in matters relating to education finance. In fulfilling this

* / The Department of Educational Research was established in 1931 within
the College of Education, the latter an affiliate of the University of Toronto. Dr
Peter Sandiford was the first head of this department, and Dr Jackson assumed the
headship in 1957.
† / Greer had been chief inspector of public and separate schools since 1925.

responsibility, he had developed a close working relationship with Dr Jackson, relying heavily on the latter's research and advice. When Greer died just one year later, the cabinet turned directly to Jackson for advice in this area. Jackson established considerable longevity in this role, serving as the major cabinet adviser through three premiers and five ministers of education.*

The triangular relationship was completed by the involvement of Professor E.B. Rideout. Rideout was intimately associated with the research activities of Dr Jackson, assisted in the development of Jackson's proposals to the cabinet committee, and, finally, was a co-opted member of the departmental grants committee.

The three elements of the decision-making structure may be illustrated as in Figure 13.

FIGURE 13
Illustration of decision-making structure involved in development of 1964 grant programme

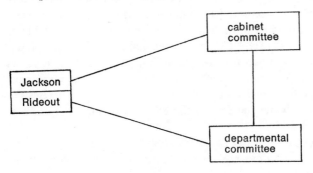

Policy preferences and objectives of participants
Since it is not possible to examine the manner in which the cabinet arrived at specific decisions involved in the determination of the grant programme (cabinet deliberations being secret) one must make inferences derived from secondary sources. With some knowledge of the advice and demands placed before the cabinet, and with the product of these and previous deliberations (the grant plans) available, it should be possible to gain some insight into the deliberative process of provincial decision making in this area.

* / Jackson's role as consultant was not limited to the area of educational finance. He played a significant part, for example, in the planning of new universities, community colleges, and the metropolitan form of educational government in Toronto.

We need not be concerned at this point with the role of the departmental committee. As was noted above, that committee was concerned primarily with the administration of the grant programme and only in an ancillary way with its development and policy implications. The role of this committee changed after 1964, however, and we shall have cause to consider its policy preferences when considering the post-1964 development of the grant plan.

In describing the policy preferences of the academic consultants, it is especially important that their participatory role be stressed. The relationship between the cabinet and Dr Jackson was an informal one. Communication was maintained between the two units throughout the deliberative process and took various forms, including research reports, memoranda, and personal contact. Jackson's advice, therefore, could be expected to take account specifically of the cabinet's preferences for certain kinds of policies or courses of action. In other words, Jackson's advice would be tendered within a framework of established cabinet policy. While it is not suggested that Jackson's academic integrity was compromised, it is likely that one would not find the ultimate preferences of the consultants embodied in the explicit advice offered to the cabinet.

It appears to be most useful to develop the policy preferences of the consultants without regard to the constraints imposed by their appreciation of the cabinet's overriding preferences. This will enable us to gain greater insight into the actual preferences of the cabinet. Otherwise, the cabinet's preferences would be lost to the extent that they were anticipated by the consultants.

There is no doubt that in the discussions preliminary to the adoption of the 1964 grant programme, the policy favoured by the academic consultants was the implementation of a 'foundation plan.' In fact, such had been their preference when the last major revision of the grant structure had been undertaken in 1958.[2] The concept of a foundation plan evolved out of a rather lengthy process of academic enquiry and practical experimentation. Some reference to the evolution of the concept is essential to an understanding of the consultants' positions.

The basis for the eventual development of the model foundation plan was laid as early as 1905 when Ellwood P. Cubberley, in a doctoral dissertation for Columbia University,[3] argued the need for grant programmes designed to achieve explicit objectives on the basis of empirical, quantitative measures. The first specific proposal of a foundation plan came in 1923 in a study of educational finance in New York by George D. Strayer and Robert M. Haig. Known as the Strayer-Haig formula, it was set forth in the following terms:

The state should ensure equal educational facilities to every child within its borders at a uniform effort throughout the state in terms of the burden of taxation; the tax burden of education should throughout the state be uniform in relation to taxpaying ability, and the provision of the schools should be uniform in relation to the educable population desiring education ...

1 / A local school tax in support of the satisfactory minimum offering would be levied in each district at a rate which would provide the necessary funds for that purpose in the richest district.

2 / This richest district then might raise all of its school money by means of the local tax ...

3 / Every other district could be permitted to levy a local tax at the same rate and apply the proceeds toward the costs of schools, but –

4 / Since the rate is uniform, this tax would be sufficient to meet the costs only in the richest district and the deficiencies would be made up by state subventions.[4]

The Strayer-Haig formula had considerable appeal in that it set forth a means of achieving virtually complete equalization by a very simple technique. Yet this simplicity contained the fundamental weakness in the formula, for there were no provisions for determining the content of 'the minimum satisfactory offering' nor for establishing the unit cost of this offering given widely varying local needs.

In overcoming this weakness in the original formula, Paul R. Mort rendered the foundation plan a viable model of intergovernmental transfer payments.[5] Beginning with the concept of a normal classroom as the standard unit, Mort designed a system of weighting pupils so as to compensate for legitimate cost differentials resulting from different pupil-teacher ratios. The foundation plan concept had thus developed into the following formula: $G = (FLE)(WADA) - (FTR)(ETA)$, where G = grant (state or provincial), FLE = foundation level of expenditure (the standard offering expressed as dollars per pupil), $WADA$ = weighted average daily attendance (the unit for measuring local need), FTR = foundation tax rate (the rate of taxation to be levied by all school districts, normally expressed in mills per dollar of equalized taxable assessment), and ETA = equalized taxable assessment (the value of the tax base in the school district, adjusted to a base comparable to all districts in the state or province).

Although the foundation plan concept gained relatively rapid acceptance in academic circles as being the most appropriate plan for intergovernmental fiscal transfers in education, it gained acceptance more slowly in state and provincial governments. The State of New York, the first to implement a variation of this model plan, made a significant contribution in its definition of the foundation level of expenditure. Under the New York plan, this level was set approximately at the average per-pupil expenditure for school districts of average revenue-raising ability in the state. 'The logic of this approach was that that would probably be the amount which the state would adopt if it were to finance the entire instructional programme as though all of the districts of the state were combined into one state district.'[6]

It took a long time before the foundation plan concept was seen as applicable to Ontario. Maxwell Cameron, writing in the mid-1930s, cited three factors which rendered the concept inappropriate. First, he argued that a reorganization of the units of local government was absolutely necessary before such a plan could be practical.

Most of the rural schools are one-teacher schools ... many of these schools are very small indeed, well over half of them having less than twenty pupils in attendance ... the current expenditure per pupil in rural schools is high, almost equal to that of cities ... the expenditure per teacher is much below that in urban areas, and ... in very small schools the cost is enormous.

This inefficiency of rural schools can be traced to the small school-section form of administration which stands in the way of all reform.[7]

Second, the inadequate system of local assessment of property militated against introduction of the plan: 'It is notorious that the ratios of the assessed to the actual values of property vary greatly throughout the province. The result is that provincial funds now flow to many local boards whose need is only apparent.'[8] Third, the division of the elementary school system into public and separate schools rendered a standard unit expenditure inappropriate.

The difficulty in the way of complete financial equalization in Ontario arises from the fact there are two widely different cost structures in the elementary schools – that of the public and that of the separate schools ...

To a large extent expenditures in separate schools are low because of the small salaries paid for teachers who are members of religious orders;* and the fact must be faced that to increase the salaries of these teachers is to subsidize the religious orders to which they belong ...

A considerable body of opinion in the province is averse to any grant system

* / Cameron estimated the proportion of religious teachers in separate schools in the early 1930s at between 30 and 35 per cent in the cities and somewhat less in the smaller urban and rural areas.

which obviously results in diverting public funds to the support of religious orders.[9]

Cameron's first two arguments have rather compelling logic. Theoretically, it should have been possible to weight the elementary school pupils in such a manner as to reflect the actual cost differential between the public and separate systems. The argument against equalizing public and separate school revenues was more emotional than logical however, and was indicative of the prevailing attitude of the political community in Ontario towards all matters pertaining to separate denominational schools.

Just two years after the publication of Cameron's thesis, a special committee of enquiry (the McArthur Committee)* also rejected any form of the foundation plan for Ontario. While citing the gross inadequacy of the prevailing system of assessing property, and going so far as to recommend a provincial equalization of all local assessments, the committee summed up its objections to the foundation plan concept in the following terms: 'It is the opinion of the Committee, however, that such differences in distribution of population and of wealth, in climactic conditions, and in facilities for transportation as are found in the Province of Ontario would make it impossible to apply any such scheme with a reasonable prospect of success.'[10] The intimate relationship between these very factors and the existing territorial organization of local government – leading to the corollary that by reforming the units of government the barriers to the implementation of a foundation plan would largely be removed, either was not considered or was rejected by the committee.†

The foundation plan concept was once again rejected by the Royal Commission on Education in Ontario (the Hope Commission), reporting in 1950. The commission based its recommended fiscal policy on a proposed reorganization of local units of government and a decentralization of policy-making responsibility. A considerable extension of equalization was expected to follow the territorial reorganization. Full equalization, under a scheme such as the foundation plan, however, was considered incompatible with effective decentralization because the local contribution would be fixed at a standard rate of taxation. The Hope Commission

*/ The chairman of the committee was Duncan McArthur, chief director of the Department of Education.

†/ The committee would go only so far as to make the following rather cautious statement: 'If, in order to obtain certain definite educational advantages, it becomes necessary to think and to make plans in relation to an area more extensive than the school section, consideration should be given to the wisdom of forming some type of larger unit of administration.'

proposed instead that provincial grants be calculated as a percentage of approved expenditure, a percentage which would vary inversely with equalized assessment per 'teaching unit.'* The proposal lost much of its attractiveness, however, when the commission recommended that the legislative appropriation be divided between public and separate schools *before* the formula was applied, so that equalization would be achieved only within, and not between,† each system.[11]

The Hope Commission report, while its fiscal recommendations do not appear to have had any direct effect upon government policy, is nevertheless of some importance because of the role the commission played in the developing positions of the two academic consultants. Dr Jackson was the secretary of the commission, while Professor Rideout gained entry into his consultative role as a research assistant for the commission. It is difficult to estimate the extent to which involvement with the Hope Commission influenced the policy preferences of Jackson and Rideout. The very fact of their participation in a five-year study of education in the province provided them with a keener appreciation of the history and problems of educational finance. Whether they shared the commission's reluctance to extend the principle of equalization to encompass separate schools more fully is less certain. Both were apparently convinced, however, that the foundation plan was feasible only if coupled with a reorganization of the territorial units of local government.

It appears fairly clear that the two consultants entered the policy formulation process with an academic committment to the concept of the foundation plan. The committment was constrained, however, by the conviction that school district consolidation was a necessary preliminary step in the adoption of such a scheme, and also by a lack of enthusiasm, if not open opposition, to the inclusion of separate schools in a system of fully equalizing grants.

Policy orientation of the provincial cabinet
The review of previous grant plans in Chapter 3 pointed up the three basic objectives which have characterized provincial policy in the financing of education in the past century: general reduction of the reliance on property taxation, equalization of fiscal burdens, and stimulation of specific educational offerings. In the postwar period, equalization and

* / The 'teaching unit' was a weighted classroom based on a sliding scale of pupil-teacher ratios for various sizes of schools.
† / This limitation was partially mitigated by the commission's recommendation that property not held by identifiable individuals be taxed for post-elementary schools only. One of the major causes of the fiscal disparity between public and separate schools would thus have been removed.

tax relief became of primary concern as a result of the increasing total burden of property taxation and the consequent increase in the magnitude of the inequities produced by its unequal incidence.

As well, however, Chapter 3 identified the intimate relationship between the inadequate and unequal units of local government and the inadequate and unequal local fiscal resources, while both chapters 2 and 3 described the provincial government's attempts to restructure these local units by encouragement rather than compulsion.

These three objectives – property tax relief, fiscal equalization, and voluntary local reorganization – appear to represent the three pillars of provincial policy in the domain of educational finance in the period under review. Together with the advice and opinion placed before the cabinet they can account for the particular design of the 1964 grant programme. What is of special interest in these objectives is the fact that local organizational reform – presumably desirable for non-fiscal reasons as well – was absolutely indispensable to an effective policy of fiscal equalization.

It is not suggested here that equalization was the predominant objective of provincial policy (although it was certainly one of the objectives) but rather that a truly effective programme of equalization was dependent upon a rather extensive reorganization (implying a consolidation) of the units of local government. This dependence resulted from two contradictory factors. First, the optimum use of resources which is possible only in a fairly large district (relatively standard pupil-teacher ratios, central purchasing of supplies, maximum use of instructional aids) allows the same, or a similar, programme to be offered at a lower unit cost in a large district than in a small district. For example, a district with but twenty pupils can not have a pupil-teacher ratio greater than twenty-to-one, even if the optimum use of the teachers' time would lead to a ratio of thirty-to-one. If the teacher's salary were $6000, the per-pupil cost in the small district would be $6000/20 = \$300$, but in a large district (capable of sustaining a thirty-to-one ratio) would be $6000/30 = \$200$. Second, however, because a much greater division of labour is possible in a large district – resulting in the employment of various specialists – it will be possible to identify a wide range of needs and to design special programmes to meet these needs. Most of these needs would not even be apparent in a small district, and even if they were, there would not be the specialized personnel to design responses to them, nor the student population sufficient to justify them. This factor leads to a greater unit expenditure in a large district as compared with a small district.

The special need of a slow-learning child, for example, is more likely to be recognized in a large school district capable of employing expert diagnosticians. Even were the need recognized in the small district, there would be so few children in any recognizable category of need that most special services would be quite impractical.

With a system of local government characterized by extreme variations in school district size, it is not possible to develop an effective measure of educational need. On the surface, weighting factors appear to compensate for both the increased cost of small teaching units and the increased cost of providing special services, but they do so by reinforcing inefficiency in the first instance and unequal recognition of educational need in the second. Thus, unless all school districts are *capable* of responding in a similar way to the defined needs of the school population, a weighting scheme becomes, in effect, not a corrective for differing needs but a subsidy for differing efforts.

In effect, then, the cabinet defined its commitment to fiscal equalization as conditional upon the success of its policy of encouraging, but not requiring, local organizational reform. And as was shown clearly in Chapter 2, that policy achieved a very modest degree of success. There were still 1121 school districts in 1964 (32.3 per cent of the total) with thirty or fewer pupils in average daily attendance.[12]

The two policy objectives were thus in basic conflict. Effective fiscal equalization required a legislated reorganization of local districts. Furthermore, because the cabinet refused to enforce school-district reorganization, and therefore accepted only a modest degree of fiscal equalization, its commitment to general property tax relief served to limit still further the effective realization of such equalization. As will be noted shortly, equalization and tax relief can be complementary in effect, but only if the tax relief is designed to supplement an effective scheme of equalization. Whenever tax relief is provided in a scheme which does not effectively equalize, the result is a diminution of the degree of equalization which would have been produced without the tax relief.[13]

The contrast between the orientations of the cabinet and its advisers is rather striking. On the one hand, the advisers favoured a scheme of effective equalization based upon a reorganized system of local districts. On the other the government, while committed to an extension of equalization, constrained this commitment by its prior commitment to general property tax relief and respect for local responsibilities in the territorial organization of school government.

This analysis clearly suggests a consistent development of cabinet policy at least throughout the two decades prior to the introduction of the 'foundation tax plan' in 1964. That suggestion appears well founded. Chapter 3 attempted to show the pattern of provincial policy which was discernible prior to the 1960s. The discussion of the 1964 programme later in this chapter will, it is hoped, demonstrate the extent to which that plan was the logical culmination of the preceding plans.

External pressures and demands
The decision-making process involving the triangular relationship of cabinet, department, and consultants was not closed to the influences of other groups and interests. The pressure of these influences was, logically, directed particularly towards the cabinet. A number of events occurred in the years just prior to and during the development of the new grant programme which likely had some effect upon the decisions finally reached by the cabinet. The importance imputed to these factors results from the political importance of the groups involved. Three of these developments have been isolated as being of special importance.

In November 1961 some 1000 delegates from fifteen provincial educational associations met in Windsor as the Ontario Conference on Education. These delegates represented the ranking leaders of the educational system of Ontario. The group dealing with finance brought forth the following recommendation regarding the structure of provincial grants:

That serious consideration be given to the adoption of the Foundation Programme both at the elementary and the secondary levels to be financed by a uniform local mill rate on the provincially equalized assessment of each municipality, with the balance of the cost for each board being provided by the province. Provision should continue to exist for local boards at their own expense to provide facilities in excess of the Foundation Programme.[14]

Recognizing the intimate link between adequate structures of educational finance and government, the recommendation of a foundation plan was followed by the statement that 'this group strongly endorses the formation of larger units of school administration.'[15] It is of some interest to note that Professor E.B. Rideout was one of the two consultants to this group.

The recommendation of a foundation plan by the Ontario Conference on Education was followed in March 1962 by a similar recommendation from the Second Canadian Conference on Education.[16] These represented highly prestigious endorsements of the foundation plan concept.

The second major development in this area was the adoption of the foundation plan in the policy platforms of both opposition parties in the provincial legislature. The New Democratic party (NDP), the smaller of the two parties, had, through its predecessor the Co-operative Common-wealth Federation, been proposing what was essentially a foundation plan (that terminology was not used, however) since at least 1954.[17] The party's position was revealed in greatest detail in a study report prepared for the 1961 founding convention of the new party. The proposal was set forth in the following six steps.

1 Reassess all property in relation to present values.

2 Divert all school taxes on commercial property to a central fund for financing secondary education.

3 Establish a fixed mill rate to be applied to all residential property throughout the province.

4 Establish a 'cost-per-pupil' figure which would represent the cost of providing education for one year for a pupil in an elementary school in a typical medium-size community.

5 Establish 'weighting' factors to adjust the cost-per-pupil in districts with a high cost of living, high travel expenses for students, high salary costs due to isolation, etc.

6 Pay provincial grants to school boards at a level which will raise the revenue collected through the standard assessments up to the weighted cost-per-pupil figure.[18]

The Liberal party adopted the foundation plan as party policy only in the autumn of 1962. Prior to that the party had proposed assumption of the full cost of elementary and secondary education by the provincial government. The specific details of the Liberal position were never spelled out publicly, but references in the legislature suggest that it was similar in principle to that of the NDP.[19]

On this issue, then, the government faced an opposition united in support of the foundation plan concept.

Finally, in a joint brief presented to the cabinet and legislature in December 1962, the two associations of separate school trustees abandoned their perennial demand for a reallocation of property assessment between public and separate elementary schools and urged instead the adoption of a full-fledged foundation programme. They put their whole case for fiscal reform in the following terms:

The solution that would correct the imbalance in the present financial structure would be the adoption of the following plan:

1 the Department of Education would determine in dollars and cents the total amount it costs to educate adequately a child in the schools of this province;

2 this cost would met in the following manner:

a) by a uniform mill rate levied province wide on an equalized municipal assessment;

b) by legislative grants.[20]

Endorsement of the foundation plan concept by the leaders of the educational 'establishment,' by the two opposition political parties, by the separate school bloc (the most politically sensitive segment of the educational system), and by the two key cabinet advisers represented an awesome coalition of forces. One need hardly be surprised, then, that the cabinet should have attempted to respond to this pressure by the adoption of some, at least, of the essential features of a foundation plan.

OVERVIEW

Consideration of a new approach to provincial grants, involving the cabinet committee and the two academic consultants, began at the close of the period of revision of the 1962 grant plan. The decision was made to make only very slight changes in the grants for 1963, thus leaving a period of nearly two years for development of the new plan if it were to come into effect, as planned, in 1964.[21]

In February 1963, at the time the grant regulations for that year were issued to the school boards, Prime Minister John Robarts presented a statement outlining the general provisions of what would be the Ontario Foundation Tax Plan of 1964.[22] At this time, a year before the plan was actually introduced, most of the essential decisions had obviously already been taken. Robarts still referred to the necessity of dividing school districts into categories on the bases of municipal status and population, however, indicating the foundation plan concept had not yet been fully accepted. This categorization had formed the basis of the previous grant plans, and was in large part a device to compensate for the government's determination to avoid a legislated consolidation of school districts – the categories comprised groups of districts in essentially similar situations, and distinct grant schedules were then developed for each of these groups. Robarts' intimation that this grouping of school districts would continue under the revised plan provided a clear indication that the cabinet continued in its opposition to enforced consolidation.

The detailed provisions of the Ontario Foundation Tax Plan were announced in January 1964.[23] By that time, a year after the original Robarts announcement, the decision to continue the categorization of districts had been dropped in favour of a scheme of weighting the pupils of differently-situated districts. This change brought the grant scheme closer to the appearance of the model foundation plan concept.

In introducing any variation of the foundation plan concept, the cabinet would have been faced with a number of difficult decisions. These difficulties were compounded, however, by the cabinet's refusal to couple the introduction of the grant plan with a provision for the reorganization of school districts, and by the insistence that the existing provisions for tax relief be given preference over an extension of equalization. The following pages will explore the nature and dimensions of the compromise effected between these conflicting objectives.

Ordinary and extraordinary expenditures

One of the most basic decisions in the whole grant programme was that limiting the foundation plan formula to what were defined as 'ordinary' expenditures. School board expenditures were to be divided into two categories: ordinary and extraordinary. The notion of extraordinary expenditure had been introduced in 1958 but at that time was used only in calculating the total grant percentage. Extraordinary expenditures consisted of those in respect of capital items, debt charges, transportation, and the capital portion of tuition fees paid by a board for the education of its pupils in the schools of another board. The notion thus embraced both direct and indirect capital expenditures as well as substitutes for capital expenditures (transportation).

There are, in effect, only two ways in which extraordinary or capital expenditures could be incorporated into a foundation plan. The first is to assume that all school boards can meet their capital requirements with a standard annual unit expenditure, with provision for the drawing of advances or building of reserves when expenditures exceed or fall below this standard in any particular year or series of years. The second method is to include in the foundation programme the full approved capital expenditure of each board, without any regard to the notion of a standard or foundation level of expenditure.

The first of these methods, embodied in the Alberta grant programme of 1961,[24] was clearly not appropriate for Ontario, given the existing organization of local districts. The simple fact was that a considerable number of districts required insignificant amounts of capital expenditure and were unlikely to develop any greater requirements in the foreseeable future, while other districts (especially in areas of rapid population growth) had large requirements which could not be expected to diminish in the foreseeable future. This alternative would have meant the accumulation of unnecessary reserve funds in some districts and the generation of ever-increasing deficits in others.

The second method – the inclusion of all approved capital expenditures in the foundation programme – was strongly opposed, for essentially philosophical reasons, by Dr Jackson.[25] The main argument against such inclusion was that it would represent too great a shift of fiscal responsibility from the school boards to the province. Assuming that the ceilings on approved expenditure were realistic (and this was not always the case at the time,* local participation in capital financing would extend only to the contribution of a standard rate of taxation and the full cost of any unapproved expenditure. Once approved expenditures equalled the yield of the standard tax rate, marginal expenditures would be financed entirely from provincial revenues. Any effective control on such expenditures, then, would have to come from the province. Thus, the most basic decisions of what facilities were to be provided, when and at what cost, would all be effectively transferred to the provincial level.

Interestingly, this was the same general argument used by the Hope Commission to reject the foundation plan concept altogether. On the basis of this fundamental decision, then, the foundation plan formula was to apply only to current, or ordinary, expenditures.

The basic foundation plan formula was described earlier in terms of the following equation: $G = (FLE)(WADA) - (FTR)(ETA)$. Thus, the provincial grant to each school district would equal the product of the foundation level of expenditure and the number of weighted pupils, less the product of the foundation tax rate and the value of the equalized taxable assessment in the district. In order to implement the formula, decisions were therefore required on the definition of each of the four factors as well as on any proposed modification of the basic equation.

Two of the four factors – the weighted average daily attendance (WADA) and the equalized taxable assessment (ETA) – while of vital importance to the impact and effectiveness of the plan, are essentially technical in nature. The province had introduced a scheme for equalizing local assessments in 1958, and this was continued unchanged under the new formula. Considerable refinements were made in the mechanics of determining the weighted average daily attendance for 1964, designed to obviate the necessity of the four-fold classification of school districts used in previous plans, but since these are to be described later as illus-

---

* / School building projects, for example, were approved up to flat ceilings of $20,000 per classroom for elementary schools and $25,000 per classroom for secondary schools. No provision was made for the recognition of increasing cost levels or of differential costs in different sections of the province.

trations of the complexity of the programme, they need not be considered here.

Given the establishment of adequate measures for these two factors, the development of the Ontario grant plan centred upon three issues: prescription of the foundation level of expenditure (FLE), prescription of the foundation tax rate (FTR), and development of a means of providing general property tax relief by a modification of the basic formula.

To show how firmly Ontario's response was grounded in the traditional wisdom of practical foundation plans, the following comments of Maxwell Cameron, written in 1936, are especially revealing. Ontario's plan followed almost exactly the pattern Cameron was able to discern in American foundation plans nearly thirty years earlier.

> The 'ideal' program is that provided by the wealthiest districts of the state. This level of expenditure being regarded as quite out of the question for the whole state, a 'defensible' program, that provided by communities of average wealth, is next taken, on the ground that these communities have been neither helped nor hindered by the existing financial system. Even this program – what the people of the state would probably spend if all communities were equally wealthy – is usually too costly to be a practical possibility in a system of state aid, and a lower level is chosen for the preliminary stages at least, the view being that eventually the state should attempt to equalize the defensible program.
>
> Then the local tax rate which would support the minimum program in the richest district is calculated ...
>
> The amount of central grant necessary is usually reduced by prescribing a standard local tax rate somewhat higher than would be ideal for complete equalization ...
>
> The scheme leaves former state aid in operation and subtracts it from the equalization grant, thus guaranteeing that no local board will lose under the new system.[26]

Establishing the foundation level of expenditure was undoubtedly the most perplexing of the three issues. Ontario was forced into the adoption of the approach outlined by Cameron (a level below the actual average expenditure) for two reasons apart from any considerations of provincial economy. In the first place, the hundreds of tiny school districts could not have made prudent use of resources equal to the provincial average. They were capable neither of employing the necessary personnel nor of organizing the necessary programmes and services. Without this capacity to recognize average need, provincial support equalizing the abilities of these districts to the provincial average would have resulted in either extravagance or discriminatory tax relief. Support to the level of expenditure in the 'wealthiest' districts would probably have provided many small districts with substantial surpluses and no local taxation at all.

The second reason for establishing a relatively low foundation level was the disparity in average expenditure levels between the public and separate elementary school systems. Using 1962 figures, the latest available when the plan was developed, one finds the average 'ordinary' expenditure of all elementary boards at $255 per pupil (of average daily attendance). However, the average in the public system was $283 and in the separate system only $178.[27] To have attempted to eliminate this disparity of $105 in one year would simply have flooded the coffers of many separate school boards.

The cabinet adopted a more prudent course – prudent within the context of its refusal to reorganize local districts – and set the foundation level at $210 per elementary pupil. The Prime Minister described this figure as lying ' ... in between the two levels that presently exist throughout the province.'[28] Actually, the $210 was almost exactly mid-way between the average expenditure levels of the separate schools and of all elementary schools, not between the levels of the public and separate schools.

For secondary schools the foundation level was set at $420 per pupil in the academic programme and at $550 per pupil in the commercial or technical (vocational) programmes. It was necessary to provide a distinct grant formula for secondary schools because of the quite different tax base as compared with elementary schools.* However, the use of separate foundation levels for academic and vocational pupils had no compelling logic as the same result would have obtained if vocational pupils had been weighted by a factor of 1.31. The use of separate levels did make the additional provincial support of vocational pupils more apparent.

The secondary school foundation levels were also considerably lower than the 1962 average expenditures. The actual expenditures averaged $480 and $670 for academic and vocational pupils respectively so that the foundation levels were $60 and $120 lower.

The second major issue in adopting a foundation plan involved the prescription of the foundation tax rate (FTR in the equation) to be used in determining the local contribution to the foundation programme. This

* / The elementary school tax base is divided between public and separate schools. At the secondary level, however, the combined base supports the single system. Thus, the per-pupil assessment of secondary schools cannot be compared with that of either public or separate elementary schools.

issue is inextricably bound up with the prescription of the foundation level of expenditure in determining the impact of the plan. The relationship between the two determines the extent to which the plan achieves both equalization and general tax relief. To illustrate this fact, we can make use of the grant equation introduced earlier.

Perfect equalization is defined as a situation in which every district can provide an equal level of expenditure with an equal rate of taxation. Under the foundation plan formula the tax rate must be examined in the light of the unit revenue produced in the district with the greatest taxing capacity (equalized assessment) as compared with all other districts.*

There are three alternatives available in establishing the tax rate: the rate may be set at a point above, equal to, or below that required to yield the foundation level of expenditure in the ablest district.

In 1964 the ablest elementary district in Ontario had an equalized taxable assessment per pupil of approximately \$28,000.[29] Applying the foundation plan formula on the basis of a single pupil, and with the prescribed foundation level of expenditure of \$210, the equation becomes: $G = (210) (1) - (FTR) (28,000)$. To achieve perfect equalization, the provincial grant (G) should be zero for this ablest district. Thus:

$$0 = 210 - (FTR) (28,000)$$
$$FTR = 210/28,000 = 0.0075 = 7.5 \text{ mills.}$$

With a tax rate of 7.5 mills, then, the ablest district would receive no grant, but every other district would receive a grant equal to the difference between \$210 per pupil and the yield of the 7.5 mills on the equalized taxable assessment. The ablest district would derive \$210 per pupil from this tax levy alone. Thus, with a tax rate of 7.5 mills, every district would raise exactly \$210 per pupil.

If the rate were set above 7.5 mills, then not only would the ablest district receive no grant, but neither would a number of less able districts. A district would not receive a grant until the yield of the prescribed tax rate fell below \$210 per pupil. Conversely, were the rate set below 7.5 mills, even the ablest district would receive a grant, since anything less than 7.5 mills would yield less than \$210 per pupil. Since the grant paid to the ablest district would also be paid to all other districts, and since that amount would be in excess of the amount needed to achieve perfect equalization, that amount of grant would become general property tax relief.

* / In order to avoid gross distortions produced by the existence of one or more very able, but very small, districts (such as resort areas), Paul Mort suggested using the ablest large district, which he called the "key" district. Other applications of the plan have used the average relative assessment of a group of the ablest districts.

Of the three alternatives, the cabinet chose the second, adopting a rate which would produce less than complete equalization. The foundation tax rate was set at eleven mills for elementary districts and seven mills for secondary districts. This meant that the per-pupil equalized assessment of an elementary district had to be less than $19,091 before the district would receive any equalizing grant (since eleven mills applied to $19,091 would produce exactly $210). This scheme by itself would thus have left not only the ablest district but a significant number of other districts without any provincial assistance in the financing of education. And it was precisely these relatively wealthy districts, containing a large proportion of the total student population, which were already spending in excess of the foundation level. For them, the actual tax rate would thus have been considerably in excess of the foundation rate.

One can only assume that the cabinet's decision to set the rate above that required for perfect equalization at the foundation level of expenditure (a level which was itself well below the actual average level of expenditures in the province) was due to an unwillingness to devote a larger proportion of provincial resources to the equalization of the burden of education. Increasing the tax rate, of course, increased the contribution of local taxation to the foundation programme and thus reduced the provincial contribution.

Having prescribed these two factors, the cabinet faced a difficult task in respect to the third issue outlined by Cameron – the guarantee that local districts would receive at least as much support under the new scheme as under the old. Under the grant plan of 1963, the highest minimum grant for elementary school boards had been $53 per pupil and 34 per cent of the recognized costs. This had been supplemented by the Residential and Farm School Tax Assistance Grant of $20 per pupil.*

As was just noted, the foundation formula would have eliminated the grant for the ablest district and all districts with per-pupil assessments in excess of $19,091, unless some modification were made. Such an adjustment was absolutely essential, for to have eliminated the provincial grant to all of these school districts (involving most of the large cities in the province) would have been politically disastrous.

The foundation plan formula was indeed modified. A minimum grant was to be payable to all school boards, calculated under two special provisions. First, every board would receive a 'Basic Tax Relief Grant' of $80 per pupil in elementary schools, $175 per pupil in an academic programme in a secondary school, and $250 per pupil in a vocational pro-

*/For an outline of the Residential and Farm School Tax Assistance Grants, see p. 49.

gramme in a secondary school. Second, abler elementary school boards would receive a special, minimum, 'equalization' grant. The amount of the latter grant would vary inversely with equalized assesment per classroom and was designed so as to increase the basic grant gradually, until it was exceeded by the regular foundation grant. Both the basic tax relief grant and the special equalization grant were designed specifically to assure that no board received less grant under the new scheme than it would have under the previous one.

The need for these provisions arose directly from the decision establishing the foundation level of expenditure and the foundation tax rate. The latter factors could have been manipulated so as to achieve the desired minimum grants without the insertion of special formulas. For example, with a foundation level of $210, and a tax rate of 4.6 mills, all districts would have received $80 per pupil in addition to that required for complete equalization. The same effect would have been achieved with a foundation level of $388 and a tax rate of eleven mills.[30] Both modifications, however, would have entailed a very substantial increase in the total provincial grant.

Quite apart from the additional provincial expenditure involved in these alternative formulas, both were essentially impractical in Ontario in 1964. Any programme of complete equalization, with or without tax relief, was impossible without a reorganization of school districts. The impact of either of the above two options would have been to make available to the less able, and small, districts the same resources as were made available to the abler, and large, districts. Such a programme could not be justified so long as the small districts were incapable of offering the same (or similar) programmes as the large districts. Thus, special grants were necessary in order to provide unequal assistance to the large districts.

Largely because the problem of unequal and inadequate units was not nearly so pronounced in the case of the secondary school districts, the foundation plan was able to achieve a much greater degree of equalization. Only a very modest amount of special assistance was required to guarantee that no district received less in provincial grants under the new formula.

The general impact of the Ontario foundation plan, including its special minimum provisions, can be seen in Figures 14 to 17. School boards were first grouped into equal classes of equalized assessment per classroom. These groups of boards were then plotted along the horizontal axes of the graphs with the distance accorded each group representing the proportion of all pupils contained within that group. The groups of boards were also placed along the horizontal axes in order of taxable capacity so that the least able boards appear on the extreme left and the ablest boards on the extreme right. The per-pupil yield of each element in the foundation grant plan was then plotted for the groups of boards along the vertical axes.

The per-pupil yield of the foundation tax rate, of course, varied directly with taxable capacity. In the case of the public elementary schools (Figure 14), a significant proportion of the districts were able to raise revenue in excess of the foundation level of expenditure from this source alone. The basic tax relief grant simply added a flat amount to the revenue produced by the foundation tax rate. The effect of this grant, then, was to enable even more districts to exceed the foundation level of expenditure. That feature was expanded for the elementary school systems by the special, or minimum, equalization grant.

The effect of the equalizing portion of the formula – the true foundation plan formula – was to bring the total revenue up to the foundation level for those districts unable to do so by means of the foundation tax rate or special grants.

As can be seen from Figure 14, public elementary school boards responsible for some 70 per cent of the pupils were able to exceed the foundation level of expenditure without benefit of an equalization grant. Thus, equalization applied to only 30 per cent of these pupils. The exact reverse situation prevailed for separate elementary school boards (Figure 15). Boards responsible for only 30 per cent of the pupils were able to exceed the foundation level so that an equalization grant was paid in respect of the remaining 70 per cent. The difference was due, of course, to the different revenue-raising capacities of the property tax base available to each of the two systems.

The secondary school boards were treated not unlike the separate school boards in that equalization encompassed the majority of pupils. In respect of both academic and vocational pupils, but especially the latter, only the very able districts were able to support levels of expenditure above the foundation level by means of the standard rate of taxation and the minimum grant.

The decision to limit the application of the foundation plan formula to ordinary expenditures left extraordinary expenditures to be treated by some form of flat or variable percentage rate formula.

The grant plan of 1964 made no change in this area from the principles of the plan adopted in 1958. What happened in 1964 was simply that mathematical formulas were substituted for the schedules or tables in determining the percentage rate of grant to be applied to the approved, or 'recognized,' extraordinary expenditure. All boards continued to receive a minimum grant of 35 per cent of their recognized expenditure, and this minimum was also termed a 'Basic Tax Relief Grant.' In addition,

FIGURE 14
Per-pupil yield of foundation tax rate, basic grant, equalization grant, and minimum equalization grant:
public elementary boards in classes of equalized assessment per classroom, 1965

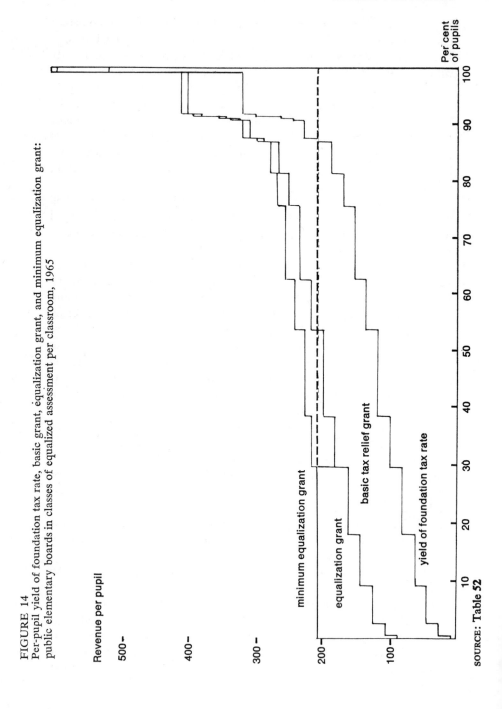

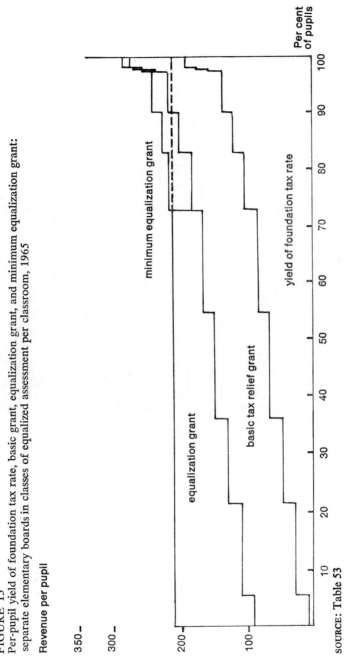

FIGURE 15
Per-pupil yield of foundation tax rate, basic grant, equalization grant, and minimum equalization grant:
separate elementary boards in classes of equalized assessment per classroom, 1965

SOURCE: Table 53

FIGURE 16
Per-pupil yield of foundation tax rate, basic grant, and equalization grant: academic pupils in secondary boards in classes of equalized assessment per classroom, 1965

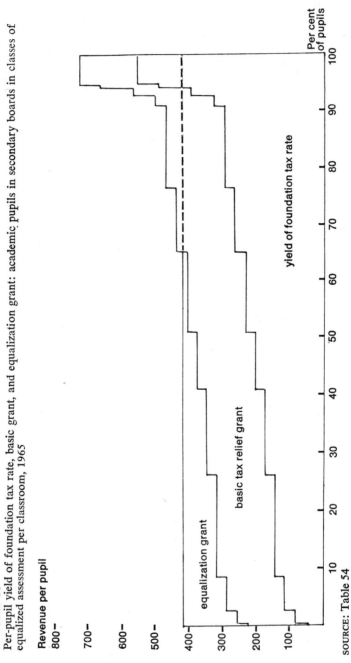

SOURCE: Table 54

FIGURE 17
Per-pupil yield of foundation tax rate, basic grant, and equalization grant: vocational pupils in secondary boards in classes of equalized assessment per classroom, 1965

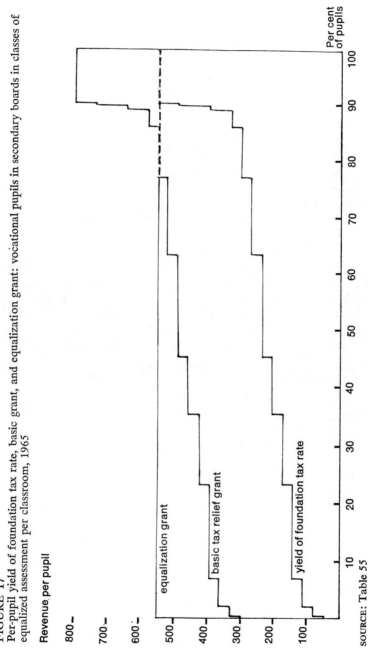

SOURCE: Table 55

qualifying boards were to receive one or both of two additional grants, the first an equalization grant, and the second a 'growth–need' grant.

For secondary boards, the equalization percentage rate was calculated as 0.1 per cent for each $2000 or fraction by which the equalized assessment per classroom fell below $1,260,000. Translated into an equation, the formula was: grant per cent $= 1,260,000 -$ ETA per classroom$/20,000$. The rate was held to a maximum of 55 per cent, reached when the assessment per classroom fell to $160,000.

The equalization formula for elementary school boards was somewhat more complicated, in that two equations were employed. Where the equalized assessment per classroom was between $230,000 and $400,000, the rate was 0.1 per cent for each $1000 or fraction by which the equalized assessment per classroom fell below $400,000, or: grant per cent $=400,000 -$ ETA per classroom$/10,000$. The maximum rate for boards in this category was 17 per cent.

Where the equalized assessment per classroom was less than $230,000, however, the rate began at 17 per cent and increased by 0.1 per cent for each further decrease of $500 or fraction in the assessment per classroom. Thus: grant per cent $= 17.0 + 230,000 -$ ETA per classroom$/5000$. The maximum rate for boards in this category was 57 per cent.

The two elementary equations were necessary in order to maintain rate differentials similar to those prescribed in the schedules under the former plan. Under those schedules, the grant rate had increased more rapidly as taxing capacity decreased for the less able school districts. To have provided these less able districts with similar rates of grant by means of a single equation which still equalized up to the $400,000 level would have necessitated paying higher rates to the abler districts. Presumably, the reason for not doing so was based on a desire to avoid increasing provincial assistance in this area or, more realistically, to channel the overall increase in provincial assistance into the foundation grants for ordinary expenditures.

The special 'growth-need' feature introduced into the rate schedules in 1958 was continued in 1964 under a distinct grant provision. In addition to the flat-rate minimum or basic tax relief grant of 35.0 per cent, and the equalizing grant of from 0.1 to 55.0 or 57.0 per cent, boards were paid a growth-need grant if their recognized extraordinary expenditure per classroom exceeded $500 (elementary) or $1000 (secondary).

The basic expenditure levels of $500 and $1000 were those which had been determined in 1958 as representing the average expenditures of boards without abnormal extraordinary expenditure requirements.

For elementary school boards, the growth-need grant rate increased by

0.1 per cent for each $50 or fraction by which the recognized extraordinary expenditure per classroom exceeded $500. The equation was thus: grant per cent = (REE per C-R) – 500 / 500. The maximum rate was the lesser of 10.0 and the difference between 95.0 and the sum of the other two percentage rates (the total grant on recognized extraordinary expenditure was thus limited to 95 per cent).

For secondary school boards the growth-need grant rate increased by 0.1 per cent for each $25 or fraction by which the recognized extraordinary expenditure per classroom exceeded $1000, or: grant per cent = (REE per C-R) – 1000/250. In this case the maximum rate was the lesser of 20.0 and the difference between 95.0 and the sum of the other two percentage rates.

In the case of all the grants for extraordinary expenditures, it is clear that the intention was simply to substitute formulas for the previous schedules. No particular extension beyond the previous plans in either equalization or tax relief was provided in this substitution.

The corporation tax adjustment grant

The fact that separate school boards have had a chronic deficiency in revenue-raising capacity in comparison with public school boards was illustrated in Chapter 4. A foundation plan formula could have eliminated this deficiency as effectively as it could have eliminated all deficiencies in revenue-raising capacity. This potential of the formula was recognized by the spokesmen of the separate school trustees and explains their request for such a formula in their 1962 brief.

In order to have fulfilled this potential completely, however, two conditions were necessary. First, the foundation level of expenditure needed to be at least equal to the highest level of expenditure then prevailing (this was what Maxwell Cameron referred to as the 'ideal' level). Second, the foundation tax rate needed to be set so as to yield the foundation level of expediture in the ablest district, reduced by any general tax relief intended to be provided. As has already been shown, the Ontario programme rejected both of these conditions. In so doing it precluded the possibility of the programme's eliminating the public-separate school revenue deficiency (this is not intended to suggest that the programme could not, or did not, reduce that deficiency).

The above argument can be demonstrated by application of the grant formulas to two hypothetical boards. The public school board is assumed to have one weighted pupil and an equalized assessment of $20,000. The separate school board is assumed to have one weighted pupil also, but an equalized assessment of only $5000.

Applying the foundation plan formula to the public school board, then, we find: $G = (210)(1) - (.011)(20,000) = 210 - 220 = 0$ (assuming no negative grants). However, the board is guaranteed a basic tax relief grant of $80 per pupil and an equalization grant of $10 per pupil. The total grant is thus equal to $90. Adding the yield of the foundation tax rate to this, the total revenue made available to the board is equal to $90 + 220 = \$310$.

Applying the same formula to the separate school board, we find: $G = (210)(1) - (.011)(5,000) = 210 - 55 = \$155$. This board would qualify for no basic tax relief grant* or special equalization grant, and its total grant would remain at $155. Adding the yield of the foundation tax rate would produce a total revenue of $155 + 55 = \$210$.

Thus, the programme would result in a discrepancy of $100 per pupil in the revenue available to the two school systems. And, as well, the discrepancy would increase as the public school expenditure level increased above $310, assuming both boards levied approximately the same tax rate. The public school board could spend $390 with a levy of fifteen mills. The same levy would enable the separate school board to spend only $230, increasing the disparity from $100 to $160.

For the first time since the Hepburn government's ill-fated 1936 amendment to the Assessment Act, the cabinet made a specific attempt to reduce this disparity. Rather than doing so within the foundation formula, however, it adopted a special supplementary grant, known as the corporation tax adjustment grant (CTAG). The special grant was based on the recognition by the province that separate schools were being treated inequitably in that they had very limited access to the taxation of the property of corporations whose ownership is not tightly held and controlled. Thus, the provincial government admitted that the disparities in revenue-raising capacities were a provincial responsibility in so far as the disparities were produced by an inequitable distribution of local taxing powers.

The corporation tax adjustment grant was designed to provide separate school boards with the revenue they would have received from local taxation had they been able to tax their 'fair share' of corporation property.[31] The political genius of the scheme, especially as compared with Hepburn's proposal, lay in the fact that it did not deprive the public schools of the revenue derived from a tax base greater than the fair share. This was defined as being equal to the proportion of non-corporation residential and farm assessment actually supporting the board. Thus, if

---

* /In actual practice, the board would receive a basic tax relief grant of $80 and an equalization grant of $75. Since the total grant would be the same, the board would gain no advantage from the provision of a basic grant.

the separate school board was supported by 30 per cent of the non-corporation residential and farm assessment, its fair share would be thirty per cent of the corporation property assessment.

If, in fact, this separate school board was supported by only 10 per cent of the corporation assessment, then the special grant provision would 'allocate' the equivalent of another 20 per cent.* This allocated assessment was then treated in two ways. First, because it represented assessment which, in equity, should have supported the board, it was added to the assessment already supporting the board in determining the equalized taxable assessment for the equalization grants. In other words, the board's taxable capacity, or ability, was increased by the allocation of this corporation assessment.

Second, and because the board was not actually given the power to tax the allocated assessment, a special grant, the corporation tax adjustment grant, was paid to the board. The grant was equal to the revenue which the board would have obtained had it been able to tax the assessment at the public school rate.[32] Use of the public school tax rate was necessary in order to prevent manipulation of the grant by separate school boards.

The intent of the grant was to correct an inequity in the local tax structure without actually interfering with that structure. Because the basic inequity was not corrected, the grant provision contained a fundamental weakness. The grant did not fully redress the fiscal disparity resulting from the structural inequity. It did not permit separate school boards to tax the allocated assessment, but paid them the equivalent of the public school commercial tax rate – a rate which was reduced by the public school board's disproportionate share of corporation property. Had the tax base been structurally reallocated, the smaller public school base would have produced a higher rate of taxation or a lower level of revenue, either of which would have reduced the revenue disparity between the two systems.

In fact, it was even possible that the public school board could satisfy its revenue requirements with a combination of provincial grants and a local tax rate of less than eleven mills. This possibility was built into the foundation plan formula, under which any board with an equalized assessment per pupil of more than $11,818 could spend at the foundation level of $210 per pupil with a tax rate of less than eleven mills. If such were the case, the separate school board would actually have been penalized by the corporation tax adjustment grant, since the board would

* / The grant was only applied when the total corporation assessment comprised at least 5 per cent of all assessment in a municipality.

receive less than the yield of eleven mills under the adjustment grant but would have the full eleven mills deducted under the equalization grant.

It was rather ironical that the special grant was introduced into the grant structure at the very time when the separate school spokesmen had dropped their claim to a reallocation of local taxing powers. That shift, however, had been predicated upon the province introducing a fully equalizing grant scheme. That the province did not do so, and that its alternative grant programme was incapable of eliminating the separate school revenue deficiency was quickly recognized by the separate school spokesmen. This recognition led to pressure on the cabinet to change the basic principles of the corporation tax adjustment grant.

Special and stimulation grants

In addition to the provisions outlined above, the 1964 grant programme contained eleven additional grant formulas – some in several parts – designed to meet particular needs or stimulate particular activities. All but one of the provisions, however, represented the continuation of provisions contained in previous grant programmes.

Since these special grants were quite ancillary to the overall grant structure, we need not devote much space to their consideration. A package of special grants was continued from early grant plans the effect of which was to ease the transition of a school board when, through municipal annexation or amalgamation, it was shifted from one grant schedule to another. Grants were paid for night school classes either at a 90 per cent rate (if the class were eligible for a federal grant[33]) or at a rate from 50 to 80 per cent. Several grants were paid to boards voluntarily joining a larger unit. An elementary school board received $300 prior to joining the unit, while the enlarged school board received $500 per year indefinitely for each smaller unit consolidated within it. Secondary school boards received $150 for each rural public school section contained within the high school district. Elementary boards received up to 50 per cent of the cost of milk distributed to pupils free of charge. Small secondary schools received up to $2000 for academic pupils and $4000 for vocational pupils as compensation for the extra cost assumed to be involved in operating a small school. Boards received up to $3 per elementary school pupil for text books and a flat grant of $12 per pupil in grades nine and ten.[34] Elementary boards received up to an additional $3 per pupil for library books. A board which offered courses in home economics or industrial arts to pupils of another board received a flat grant of $7.50 per pupil per term. Boards received up to 50 per cent of the cost of a school site. Grants were paid to defray part or all of the cost of a board's membership in the Ontario School Trustees' Council and one of its affiliated associations.[35]

The only grant of this type added in 1964 was one covering the salaries of locally employed inspectors. Boards received from 35 to 95 per cent of the salaries up to a maximum salary of $800 per month.

Complications in the grant programme

The above description represents the essential provisions of the Ontario Foundation Tax Plan of 1964. It does not, however, give the full flavour of the plan's complexity.

Little would be gained from an exhaustive description of all these complications save, perhaps, a feeling of sympathy for those who developed and worked with the scheme. It is important, however, that the reasons for such complications be appreciated. Two examples should suffice for this purpose: the calculation of the weighted classrooms and pupils, and the limitations on the total grant. The reader whose interest lies only in an appreciation of the principles of the grant structure might choose to exercise his prerogative at this point and move directly to Chapter 9.

The foundation plan used two formulas for calculating and weighting the average daily attendance. One was used for the basic tax relief grant (the minimum grant for ordinary expenditures) and the other for the equalization grant.

The first formula began with the basic pupil load of a school district — the actual average daily attendance of all pupils for whom the school board was legally responsible. This basic load was then weighted by adding a factor representing the additional burden imputed to pupils receiving special instructional services. The grant regulation set out a table of weighting factors for various categories of special pupils. For example, an approved class for hard-of-hearing children carried a factor of ten. The total average daily attendance of the school board was then increased by ten for each hard-of-hearing class it operated.

The basic tax relief grant was calculated directly from this weighted enrolment. If the figure for a particular elementary school board were 150.65, for example, the minimum grant would be (150.65) $(\$80.00) = \$12,052$.

The second weighted pupil figure was calculated as a function of the number of weighted classrooms. The latter was determined under a formula designed to take a number of varying situations into account.

The way in which the number of classrooms was calculated for any particular board thus depended on the particular situational category into which the board fell.

Secondary schools, being almost entirely under the jurisdiction of boards of fairly large districts, were all treated uniformly. The number of weighted classrooms was equal to the actual average daily attendance of all resident pupils divided by twenty-two. Elementary school boards were placed in one of four categories, with a distinct formula being applied to each. The four categories were: boards with 1000 or more pupils (in average daily attendance) in a single school section or separate school zone, boards with 1000 or more pupils in an enlarged district (township school area or combined separate school zone), boards with fewer than 1000 pupils in a single section or zone, and boards with fewer than 1000 pupils in an enlarged district.

Boards with 1000 or more pupils in a single section or zone were considered the standard, or normal, boards. For such, the number of classrooms was simply the lesser of the number actually operated on the first school day of January in the current year and the number of resident pupils divided by thirty. Boards with fewer than 1000 pupils were considered to have legitimate need (small enrolments per grade, sparse settlement) for operating classrooms with fewer than thirty pupils. For such boards in a single section or zone, the number of weighted classrooms was taken as the *greater* of the number actually operated and the number of resident pupils divided by thirty. The number of weighted classrooms could not exceed the number of pupils divided by twenty, however.

For boards responsible for enlarged districts, the appropriate one of the two above calculations was used, but a special weighting factor was added. The reason for the supplementary weighting can be appreciated by reference to Figure 18, which represents a hypothetical township school area composed of six school sections each of which formerly had its own school board operating a one-room school for twenty pupils. While each of these six sections was a distinct unit, the second of the two basic calculations would have applied and each district would have been credited with one weighted classroom – a total of six weighted classrooms for the whole township.

If the six sections were combined into a township school area, and a single central school erected, that school would likely have only four classrooms (thirty pupils in each room). The same formula would then credit this enlarged district with only four classrooms, the greater of the number operated (four) and the average daily attendance divided by thirty ($120/30 = 4$). The act of consolidation and centralization would thus

FIGURE 18
Hypothetical township school area composed of six former school
sections

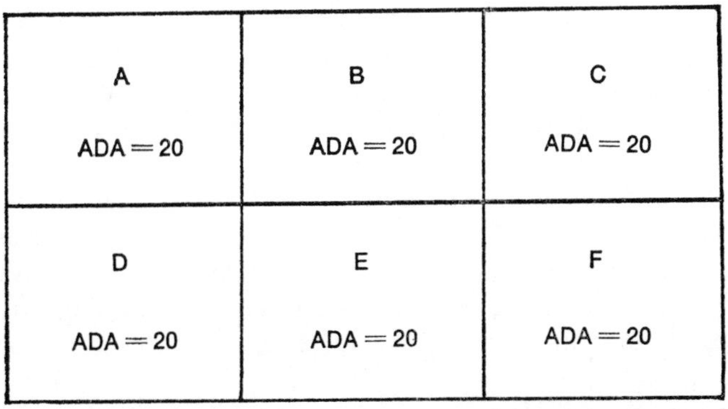

A ADA = 20	B ADA = 20	C ADA = 20
D ADA = 20	E ADA = 20	F ADA = 20

have reduced the number of weighted classrooms credited to the township by one-third, or two. Because both the current and capital equalization grants were to be determined from this factor, the combined grant to the enlarged district could well be less than the sum of the grants to the individual sections. This would have run counter to the provincial government's policy of encouraging the formation of larger districts.

The additional weighting factor was designed to correct this anomaly. Boards of enlarged districts were credited with a number of classrooms equal to the lesser of one-half the number of dissolved sections or zones (in which no schools were being operated) and one-sixtieth of the resident pupils living in rural areas within the district.

The effect of the additional weighting can be seen by reference again to the hypothetical example illustrated in Figure 18. That board would have been credited with a special weighting factor of the lesser of $5/2 = 2.5$ and $120/60 = 2.0$. Thus, the factor would be 2.0 which, when added to the basic 4.0, would credit the board with six classrooms, exactly the number calculated without the consolidation.

For all school boards, elementary and secondary, the number of weighted classrooms could not be less than 1.0 for a board operating a school or less than 0.5 for a board educating all its pupils in the schools of other boards.

Having thus determined the number of classrooms, the weighted average daily attendance to be used for the equalization grant was calculated as the greater of two figures: first, the relevant number of classrooms as calculated above multiplied by thirty, plus the factor for pupils receiving special instruction, or, second, the weighted average daily attendance used for the basic tax relief grant plus the number of classrooms added for enlarged districts multiplied by thirty.

The second alternative used to determine the weighted average daily attendance for the equalization grant was included to protect one particular group of school boards – boards with 1000 or more pupils having a pupil-teacher ratio of more than thirty-to-one. For these boards the number of weighted classrooms was limited to the actual number of pupils divided by thirty. If that quotient had then simply been multiplied by thirty, the number of weighted pupils would have been the same as the actual number of pupils, and the board would have derived no benefit from the intermediate calculation of weighted classrooms. This alternative calculation, therefore, assured such boards of the benefit of the weighting produced by consideration of the number of closed school sections or zones.

The weighted attendance figure produced by this second rather tortuous exercise was then multiplied by the equalization portion of the foundation level ($130 for elementary schools) and from this product was subtracted the yield of the eleven mill foundation tax rate to arrive at the equalization grant.

The weighting of pupils in the above manner created a problem in the calculation of the actual grants. Since all of the additional pupils credited to a board on the basis of its size or location were only devices for taking account of assumed need, there was no guarantee that this need would, in fact, exist in the form of necessary greater unit expenditure. Referring again to the hypothetical district depicted in Figure 18, the weighting calculation produced a weighted average daily attendance of 180 pupils whereas there were actually only 120 pupils. The effective foundation level of expenditure for this board would not have been $210 ($80 + $130), but $275 ($80 + 180/120 × 130). There would be no guarantee that this board actually required $275 per pupil to provide the level of service others could provide for $210. A maximum limitation was therefore placed on the equalization grant for current operations.

The maximum grant was equal to the sum of the capital basic tax relief and equalization percentage rates applied to a figure termed the 'net recognized current cost of operating.' The latter was equal to the total of all current expenditures less the current basic tax relief grant and a number of stimulation grants – it was, therefore, the current expenditure which remained to be supported by the current equalization grant.

In addition to that maximum, three limitations were applied to the total grant paid to each school board. Two of these, one applying a minimum and the other a maximum, were based on the decimal fraction that the 1963 grant was of the recognized expenditure for 1962 (upon which the 1963 grant was, in large measure, based). The 1964 grant, as a decimal fraction of the 1963 recognized expenditure, could not increase by more than 120 per cent, nor decrease by more than five percentage points. The intent of the provision was simply to smooth out any radical changes in the magnitude of grant paid to a board as a result of the transition to the new plan.

Finally, an overriding maximum limitation was imposed on the grant, calculated as a percentage of a board's total expenditure (not just the recognized expenditure) in the preceding year. Special formulas were prescribed for the calculation of this percentage rate. For elementary boards, the rate began at 35.0 per cent and increased by 0.1 per cent for each $1000 or fraction by which the equalized assessment per classroom fell below $620,000, to a maximum rate of 95 per cent. For secondary boards, the rate began at 35.0 per cent and increased by 0.1 per cent for each $2000 or fraction by which the equalized assessment per classoom fell below $1,260,000, again to a maximum rate of 95 per cent. The total grant, then, could not exceed this rate applied to the total expenditure in the preceding year.

The basic provisions of the Ontario Foundation Tax Plan were, as has been revealed in the preceding pages, simple in concept but highly complex in application. The plan was described by the Ontario Committee on Taxation as one exhibiting '... that quality to which every part of a provincial and local revenue system should aspire – fiscal sophistication in a framework of simplicity.'[36]

The reaction of the layman was probably summed up better by the Toronto *Star* in an editorial written at the time the plan was first introduced. 'The Education Minister's statement was so complex that MPP's jeered, unable to understand what he was talking about. And the system of grants is so complicated that it will take ... [the] executive secretary of the Metro School Board another week to work out how much it means in dollars and cents to Metro schools and taxpayers.'[37]

One of the very real advantages of the 1964 grant programme was the ease with which adjustments could be made in any of its components. Both the process by which such adjustments were made and the nature of the actual adjustments are to be the subject of the following chapter.

9

The Ontario Foundation Tax Plan, 1965-8: the process of change and overall impact

The Ontario Foundation Tax Plan was subjected to annual revision following its inception. This revision, however, took place within a decision-making structure which differed in certain major respects from that which existed during the original development of the plan. Before examining the nature of the changes in the plan, then, we shall examine the nature of the changes in the process.

POLICY-FORMULATION PROCESS
Changes took place in the personnel of two of the three units in the policy-formulation process and in the roles of all three. The three units, described in the preceding chapter, were the cabinet, the departmental committee, and the academic advisers or consultants.

The educational grants committee of the cabinet simply ceased to function. The role it had formerly performed was delegated to two others. The departmental committee, with the assistance of the consultants and subject to review by the minister and deputy minister, was to be responsible for the development of new and revised grant programmes. The Treasury Board, itself a committee of cabinet, was to be responsible for exercising a general fiscal control over provincial grants and for the development of broad fiscal policies to be implemented by means of specific grant programmes. Some time elapsed before the Treasury Board staff developed the competence and experience necessary for the performance of its second function. As a result – and the following chapters will provide considerable documentation of this point – the Department of Education grants committee proceeded to develop and expand the foundation tax plan without clearly defined policy objectives and without an adequate mechanism for integrating this plan with other elements of provincial assistance to school boards. The Treasury Board did, however, exercise its function of general fiscal control.

Changes at the consultant level were also of signficant proportions. On 1 July 1965 Dr Jackson assumed the directorship of the newly-formed Ontario Institute for Studies in Education (OISE). Reference will be made to this institution at a later point, but it was designed to be a large centre undertaking research, development, and graduate instruction in almost all areas of education. The increased administrative responsibilities incumbent in this position forced Jackson to relinquish his active participation in the research and development project he had previously carried on with Professor Rideout. Dr Jackson remained a close confidant of both the Prime Minister and the Minister of Education, but he was no longer involved in the generation of detailed grant proposals. The major responsibility in this area fell upon Professor Rideout.* And while Jackson lost none of his access to the provincial cabinet, this access came more and more to be shared with Rideout. In January 1966 the author was employed by OISE,† specifically to assist Professor Rideout in his research and development programme. In the following September, the author was invited to sit on the Department of Education grants committee. To a considerable extent, then, the relationship which had previously existed between Jackson and Rideout had been replaced by that between Rideout and the author. The difference lay in the over-shadowing presence of Dr Jackson in the latter situation.

The departmental committee probably experienced the least change in appearance but the greatest change in function. Previously an administrative unit, the committee was delegated major responsibilities for the examination of policy issues and the formulation of recommendations to the minister and deputy minister. While the committee was always careful to avoid trespassing on areas of cabinet responsibility (policy making), it nevertheless became a powerful unit in the total process. The committee's strength lay in the extent of its control of the flow of information to the more senior officials of the department, the minister, and the cabinet as a whole.

Because of the elevation of the committee's role, some examination of its membership is now essential. Disregarding the co-opted consultants for the moment, the committee consisted of six departmental officials in 1968.[1] Four of these members had served consistently since before the

* / Professor Rideout became a member of the Department of Educational Administration within OISE when the latter was established.

† / The author was appointed as research associate and then as lecturer in July 1967.

inception of the grant programme in 1964. These four were P.H. Cunningham, F.S. Wilson, J.R. Thomson, and W.G. Chatterton. Cunningham, the chairman of the committee, became director of financial administration in 1966 (a staff position in the office of the assistant deputy minister, administration). Previously, he had been director of the departmental business administration branch (1965), superintendent of business administration (1958–65), and chief of the grants office prior to 1958. Wilson assumed the latter office[2] in 1958, prior to which he was assistant to the superintendent of business administration (Cunningham). Thomson and Chatterton were both assistant superintendents in the supervision division of the department. Prior to the departmental reorganization of 1965–6, Thomson had been in the secondary school section and Chatterton in the elementary school section. The reorganization eliminated that distinction.

The two more recent additions to the committee were G.D. Spry and R.K. Fletcher. Spry had been comptroller of finance for the Toronto Board of Education and was appointed to the newly-created post of director of the school business administration branch of the department in 1966. He joined the committee at that time. Fletcher joined the committee in 1967, upon his appointment as assistant supervisor of the grants section. Both Wilson and Fletcher were responsible to Spry in the departmental hierarchy.

One of the most interesting aspects of this membership was the concentration of experience and expertise in the areas of accounting, budgetting, and school administration. Four of the six members (Cunningham, Spry, Wilson, and Fletcher) were chartered accountants. The remaining two (Thomson and Chatterton) were former school inspectors. In order to fulfil its new responsibilities in the policy-formation process, however, the committee required a competence in intergovernmental finance generally and education finance specifically. For this it turned to its co-opted academic consultants. Thus, while the character of the policy-formation structure changed markedly after 1964, the constant element was the central role played by the academic consultants. The changed process may be characterized by Figure 19.

The process of annual review of the provincial grant programme took place according to a relatively consistent time-table. During the months of February through August, the data necessary for the calculation of the grants were collected from the school boards by the Department of Education. During September, the process of review began simultaneously with the calculation of the current year's grants. From September until late October or early November (the length of time usually depending upon the extensiveness of the proposed revisions) the departmental

FIGURE 19
Illustration of decision-making structure involved in development of post-1964
grant programmes

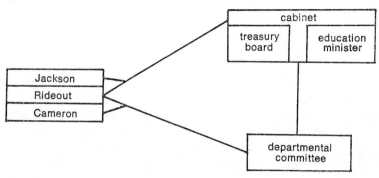

committee considered problems in the grant programme and proposals
for their resolution. The identification of the problems might come from
any of the three units in the system or from outside (briefs from school
boards, associations). Proposals for resolving the problems might come
from the same source, but most often were developed in the deliberations
of the committee – often in response to tentative suggestions from the
consultants. At the conclusion of this phase, the committee drafted a
summary of its proposed changes in the grant plan for the subsequent year,
together with an estimate of the cost of these changes and of the total
grant programme. This summary was forwarded through the senior
officers of the department to the minister and incorporated in the departmental estimates submitted to the Treasury Board.

During November, and sometimes into December, the proposals were
reviewed by these persons or groups. The proposals might be accepted,
rejected, modified, or referred back for further study. Because of the
informal channels of communication within the department, including
the minister, approval was virtually certain when the process reached
the final stages. The Treasury Board, however, might well prescribe the
elimination of one or more proposed changes or the reallocation of
incremental spending into a preferred proposal – although the departmental committee would participate in establishing priorities when all
proposals were not accepted.

Once the major proposals had been reviewed and approved at these
levels (minor administrative changes were not reviewed), the departmental committee transcribed them into a departmental regulation. This
was usually completed in late December or early January. The completed regulation was then forwarded to the minister, approved by the

cabinet, and released at the minister's discretion. Public release – and distribution to the school boards – usually occurred in late January or early February. Thereafter, the collection of data began and the cycle renewed.

GRANT PROGRAMME

The major changes which were made in the grant programme between 1964 and 1968 will be discussed within several categories, designed to illuminate the kinds of changes more than the specific details subjected to change. In addition, however, one particular set of changes will be examined in considerable detail in order to explore the nature of the relationship between the policy-formation process and the specific changes.

Equalizing local assessments
In 1966 the Department of Municipal Affairs changed the basis upon which local assessments were equalized. Rather than standardizing assessments to their equivalent value in 1940, they were henceforth to be standardized to their full value in the current year. Even though the foundation tax plan represented the major use to which this assessment equalization scheme was put, the Department of Education was not involved in the decision to make this change. The use of current values provided a more exact measure of taxable capacity and therefore would hardly have been opposed by those responsible for the education grants. However, the change in standard base created two problems for the grant plan.

The first problem was the rather simple administrative one of amending the relative assessment figures used in the grant formulas. The change in assessment base increased the nominal value of equalized assessments in the province by approximately 3.5 times. Maintenance of the same relative treatment of school districts thus required an equivalent adjustment of all formulas using equalized assessment. This was done by reducing the foundation tax rate from eleven to three mills for elementary boards and from seven to two mills for secondary boards.* The formulas used to determine the percentage rates for the equalization grant on extraordinary expenditure were also amended, and the opportunity was used to substitute a single formula for the two previously used in respect of elementary boards. The elementary rate increased by 0.1 per cent for

* / The change in the elementary rate represented a modest extension of equalization in that the tax rate was reduced by 3.67 times while the assessment had been increased by 3.5 times.

each $2500 or fraction by which the assessment per classroom fell below $1,500,000. As an equation, the formula became: grant per cent = 1,500,000 − ETA per classroom/25,000. In the formula for secondary boards, the percentage increased by 0.1 for each $7000 or fraction by which the assessment per classroom fell below $4,410,000. Again as an equation, the formula became: grant per cent = 4,410,000 − ETA per classroom/70,000.

The second problem resulting from the adoption of a new standard for equalizing assessments was partly a product of the change itself but more importantly a product of the lack of consultation between the two departments involved. If the basis of assessment equalization were to be full value in the current year, it would follow that the equalizing factors would have to be completely revised each year. Given the volatile nature of the real estate market at the time, these revisions could involve substantial changes in the total value of equalized assessment.

In 1968, however, the Department of Municipal Affairs did not complete this revision. Some municipalities were left with the equalizing factor established for 1967, while others were assigned new factors based on the changes in property values during the year. The Department of Education was not informed that the revision was incomplete.[3] The effect of the partial revision was to produce a rather dramatic, and largely artificial, change in the relative taxing capacities of school districts (and thus in the equalization grants to which they would be entitled). When the grants committee discovered the dimensions of this situation, and determined the cause (by initiating communication with the Department of Municipal Affairs on the issue), it was forced to recommend the use of either the 1967 or 1968 equalizing factors in the 1968 grants, depending on which was more favourable to the school board.

The result was a serious imbalance in the equalization formula embodied in the foundation plan. Where a revised factor decreased the relative taxing capacity of a school district, this was translated into a relatively higher provincial grant. But where the new factor increased the relative capacity, the change was not reflected in a relatively reduced grant. However, where the factor remained unchanged, the relative grant treatment remained unchanged, regardless of whether taxing capacity had actually increased or decreased. The latter problem would not have arisen had there been adequate channels of communication and co-ordination between the two departments of the provincial government.

Foundation levels of expenditure
No changes were made in the foundation levels of expenditure in the second year of the grant programme (1965). This was a deliberate step

designed to permit the original levels to become fully operational – the limitations placed upon increases and decreases in total grant prevented a number of boards from reaching their proper levels of provincial support in one year. In 1966, 1967, and 1968, however, significant increases were made in these levels. The elementary foundation level was raised from $210 to $220 in 1966, to $260 in 1967, and to $280 in 1968. The academic secondary level was increased from $420 to $440 in 1966, to $450 in 1967, and to $465 in 1968. Finally, the vocational secondary level was increased from $550 to $570 in 1966, to $580 in 1967, and to $600 in 1968.

The manner in which these increases were distributed between the equalizing and minimum provisions of the foundation plan formulas is highly interesting. In 1966 the basic tax relief grant and the equalization grant were both increased by $5 for elementary boards and by $10 for secondary boards. Increasing the minimum grant benefited all school boards regardless of their relative taxable capacities. Increasing the equalization grant, of course, benefited only those boards with relatively small taxing capacities. The changes in the secondary panel in 1967 were similar but less generous. Both the minimum and equalization grants were increased by $5, producing an overall increase of $10 in the foundation level. For elementary school boards, however, the foundation level was increased by $40, all of the increase being put into the equalization grant. This was one of the two responses of the government to a particularly well-argued brief submitted by the separate school trustees' associations (the second was a change in the corporation tax adjustment grant, to be described shortly). This change produced a dramatic extension in the equalization achieved by the foundation plan. Limiting that extension somewhat, however, was a simultaneous increase in the foundation tax rate from three to 3.5 mills.

Under the original elementary school foundation plan formula of 1964, equalization had extended only to districts with equalized taxable assessments per pupil of $11,818 or less. Substituting the revised method of equalizing assessments introduced in 1966, this amount would have been $41,363. With the foundation level and tax rate introduced in 1967, however, equalization was extended to all districts with equalized taxable assessments up to $50,000 per pupil. Without the increase in the tax rate, the level of equalization would have been increased to an equalized assessment of $58,333 per pupil.

The changes in the foundation levels for 1968 were dramatically different. The elementary school level was increased to $280, but the full $20 increase was put into the minimum, or basic tax relief, grant. This had the effect of increasing the provincial grant to all districts – without regard to taxable capacity. Unlike the 1967 increase in the foundation level, it provided additional support for the abler districts. For these abler districts, however, at least one-half the increase was illusory. Coupled with the increase of $20 in the minimum grant was the elimination of the minimum equalization grant.*

The minimum equalization grant – a transitional feature of the 1964 programme – was eliminated on the advice of the consultants when it was determined that the maximum net benefit of the grant would be $20 per pupil. By increasing the minimum grant by $20, then, no board could suffer a loss in total grant from the elimination of the special provision. The net benefit of the increase in the minimum grant varied from zero to $20 per pupil. And since the benefit varied inversely with taxing capacity – that is, since the discontinued special grant had been of benefit only to the abler districts – there was a certain amount of equalization incidental to this change.

The foundation level increases for secondary school boards affected both the basic and equalization grants, but were weighted in favour of the basic. The level was increased from $450 to $465 for academic pupils, $10 of this increase being channelled through the basic grant and $5 through the equalization grant. The vocational level was increased by $20 to $600 – $15 through the basic, and $5 through the equalization, grant. The above changes in the foundation levels of expenditure are summarized in Table 26.

TABLE 26
Increases in foundation levels of expenditure

Type of pupil	Increase over previous year							
	1965		1966		1967		1968	
	BTRG[a]	EG[b]	BTRG	EG	BTRG	EG	BTRG	EG
Elementary			$5	$5		$40	$20[c]	
Secondary-academic			10	10	$5	5	10	$5
Secondary-vocational			10	10	5	5	15	5

[a]/BTRG = basic tax relief grant
[b]/EG = equalization grant
[c]/Effect reduced by elimination of the minimum equatization grant.

*/ As described earlier, this grant had increased from $10 per pupil in inverse relation to taxable capacity until it was exceeded by the normal equalization grant.

From ADA *to* ADE

In 1967 the concept used in measuring the number of pupils was changed from average daily attendance to average daily enrolment. This change automatically increased the pupil-load (and therefore the grant) of all school boards, since it ceased to reduce the load for absent pupils. The change was made for two purposes: to relieve teachers of some of the clerical responsibilities involved in keeping daily registers, and to cease penalizing school boards for abnormal numbers of absences produced by such disruptions as epidemics of influenza. The change was made at the direction of the deputy minister of education but had the unanimous support of the grants committee because it was considered a more adequate measure of local need.

Corporation tax adjustment grant

In Chapter 8 it was noted that the corporation tax adjustment grant could work to the disadvantage of separate school boards when the public school tax rate on commercial assessment was less than eleven mills (since the grant was equal to the yield of the public school rate on the allocated assessment while the yield of eleven mills was deducted under the foundation plan formula). A simple correction was made in the provision for 1965, which provided that the grant would equal the greater of the public school rate and eleven mills applied to the allocated assessment. Even this did not fully rectify the problem, however, since the percentage rate for extraordinary expenditures would be reduced by the allocated assessment with no compensating increase in the special grant.

In 1966 another adjustment was made. As was noted above, the introduction of a new system of standardizing assessments in 1966 necessitated the reduction of the foundation tax rate from eleven to three mills. But rather than holding the CTAG to a floor of three mills applied to the allocated assessment, the grant was made the product of the greater of the public school rate and four mills on the allocated assessment. The net grant was thus to be at least equal to the yield of one mill – less the net reduction in grant on extraordinary expenditure (which was very unlikely to be as great as the increase in the nominal grant).

In October 1966, at the time the departmental committee was considering changes in the grant programme for 1967, the two separate school trustees' associations submitted a brief setting forth quite clearly the magnitude of the discrepancy in total revenue available to the public and separate schools.[4] The trustees called for an increase in the equalization portion of the foundation level of expenditure, and a revised formula for calculating the allocated assessment used in the corporation tax adjustment grant. The foundation level was, in fact, increased by $40 – all in the equalization grant. The response to the second request was not so straightforward.

The trustees' brief argued that the definition of 'fair share' of corporation assessment should be changed so that it would be the corporation assessment per pupil of the abler board in the municipality rather than the proportion of residential and farm assessment of the less able board. Thus, for example, if the public school board had access to $10,000 of corporation assessment per pupil, then the fair share of the separate school board would also be $10,000. If, in fact, the separate school board had access to only $2000, then it should be allocated the equivalent of $8000 per pupil. This request, if granted, would have removed the advantage accruing to public school boards by virtue of the fact that they continued to be able to tax all of their corporation assessment, while the separate school boards were given only the equivalent of their proportion of residential and farm assessment.

The cabinet, on the recommendation of the departmental committee, responded with a compromise provision. Instead of accepting the separate school trustees' position, the amended provision defined the fair share of corporation assessment as being the proportion of all elementary pupils in a municipality attending the separate schools. This compromise provision retained the relative advantage of public school boards, however. For while the separate school board would have its tax base adjusted to the equivalent of its fair share, the public school board would lose none of the disproportionate share of corporation assessment which it was able to tax. While the provision did not provide all that had been requested, it did work to the advantage of the separate school boards. This was so because, without exception, separate school boards have a greater proportion of the total enrolment in a municipality than of the total assessment, and especially of the total corporation assessment.

A second change was also made in the provision in 1967 which further increased the special grants paid to separate schools. The tax rate used in determining the actual corporation tax adjustment grant was increased from the greater of the public school rate or four mills to the greater of the equalized public school rate* plus one mill and 4.5 mills. Thus, the grant not only guaranteed the yield of one mill on the allocated assessment (the foundation tax rate had been increased from 3.0 to 3.5 mills so that 4.5 mills represented a net grant of one mill) but also assured

*/The local public school rate was adjusted to what it would have been if calculated on the basis of fully equalized assessment.

separate school boards of corresponding revenue whenever the public school tax rate exceeded the floor of 4.5 mills.

As will be illustrated shortly, these changes in the corporation tax adjustment grant, coupled with the general extension of equalization effected through the increased foundation level, produced a dramatic increase in separate school revenues and reduced the revenue disparity between public and separate schools to its lowest point since about 1952.

As the general level of equalization was broadened, however, the basic inequity of the corporation tax adjustment grant became more apparent. For while the provision worked towards the equalization of public and separate school revenues within the same municipality, it did nothing to equalize revenues between municipalities. As was noted in Chapter 8, complete and general equalization would have obviated the need for the special grant since all school boards would have had access to the same revenue per pupil with the same effort in taxation.

Logically, then, the need for the grant should have decreased as the general level of equalization increased. That the two were extended simultaneously indicates the success of the separate school trustees' political pressure, for the effect of these increases was to provide a greater increase in the level of support to a particular group of separate school districts (in municipalities with substantial amounts of corporation assessment) than was provided to all other districts – public or separate.

The enrolment growth grant

One of the basic problems in the foundation plan was its use of enrolment and expenditure data for the previous year (with the single exception of debt charges which, because they are predictable, were included for the current year). For boards with average, or less than average, rates of growth in enrolment and expenditure this created no serious problem. It simply meant that the effective rates of grant were lower than the nominal rates. For example, a grant of $15,000 calculated in respect of 100 pupils, but paid when the enrolment had increased to 105, represented a nominal grant of $150 per pupil but an effective grant of $143 per pupil. If enrolments increased uniformly for all boards, the effective grants would be uniformly lower than the nominal grants.

Where the enrolment was increasing more rapidly than the average, however, a board was placed in a position of relative disadvantage. The board received no grant in respect of additional pupils in excess of the average increase. As was shown in Chapter 5, enrolment growth was most rapid in the suburban municipalities. Thus it was in these areas that the grant formula worked most inequitably. And it was from a suburban board that pressure was exerted on the government to rectify the inequity.[5]

There were two rather obvious ways in which the problem could have been resolved. The first would have been to calculate the grants on the basis of estimates of the current year's enrolment, and to recalculate them when the final, audited, figures were available. The second would have been to substitute the attendance or enrolment of a specific date (the first school day in January, for example) for the average daily attendance or enrolment for the full year. The departmental committee, however, refused to recommend either of these solutions. In part this was based on an assessment of the benefits in increased equity as compared to the costs in administration. In part, as well, it was a function of the timing of the deliberative process.

Using the actual enrolment on a specific date would only partially correct the existing inequity. The date would have had to be in the January to June school term since a later date would not allow time for collection of data and calculation of grants within the calendar year. As a result, increases in enrolment for the September to December term would still not be reflected in increases in grant. Yet even to achieve this limited advantage would have involved the development and administration of a completely new system of collecting and checking enrolment or attendance. The alternative of using estimated enrolments was not seriously considered. The large number of school boards rendered it administratively impossible.

Probably the more compelling reason for the rejection of these alternatives was simply the timing of the deliberations. This was a case in which the minister of education directed the committee to develop a response to the particular problem. However, the direction came early in 1966 – after the grant regulations for that year had been approved and distributed. If the solution were to be effective in 1966, and this was the intent of the minister, it was essential that it be developed within the framework of the existing grant programme. Changes in the method of determining enrolment or attendance – one of the key factors in the grant formula – would have necessitated a rewriting of major sections of the regulation, and therefore were not practical until at least the following year. The committee therefore recommended the addition of a special supplementary provision in the grant programme. The general nature of this provision was developed by Professor Rideout in collaboration with Dr Jackson. The provision was issued in April 1966 as an amendment to the 1966 grant regulation.[6]

This provision, known as the attendance growth grant in 1966, placed the responsibility on any school board anticipating an above-average enrolment increase in the current year to make application for special assistance. If an elementary school board estimated that its average daily attendance for 1966 would exceed that for 1965 by at least thirty pupils and 5 per cent, then it would qualify for a grant of $100 for each estimated pupil in excess of the 'normal' increase.[7] Where a secondary school board had an average daily attendance of at least 400 in 1966 and estimated an increase of at least 10 per cent over 1965, it qualified for a special grant of $200 for each estimated pupil in excess of the 10 per cent 'normal' increase.[8] The grants were to be recalculated in 1967 when the actual increases were established. Any discrepancy between the estimated and actual increases would be reflected in an increase or decrease in the total grant for 1967.

In 1967 the name of the special provision was changed to the enrolment growth grant, simply reflecting the shift from average daily attendance to average daily enrolment throughout the grant programme. This was the only change in the provision between 1966 and 1968.

A major revision had been proposed for 1967 but was rejected by the Treasury Board.[9] The special grant contained no equalization; it provided a flat grant of $100 or $200 per pupil irrespective of taxing capacity. Professor Rideout had proposed that for 1967 the grant should begin at these flat amounts but increase thereafter in inverse relation to taxing capacity. Rideout's proposal was to pay an additional $1.00 (elementary) or $2.00 (secondary) for each percentage point in a board's equalization grant rate for extraordinary expenditures. When this proposal was rejected the provision reverted to its original formula. The proposal was not repeated in the following year.

Northern assistance grants

Chapter 8 noted the extent to which the potential equalization of a foundation plan formula was constrained in Ontario by the existing territorial organization of local educational government and the province's unwillingness to mandate a reorganization of the local units. This constraint was most pressing in the frontier and developing areas of northern Ontario. In these areas, beyond the reaches of municipal organization, school districts were organized on the recommendation of the provincial inspector (subject to the approval of the cabinet) in the case of public elementary schools, or by ten heads of families in the case of separate elementary schools. Secondary education was simply not provided in most of this area.

School districts were generally extremely small, often with fewer than twenty-five pupils in the entire district. The tax base was often so small and unstable that the school board could not, without a confiscatory rate of taxation, support more than a minimal educational offering. Besides these unique factors, they shared in the problem of a higher cost structure for goods and services typical of the whole northern region of the province. During 1966 the Department of Education undertook an extensive analysis of the problems of the remote northern school districts. The results of this analysis were made public by the minister in April 1966.[10] The study concluded that of the 156 one- and two-room school districts examined, at least 100 ought to be amalgamated with neighbouring districts. Some forty of the remaining were also deemed to require special assistance, but were too isolated to amalgamate with a larger district.

A comprehensive response was designed to resolve the problems of the two categories of northern districts. The fiscal aspects of the response were incorporated into the foundation plan programme by means of another amending regulation in 1966.[11] With respect to the first category of school districts – those which were deemed to be in a position to consolidate with neighbouring districts – the government showed itself unwilling once again to legislate larger school districts. Instead, it chose to encourage voluntary consolidation by providing attractive fiscal incentives. Two distinct types of consolidation were to be encouraged: the first involved the incorporation of a district into a larger unit, and the second involved the abandonment of existing schools in the small districts and the negotiation of an agreement with a larger district for the education of the smaller district's pupils (with the smaller district paying tuition fees and transportation costs).

In the first type of consolidation, involving the dissolution of the district, the province contracted to guarantee for five years the normal incentives to consolidation (extra weighted pupils plus $500 per former school section or zone) without limitations based on the number of rural pupils. In addition, the province would pay – and herein lay the real incentive – the full approved cost of any additional accommodation required by the enlarged district.

In the second type, involving the education of pupils under a formal agreement, the province provided special assistance to both the sending and the educating boards. For the educating board, the province agreed to pay the full approved cost of any necessary capital construction. For the sending board, the province agreed to pay the full excess of the cost of tuition fees and transportation in the current year over the yield of seven mills on the local equalized assessment (90 per cent of the grant would be paid in the current year and the remainder in the subsequent year when audited financial statements were available). The maximum levy (seven mills) was approximately double the foundation tax rate prescribed for normal elementary boards under the foundation plan formula.[12]

The high local tax rate was required, however, to avoid extending an undue advantage to non-educating districts and thus negating the effectiveness of the first category of incentives designed to encourage amalgamation of districts. In so doing the provision embodied a recognition of the inability of the larger northern school districts to provide educational services at the foundation level of expenditure, and therefore at the foundation tax rate. This recognition was not embodied in any general revision of the grant structure, however.

The primary problem of the remaining isolated districts was recognized as the inability to attract and retain competent teachers, given the district's isolated location and limited resources. The province therefore undertook to recruit a group of qualified teachers willing to serve in these communities,[13] to be known as the Northern Corps of Teachers. They were to receive special travel and isolation allowances from the province.

A small group of the isolated districts (eleven in 1966 and 1967, and eight in 1968) were considered to be in need of additional financial assistance in employing these specially recruited, or other qualified, teachers. The districts were identified in a schedule appended to the grant regulations, and a special salary grant was provided. The grant was calculated under a rather complicated formula in 1966 and 1967, but this was simplified considerably in 1968. In the latter year, the special grant varied up to $4800 per teacher, depending upon the teacher's salary, certification, and years of experience. The grant was limited, however, so as not to reduce a school board's tax rate to less than seven mills on equalized assessment.

All of these northern assistance grants can be seen as representing fiscal substitutes for legislated changes in the organization of local government. In the first two cases, grants were provided as substitutes for mandated territorial consolidation. In the third case, the grant was a substitute for provincial assumption of responsibility for education in areas unable to provide an acceptable standard of education within the constraints imposed by the existing distribution of authority, responsibility, and resources.

In the latter regard, the provincial undertaking to recruit teachers and pay all but a fixed amount of their salaries left almost no discretionary authority to the school board. It did, however, permit the province to maintain *de jure* respect for local autonomy.*

The revised capital approvals scheme

In 1967 the method of approving capital expenditures was radically altered. The change grew out of a comprehensive study of school building construction undertaken by the Department of Education. The former imposition of fixed ceilings on approved expenditures was replaced by a formula which related the approval to the type of accommodation (classroom, laboratory, gymnasium), the size of the area constructed, the size of the total project, and the geographical location of the project within the province.

School buildings were divided into four categories: elementary (kindergarten to grade eight), senior elementary (any combination of grades seven to ten), secondary (grades nine to thirteen), and vocational secondary. Within each of the four categories, each distinct type of accommodation was assigned an 'accommodation unit factor' on the basis of the square footage of the room (the larger the room the greater the factor). The factors for each unit in a project would then be totalled to produce an 'accommodation unit total' for the project. The accommodation unit total would then be multiplied by an 'accommodation unit value' to arrive at the approved cost of the project. The accommodation unit value varied with two factors: the number of units in the project (the unit value decreased as the number of units increased), and the geographic 'zone' in which the project was located.[14]

The approved cost arrived at by this highly sophisticated formula (the unit factors and unit values were based on actual cost figures and were to be adjusted annually) was designed to recognize for grant purposes between 80 and 100 per cent of the cost of all capital projects. If the actual cost were less than the approval, the lesser figure would, of course, be used. The new formula was announced on 20 February 1967, to take effect for all projects undertaken after 1 January 1967.[15] After pressure from a number of school boards, however, the much more generous plan was made retroactive to cover all projects undertaken after 1 January 1965.[16] Boards subject to this retroactive adjustment received a lump-sum, 'windfall' grant in 1967.

The growth-equalization grant

The introduction of the growth-equalization grant in 1968 provides an

* / The school board retained the legal responsibility for employing the teacher and was legally free, of course, to reject the special assistance offered by the province.

opportunity to describe the policy-formation process more fully. While this provision is not necessarily representative of all new grants, it is the one with which the author was most intimately concerned and for which the most detailed information is available. The development and implementation of the provision will therefore be described in considerable detail.

The developmental process began as early as January 1966 when the author was first employed as Professor Rideout's research associate in the Ontario Institute for Studies in Education. Rideout requested a study of the extraordinary expenditure levels of school boards with a view to determining the adequacy of the existing 'normal' levels used in the growth-need grant ($500 per classroom for elementary boards and $1000 per classroom for secondary boards). Upon examination of the distribution of expenditures, it was apparent that while the secondary level remained reasonable, the elementary level was too low. There was, in fact, very little difference between the per-classroom expenditures in the two panels. The conclusion was therefore drawn that $1000 should be used as the normal expenditure level for both elementary and secondary boards.

The author continued the study, however, and undertook an analysis of the impact of the three grants for extraordinary expenditure. By calculating the tax rates required of variously situated districts, it was discovered that the growth-need grant had a marked over-compensating effect for a certain group of districts. The nature of this effect is shown graphically in Figure 20 for three hypothetical secondary school districts. Recognized extraordinary expenditure per classroom from zero to $6000 is measured on the horizontal axis. The vertical axis indicates the local tax rate (in mills) required to support a given level of expenditure after payment of the three grants (basic tax relief, equalization, and growth-need grants). Tax rates are shown here for districts with equalized assessments per classroom of $1,000,000, $2,000,000, and $4,000,000.

The path traced by the local tax rate is hyperbolic in each case. For the ablest district (assessment per classroom of $4,000,000) the tax rate continues to rise, but at a decreasing rate, for the full range of expenditure levels. For the middle district, however, the tax rate declines as expenditure increases beyond $4550 per classroom. This district could spend at the level of $6000 per classroom and its tax rate would be 15 per cent lower than if it spent only $4550. In the third case, where the assessment per classroom is $1,000,000, the same over-compensating feature is apparent, although the total grant rate reaches its maximum of 95.0 per cent when the expenditure reaches a level of $3800 per classroom (indi-

FIGURE 20
Effective local tax rates of three hypothetical secondary school boards with varying levels of recognized extraordinary expenditure per classroom: 1966 grant formula

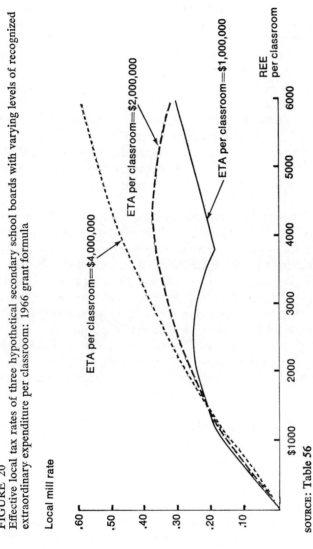

SOURCE: Table 56

cated as point x on Figure 20). For this board, an expenditure of $3800 would entail a tax rate 25 per cent lower than an expenditure of $2500.

The flaw in the growth-need formula was the calculation of the percentage rate independent of that determined under the equalization formula. The growth-need grant was designed to reduce the burden imposed on school districts by above-normal expenditures. The grant percentage was calculated as a function of total expenditure, however, and not the local burden. Thus, with a given growth-need grant, the proportion of the local burden that was relieved by the grant increased as the equalization grant increased (or as the taxing capacity decreased).* For any board a point would be reached beyond which the burden was reduced at a faster rate than the expenditure increased.

During the spring of 1966 the author prepared a report of this study, outlining the problem investigated, the expenditure patterns of school boards, and the weakness in the growth-need grant. An attempt was made to suggest a remedy for this weakness. Three possible remedies were considered: a modification of the existing formula (designed to 'flatten-out' the tax curve), the use of a graduated local tax rate (the grant percentage would increase directly with the tax rate), and the use of a foundation-plan formula for extraordinary expenditure. The use of a foundation plan formula was favoured because it appeared to be the most equitable of the three alternatives. It was argued that since only necessary expenditures were recognized for grant purposes, there was good reason to require only a standard rate of local taxation to support such expenditures.

A special problem was encountered in proposing a method which could deal with both capital expenditures from current funds and debt charges. Use of a single foundation tax rate would have provided an unrealistic incentive to adopt a pay-as-you-go method of financing in virtually all cases. The province would have paid the difference between the full expenditure and the yield of the standard tax rate in only one year, rather than the difference between the annual principal and interest charges and

---

* / For example, an REE per classroom of $3000 would have entitled a secondary school board to a growth-need grant at 8 per cent of its total REE. One board, with an ETA per classroom of $4,000,000 would have had a local burden of $1773 per classroom before the application of the growth-need grant. Another board, with an ETA per classroom of $2,000,000 would have had a local burden of $915 per classroom before the application of the grant. The growth-need grant, payable on the full $3000 in each case, would have reduced the burden by $240 in each case. This reduction, however, would represent a reduction of 13.5 per cent in one case and 26.2 per cent in the other. The relative magnitude of the reduction in local burden was thus a function not only of the level of expenditure but also of the level of taxing capacity – the latter having already been compensated for by the equalization grant.

the tax rate, spread over the life of the indebtedness. The author could find no simple solution to this problem, and recommended that for large capital expenditures from current funds the foundation tax rate be twenty times the normal rate, thus paying the same grant in one year as would have been paid over twenty years had the expenditure been financed through borrowing.*

The report was given to Professor Rideout, who forwarded a copy to Dr Jackson for the latter's information. Early in October 1966 the report was placed on the agenda of the Department of Education grants committee for consideration (the author had by this time joined the committee). The committee was not persuaded of the desirability of a foundation plan for extraordinary expenditures. The consensus appeared to be that the problems encountered with expenditures from current funds outweighed the problem existing in the growth-need grant. The committee did accept the recommendation to increase the 'normal' expenditure level for elementary school boards from $500 to $1000 per classroom, however. Having accepted that proposal, and thereby standardizing the elementary and secondary normal levels of expenditure, the committee decided to standardize the formulas as well. As a result, the 1966 formula for secondary school boards was applied to both panels in 1967. While this simplified the grant structure, it also extended the over-compensating feature of the secondary formula to elementary boards where the problem had previously been less severe.

In the seven months between completion of the 1967 grant programme (January) and the beginning of deliberations regarding changes for 1968 (September), the author continued a periodic analysis of the problem. Because there had been no clear indication of support for a foundation-type formula from either Rideout or Jackson, the author was especially concerned with the theoretical arguments for and against such a scheme. It had been quite clear that any proposal initiated by the author would require the support of Rideout, and at least the approval of Jackson, if it were to be accepted by the departmental committee.

It was just at this time (specifically, on 20 February) that the minister of education announced the introduction of the new scheme for approving capital expenditures – described earlier in this chapter. This scheme, designed to approve nearly the full expenditure on capital projects, was to have considerable impact upon the author's support of a foundation plan. In March the author was requested by the departmental committee to prepare a report on the newly-announced foundation plan in Manitoba.

* / A smaller factor would be used where the normal term of debt on a particular item would be less than twenty years.

The Manitoba plan, while differing in certain basic respects from the Ontario plan, provided for the inclusion of all approved extraordinary expenditures in the regular formula. Commenting on this feature provided an opportunity to raise once again the argument in favour of similar treatment of extraordinary expenditures in Ontario.

The report was completed in March, approved by Professor Rideout, and forwarded to Dr Jackson. Jackson expressed some concern over the comments related to a foundation plan and asked the author for an elaboration of his views. This was done in an exchange of memoranda. In preparing a statement for Dr Jackson, the author was compelled to examine the case more closely. Several discussions were held with Professor Rideout, the result of which was essentially the realization that the situation had been radically changed by the new capital approvals scheme. A programme which recognized the full expenditure on most projects and then required only a standard rate of local taxation would shift all effective control over expenditures to the provincial level of government. Under the previous approval scheme only the rudimentary essentials of a project were approved and thus all optional expenditures would have remained a local responsibility, even with a foundation type grant formula.

The author then attempted to develop an alternative grant formula – one which would retain an element of local responsibility for marginal expenditures, but would still provide additional provincial support for districts with above-normal need. The alternative developed was a rather complicated formula to replace the growth-need grant. The essential difference from the existing growth-need grant was that the proposed grant would be calculated as a function of the relative burden remaining after the calculation of the basic tax relief and equalization grants (as opposed to the relative burden of the total expenditure before the calculation of these grants).

This proposal was then drafted as a report, and submitted to Professor Rideout, and through him to Dr Jackson. In contrast to the original report, Jackson responded this time with a statement to the effect that this, or some similar proposal, would have to be accepted in order to correct the basic weakness in the growth-need grant. The proposal had thus earned at least the tentative approval of the two senior consultants.

This report was submitted to the departmental committee in October, during the process of considering changes for 1968. While the committee balked at the complexity of the author's proposal, it appeared to be resigned to the necessity of the change, unless a simpler formula was proposed. During the informal discussions in committee, the author came to the realization that the intent of the proposal could be realized as effectively but more simply by combining the equalization and growth-need grants into a single modified foundation-type grant using a variable 'foundation' tax rate. The author requested a postponement of the deliberations until a revised proposal could be presented.

In early November the new proposal was presented to the committee. It recommended a 'growth-equalization' grant which would equal the difference between a board's recognized extraordinary expenditure and a tax rate which varied directly with expenditure. The grant would retain the notion of a 'normal' expenditure level of $1000 per classroom. Up to the normal level, the 'foundation' tax rate would increase proportionately with expenditure, reaching .433 mills for elementary school boards and .147 mills for secondary school boards when the expenditure reached the $1000 level. Thus, boards would be required to levy .000433 mills or .000147 mills for each dollar of expenditure per classroom up to the normal level. These rates were determined as those applying to the most favoured boards under the existing scheme. Above the normal expenditure levels, however, the tax rate would increase at a much slower rate. Specifically, the rate would increase by .00015 mills for elementary school boards and by .000075 mills for secondary school boards for each dollar of expenditure per classroom above the $1000. These rates were determined as most closely approximating the average rates under the existing scheme. It was proposed that the basic tax relief grant be retained unchanged in order to continue the existing protection for the larger, abler school districts.

This proposal was not expected to involve any substantial increase in provincial expenditures. Some boards would receive less grant under the formula (those which had been over-compensated) while others would receive more. This followed from the selection of tax rates which reflected the average situation under the existing formula. The author had adopted this objective on the grounds that any proposal for increasing the level of provincial support should be raised as a separate issue and defended on different grounds.

The grants committee offered no objections to the proposal and therefore accepted it for recommendation to the minister. All of the proposals for change in the grant structure were then consolidated and forwarded through the departmental hierarchy, together with an estimate of expenditure for consideration by the Treasury Board. These proposals and estimates were accepted by both authorities during November, and the committee proceeded to draft the 1968 grant regulation.

At this point, however, the results of a test calculation of the proposed changes (using data from the previous year's grants) became available.

The calculation indicated an increase in grants on extraordinary expenditure of some $10 millions, due to the change in the growth-need formula. This unexpected increase would occur because it turned out that it was the larger school districts (with large absolute expenditures) which tended to be treated more favourably under the new scheme. The decreased grants to the smaller boards did not balance these increases for the larger boards.

The committee was then faced with two alternatives: to retain the new formula – requiring either a request for additional funds or a reduction in some other grant feature – or to amend the formula to eliminate the unexpected increase in expenditure. On the advice of Professor Rideout, the committee adopted the second alternative. Rideout determined that the effect of the new capital approvals formula – announced in 1967 but made retroactive to 1965 – had been to increase the normal expenditure level to approximately $1500 per classroom for both elementary and secondary boards. He proposed, therefore, that $1500 be substituted for $1000 in the growth-equalization formula, and that the local tax rate be allowed to rose proportionately with expenditure up to this level. The rates would thus reach .65 mills for elementary school boards and .221 for secondary school boards at expenditures of $1500 per classroom (instead of .433 and .147 at $1000). Beyond the $1500 level, the rates would increase in the same manner as in the author's proposal. Rideout's proposal effectively eliminated the estimated increase in expenditure.

The committee accepted this change and incorporated it in the draft regulation. The latter was duly ratified and issued in January 1968. Thus, after two years of analysis and discussion, the process of changing the grant formula for extraordinary expenditures had been completed.

It is hoped that this rather detailed examination of one change in the grant structure has revealed something of the nature of the process of change itself. Proposals for change generally originated in the group of academic consultants. These proposals were then discussed by the departmental committee, which brought to bear insights gained from administrative and supervisory experience and a greater familiarity with the actual operation of educational government. Finally, the recommended changes were reviewed by the minister and Treasury Board.

It was possible for other groups, such as school boards or their spokesmen, to gain access to this process, but this tended to be the exception rather than the rule. Where such access was effective, it was almost always the case that the group was accorded some authority in speaking to the issue being raised – such as the representations by separate school trustees for changes in the corporation tax adjustment grant. Access of this kind was normally gained through the minister of education, as was the case with the pressure for special treatment of boards experiencing rapid enrolment growth (resulting in the enrolment-growth grant). Alternatively, as with several stimulation grants to be discussed below, access was granted to other branches of the Department of Education to make special cases for particular additions or amendments to the grant programme. Such access was generally effected directly through members of the grants committee.

Other changes
While the above represented the major changes in the Ontario Foundation Tax Plan between 1964 and 1968, they by no means comprise the total number of changes. Virtually all of the remaining changes were based on one or more of four objectives: to simplify the grant structure, to recognize newly emergent or previously neglected needs, to improve the measure of need and capacity, and to refine the techniques of bridging the gap between need and capacity.

Of the eleven special or stimulation grants provided in 1964, six remained substantially unchanged in 1968.[17] Two of the original grants were incorporated into other areas of the grant programme.[18] A grant for the education of deaf children was introduced in 1965 but incorporated into a comprehensive special education grant in 1968. The grant for small secondary schools was eliminated in 1968. The textbook and library book grants were extended to grade twelve in 1965 and 1967 respectively. In addition, the formulas for both were amended to incorporate an element of equalization.

The treatment of pupils receiving special education was changed several times. A special grant was paid in 1965 in place of weighting such pupils. This served only to make the funds received by a board more apparent. The basis of the special grant was changed slightly in 1967 and the amounts increased substantially in 1968. A new grant was introduced in 1966 covering the cost of television receiving sets for elementary schools. This was extended to secondary schools in 1967 and somewhat liberalized in 1968.

Two special grants were introduced in 1968. The first was designed to meet part of the cost of abnormally high fees paid by one board to another. The second extended the principle of the enrolment growth grant to secondary school boards whose enrolment would jump (but not sufficiently to qualify for the existing grant) as a result of the closing of a private school and the transfer of pupils into the public secondary school.[19]

A number of changes were also made in the detailed calculation of the grants. Most of these were designed either to simplify the calculation (as when the two formulas for weighting pupils were consolidated in 1967) or to remove protective features no longer deemed necessary (as when the extra weighting of pupils for enlarged elementary districts was reduced in 1968).

The extent to which the foundation plan could be modified and expanded was always constrained by the necessity of prescribing a single grant programme responsive to the tremendously varied educational needs and both educational and fiscal capacities of the existing school districts. There was a limit, in other words, to the extent that grants could achieve provincial objectives and beyond which only a major restructuring of local government could be effective. We shall turn shortly to a consideration of the policy emerging from the provincial government's recognition that this limit had finally been reached.

IMPACT OF THE FOUNDATION PLAN

The Ontario Foundation Tax Plan was a complex programme of provincial grants. Space does not permit an exhaustive analysis of its impact upon the financing of education in Ontario. There are, however, several significant aspects of this impact which can be explored in this context.

The initiation of the grant plan involved a substantial increase in the commitment of provincial resources to elementary and secondary education. Table 27 shows the total amount of provincial grants from 1958 to 1968, with the percentage increase each year. The total grant was increased by 24.8 per cent in 1964 as compared with 1963. The increases for the subsequent two years were similar to the annual increases prior to 1964. In 1967, however, the total grant increased by 26.5 per cent, an even greater relative increase than in 1964. The large increase in 1967 can be attributed to the increase of $40 in the elementary foundation level and the change in the formula for the corporation tax adjustment grant. There was a substantial, but more normal, increase of 17.1 per cent in the total grant for 1968.

Relating these grants to the expenditures of school boards, as in Table 28, places the relative increases in a better perspective. It can be seen here that while the proportion of school board expenditure met by provincial grants stood at 39.2 per cent in 1963, the proportion was increased to 42.4 per cent for 1964. This proportion increased further to 43.7 per cent in 1965 but dropped to 42.7 per cent in 1966. The large increases in grants in 1967 brought this percentage to 45.3 per cent, the highest point in the ten-year period illustrated. Something of the magnitude of the

TABLE 27

Provincial grants to school boards: amount and
relative increase, 1958–68

Year	Amount ($000)	Increase over previous year
1958	128,168	
1959	148,186	15.6
1960	158,741	7.1
1961	181,278	14.2
1962	201,147	11.0
1963	228,679	13.7
1964	285,497	24.8
1965	328,528	15.1
1966	373,057	13.6
1967	472,040	26.5
1968	552,840	17.1

SOURCE: Minister's Reports

TABLE 28

Provincial grants to school boards and school
board expenditures, 1958–67

Year	School board expenditure ($000)	Provincial grants ($000)	Grants as percent of expenditure
1958	327,728	128,168	39.1
1959	382,954	148,186	38.7
1960	429,932	158,741	36.9
1961	474,856	181,278	38.2
1962	532,217	201,147	37.8
1963	583,161	228,679	39.2
1964	673,653	285,497	42.4
1965	752,555	328,528	43.7
1966	873,015	373,057	42.7
1967	1,041,264	472,040	45.3

SOURCE: Minister's Reports

resources required to increase the provincial share of educational expenditures is indicated here. To accomplish the increase of only 2.6 percentage points in the provincial proportion required an increase of 26.5 percent in the total grant.

The basic element in the grant programme was, of course, the foundation plan for operating expenditures. Table 29 shows the per-pupil foundation levels of expenditure used in the grant plan from 1964 to 1968 and compares these with the actual average per-pupil operating expenditures in the preceding year.[20] In 1964 the foundation levels represented

TABLE 29
Comparison of foundation levels and actual average expenditure levels, 1964-8

Grant year	Foundation level			Average expenditure[a]			Foundation level as % of expenditure		
	Elementary	Secondary academic	Secondary vocational	Elementary	Secondary academic	Secondary vocational	Elementary	Secondary academic	Secondary vocational
1964	210	420	550	268	527	634	78.4	79.7	86.8
1965	210	420	550	288	562	679	72.9	74.7	81.0
1966	220	440	570	300	610	718	73.3	72.1	79.4
1967[b]	260	450	580	319	644	750	81.5	69.9	77.3
1968	280	465	600	363	684	867	77.1	68.0	69.2

[a] /'Ordinary' expenditure (excludes capital, debt charges, and transportation) in the preceding year.
[b] /The measure of pupils was changed from ADA to ADE in 1967.
SOURCE: Grant Regulations and Minister's Reports

78.4, 79.7, and 86.8 per cent of the expenditure in the elementary, secondary academic, and secondary vocational panels respectively. Since the foundation levels were held constant in 1965, this proportion naturally declined in that year. Both of the secondary school proportions continued to decline, however, reaching lows of 68.0 per cent and 69.2 per cent of expenditure in the academic and vocational panels respectively in 1968. The elementary proportion increased slightly in 1966, and increased substantially in 1967, reaching 81.5 per cent of expenditure in that year. It declined slightly in 1968 to 77.1 per cent. Whereas the elementary level had been the lowest of the three in relation to expenditure in 1964, it was the highest in 1967. All of these proportions would have been considerably lower if the foundation levels had been compared with expenditure in the same year. That was not the basis upon which the grants were calculated, however.

The introduction and development of the foundation plan had a marked impact upon the relative revenue deficiency of the separate school system. Table 30 shows the amount of revenue per pupil derived from local taxation and provincial grants in the public and separate systems from 1958 to 1967, and the resultant deficiency of the separate system. This deficiency had increased from $80 per pupil in 1958 to $94 in 1962, and had then decreased to $83 in 1963. In 1964 the deficiency was reduced to only $70 per pupil. This increased again, in both 1965 and 1966, however, so that in 1966 it had almost regained the magnitude of 1958

TABLE 30
Per-pupil revenue from provincial grants and local
taxes: public and separate elementary schools in
Ontario, 1958–67

	Revenue per pupil						Separate school deficiency
	Public			Separate			
Year	Grants	Taxes	Total	Grants	Taxes	Total	
1958	$ 85	$145	$230	$ 87	$63	$150	$80
1959	91	161	252	99	66	165	87
1960	93	175	268	103	72	175	93
1961	97	184	281	112	75	187	94
1962	98	185	283	118	77	195	88
1963	100	189	289	128	78	206	83
1964	130	205	335	189	76	265	70
1965	138	216	354	204	77	281	73
1966	151	241	392	227	86	313	79
1967	172	274	446	299	96	395	51

SOURCE: Minister's Reports

in absolute terms. The large increase in the equalization portion of the foundation level and the liberalization of the corporation tax adjustment grant combined in 1967 to reduce the revenue deficiency by an incredible $28 per pupil, bringing the total to only $51. While data are not yet available to assess the impact of the 1968 changes, the fact that the increase in the foundation level was placed entirely in the minimum provision would almost certainly have resulted in a widening of the disparity between the two systems once again.

The foundation plan formula used in the Ontario grant plan had the effect of equalizing the burden of supporting a standard level of expenditure for the school districts with relatively small taxing capacities. The abler districts were placed in a position to choose between two alternative types of spending and taxing policies. First, they could spend at or near the foundation level of expenditure and thereby levy a rate of taxation lower than the foundation tax rate. Second, they could levy a rate at or near the foundation tax rate and thereby spend in excess of the foundation level of expenditure. The normal response of the abler boards was clearly to choose the second alternative. Figures 21, 22, 23, and 24 illustrate this response quite clearly. School boards were grouped into classes of equalized assessment per classroom and placed along the horizontal axes in ascending order of taxing capacity (that is, the least able group is shown on the left, and the ablest on the right). The bars on the graphs then represent the mean current expenditure per classroom[21] and the mean 'calculated' mill rate[22] of the boards in each class. Regression

FIGURE 21
Mean current expenditures of elementary boards in classes of equalized assessment per classroom, 1964

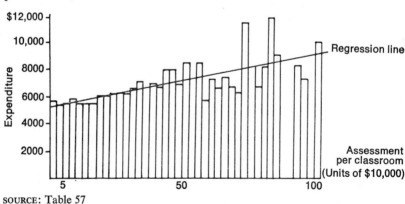

SOURCE: Table 57

FIGURE 22
Mean calculated current mill rates of elementary boards in classes of equalized
assessment per classroom

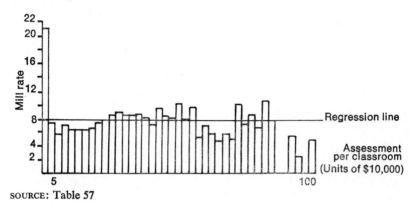

SOURCE: Table 57

FIGURE 23
Mean current expenditures of secondary boards in classes of equalized assessment
per classroom, 1964

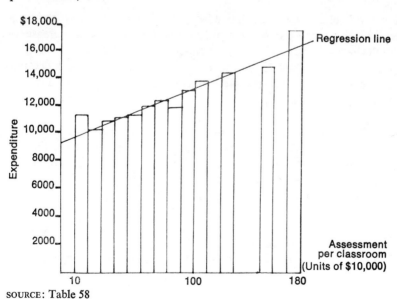

SOURCE: Table 58

FIGURE 24
Mean calculated current mill rates of secondary boards in classes of
equalized assessment per classroom

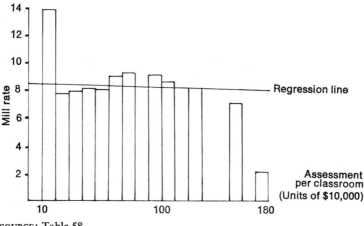

SOURCE: Table 58

lines (fitted by the 'least squares' method) have been plotted in each case
to indicate the trends in the relationships without the individual fluctuations.[23]

For both elementary and secondary boards, the mean expenditures
increased in direct proportion to taxable capacity. Each increase of
$25,000 in equalized assessment per classroom resulted in an increase of
approximately $100 in expenditure per classroom. The local tax rate
was virtually unrelated to taxable capacity. In the elementary panel, the
rate decreased by only 0.065 mills over an increase in assessment per
classroom of $1,000,000. The secondary rate decreased at a slightly
faster rate, but still fell by only 0.345 mills over an increase in assessment
per classroom of $1,000,000. It is also apparent from the charts that for
both elementary and secondary boards, the mean local tax rates of boards
at either of the extremes of taxable capacity departed significantly from
the path described by the regression lines.

The Ontario Foundation Tax Plan of provincial grants to school
boards did not, and had not been intended to, create any radical changes
in the level of provincial support of education or in the distribution of
provincial grants to the variously situated school districts. It could not
have done so because it was designed to resolve or ameliorate the symp-
toms of the basic problems and not the problems themselves. Thus, while
the plan placed greater emphasis on equalization than had earlier plans,

it resolved neither the structural weaknesses of the local tax base nor those of the territorial units of local government, from whence arose the fiscal problems of inadequate and unequal resources.

It is in the very nature of intergovernmental transfer payments, however, to compensate for weaknesses in the resources that would otherwise be available to the lower level of government. The problem encountered in the foundation plan was not that this compensation was ineffective, but that the effectiveness has been limited by the constraints imposed, above all, by the inadequate and unequal units of local government. Given those constraints, the grant plan proved to be a sophisticated and flexible device for channelling provincial resources to local school boards.

PART III

Federal–Provincial fiscal responses

10

The Federal–Provincial Technical and
Vocational Training Agreement

Few fiscal transfer arrangements have had as dramatic an impact upon the provision of elementary and secondary education as did the capital grants for vocational school construction under the Federal-Provincial Technical and Vocational Training Agreement in effect from 1961 to 1967. In 1960, 23.7 per cent of the secondary-school pupils in Ontario were enrolled in vocational programmes. Seven years later, in 1967, this proportion stood at 46.4 per cent.[1] And perhaps the most striking feature of this enrolment shift was that it was clearly not envisaged when the federal government made the original offer of the conditional grant.

The Technical and Vocational Training Agreement contained a comprehensive programme of federal grants, including grants for current expenditures under ten specified programmes. The majority of the current grants were simply continued from an earlier grant package[2] and the additional provisions of 1961 did not represent any basic change in federal policy or in federal-provincial fiscal relations. What was significant about the new agreements of 1961 was the extension of federal conditional grants for capital expenditures on vocational training facilities.

While the British North America Act clearly assigns responsibility for education to the provincial governments, it also places a general responsibility for economic growth and development in the hands of the federal government. The latter concern has led to a growing involvement of the federal government in matters pertaining to manpower – manpower policy in general and training in particular.

The federal Department of Labour, through its technical and vocational training branch, became the centre of the federal concern for the initiation and co-ordination of programmes intended to meet the manpower requirements of the national economy. (In 1966 this function was transferred to the new Department of Manpower and Immigration.[3]) In a continuing series of studies and surveys, the branch attempted to identify manpower needs and stimulate provinces into responding to them. For example, a 1960 study of the level of education and training of the Canadian labour force pointed to a rather startling inadequacy in the training facilities available within the country. It was discovered that in a sample of five industries, 35 per cent of the skilled workers had been trained outside Canada.[4] Furthermore, of all secondary-school pupils in Canada, only 15 per cent were enrolled in vocationally-oriented programmes.[5]

The general attitude of those concerned with manpower training at the federal level was perhaps best summed up by the director of the technical and vocational training branch, C.R. Ford, in 1961: 'The responsibility for the direction, administration, and co-ordination of the programs for training manpower is much more important than some Departments of Education realize.'[6] The federal branch thus had a clear interest in developing a programme which would produce a change in provincial priorities. At the same time that the federal technical and vocational training branch was becoming increasingly concerned with provincial inaction in the area of vocational training, the federal cabinet was facing a severe problem of unemployment in the Canadian labour force. The average annual rate of unemployment in Canada had increased from 3.4 per cent in 1956 to 7.0 per cent in 1960.[7]

While the origin of the federal proposal under study appears to have lain in the concern of a branch of the federal public service over facilities for vocational education, the support of the proposal by the cabinet was probably due at least as much to a concern over unemployment. Michael Starr, minister of labour, made the following statements in introducing the proposal in the House of Commons: 'It is designed to undergird the government's programme to increase employment and foster national development ... The need for more training facilities ... is further substantiated by the facts of the present unemployment situation.'[8] This concern for unemployment was obviously shared by other members of Parliament. Indicating support for the proposal by the Liberals, Alexis Caron stated that: 'Ever since 1957 ... we have repeated to the Minister of Labour and to the government that something special had to be done to keep the economic recession from taking alarming proportions.'[9]

The argument that the capital grants were designed with immediate economic problems in view does help to explain the nature of the original federal offer. The Technical and Vocational Training Assistance Act,[10] as introduced and passed in 1960, provided a federal grant of 50 per cent of approved provincial capital expenditures on vocational training and retraining facilities that were made before 31 March 1967. The grant was to be increased to 75 per cent, however, for expenditures made before 31 March 1963. 'This legislation is designed for the immediate present. That is why we have the cost of these schools terminating on 31 March 1963 for participation to the extent of 75 per cent by the federal government in the expenditures made by the provinces.'[11]

Even clearer than the federal cabinet's intentions in proposing the new capital grants was its anticipation of the cost, as Mr Starr estimated that the current manpower requirements called for an increase of 50 per cent in the provincial technical and vocational training facilities. When queried on this estimate during consideration of the bill in committee, he stated:

In this respect I am advised that all we can do is to take the word of the provinces. They are the ones who advise us in respect of these matters and it is the provinces who say that they feel that a 50 per cent increase in present capacity is necessary over the coming years.

J.W. Pickersgill, pursuing the matter, asked: 'Is the Minister really telling us that his department does not know what the present capacity [for vocational training] is in this country?' To which Mr Starr replied: 'I do not want any misunderstanding; that is exactly what I told you.'[12] This estimate of needed capital expansion, based entirely on provincial data, came to a total cost of $90,000,000 for the six years of the proposed agreements (1961 to 1967). The figure obtained from Ontario was a mere $15,000,000.[13]

After passage of the Act, the Department of Labour estimated that the federal payments for the first fiscal year (1961–2) would be $14,775,-000.[14] During that first year, however, the department approved projects with a total estimated cost of $332,829,844.[15] It was necessary for the department to submit supplementary estimates twice during 1961, just to meet the obligations in that first year. The basic reason for the dramatic increase in approved expenditures and federal grants over what had been anticipated rests more than anywhere else on the use Ontario made of the programme. Of the $332,829,844 in approved projects for 1961–2, Ontario accounted for $229,829,114 (69.1 per cent of the total).[16]

The original federal proposal was clearly designed to stimulate expenditures at the provincial, and not at the school-board or municipal, level. Asked specifically whether the federal grants would be paid in respect of local expenditures or only those portions of local expenditures financed by the provinces, the Minister of Labour replied, 'It is 75 per cent of the provincial contribution.'[17] This intent was clear at the provincial level as well. Answering essentially the same question in the provincial legislature, John Robarts stated in December 1960: 'This scheme is set up to establish a financial partnership ... between the federal government and the provincial government ... not between the federal government and any municipality.'[18]

What this implied was a scheme of federal grants to assist in the construction of provincial trade schools and institutes of technology. As late as February 1961 Robarts indicated that this was the underlying assumption by referring to the capital grant programme as ' ... the capital grants that are made available for technical institutes.'[19]

An intimation of Ontario's response to the federal offer came only one month later, in March 1961, when Robarts announced that the federal government had agreed to include provincial grants to school boards for the construction of vocational high schools, and the vocational components of composite high schools, in the definition of provincial expenditure on vocational training facilities.[20] As will be described shortly, it was Ontario's use of this provision that so changed the nature of the federal-provincial conditional grant programme. The federal estimate of a $15 million expenditure by Ontario over six years was thus based on an anticipated expansion of facilities in the provincial institutes of trade and technology. It did not anticipate a complete transformation of the secondary-school system as well.

The Technical and Vocational Training Assistance Act was given effect through agreements signed with each of the ten provinces. It was these agreements, and their appended schedules, which set out the conditions and terms of payment of the federal grants. Capital expenditures were to be approved if the facilities being provided were to be used for any of the ten programmes supported by the operating grants. Secondary school facilities would be approved if they were to be used for ' ... those courses, given as an integral part of high school education, in which at least one-half of the school time is devoted to technical, commercial and other vocational subjects or courses designed to prepare students for entry into employment by developing occupational qualifications.'[21] Facilities would also be approved if used for ' ... courses which provide students with an essential basis for further training after leaving regular high schools ...'[22] Specific items subject to approval within the above framework were defined as: 'The cost of approved construction, purchase, addition or alteration of buildings or physical plant, the whole or that part of which has been completed or put in place, and approved machinery and equipment which has been delivered and put in place ...'[23] Specifically excluded were expenditures for the purchase of land, for the costs of capital financing, or for general shops or facilities used for industrial arts classes.[24] The provinces were required to submit every capital project to the federal Department of Labour for approval prior to any commitment of funds. Audited statements of expenditure had then to be forwarded upon completion of the project.

The Ontario cabinet announced its decision to accept the federal offer on 28 March 1961, and formally signed the agreement on 26 June 1961. The grants took effect as of 1 April 1961.

The cabinet's decision, however, was to place the emphasis of its response on the secondary schools rather than the provincial institutes. According to the provincial director of vocational education, the major reason for this was the fact that projects would then be contracted by the school boards rather than by the provincial Department of Public Works.[25] The latter body was capable of undertaking only a small number of projects in any one year. In order to take maximum advantage of the federal-provincial agreement, however, it was essential that the building programmes be concentrated in the initial two years of the agreement, when the federal rebate would be 75 per cent. Channelling the programmes through the school boards would make it possible to undertake a great many projects simultaneously, under contracts with private construction companies.

Before launching this response, the cabinet sought assurance from officials of the Department of Education that the secondary school course of study could, in fact, be revised in such a way as to make possible the channelling of a provincial programme of technical and vocational education through the secondary school system.[26] It was only after receiving that assurance that the cabinet decided to proceed with the programme in this manner.

As well as authorizing a radical reorganization of the secondary school course of study, the cabinet decided to remove any financial responsibility for the resultant building projects from the school boards. This was a logical decision in so far as the emphasis on vocational training was a provincial project, developed in response to a federal conditional grant. It was also a very practical decision in that since the federal grant was paid in respect of provincial expenditures only, and not school board expenditures, provincial assumption of the full cost of the programme maximized the federal contribution to Ontario.

As was noted above, the Department of Education was directed to develop a revised course of study for the province's secondary schools which would permit those schools to take advantage of the federal-provincial programme of technical and vocational training. The Minister of Education announced the essential features of this revision on 28 August 1961, barely one month after he had formally signed the federal-provincial agreement on behalf of Ontario.[27]

The new course of study – known familiarly as the 'Robarts Plan'* – was to contain three basic streams in the school programme: arts and science, science, technology, and trades, and business and commerce. Each stream would contain a five-year course, completed in grade thirteen, and a four-year course, completed in grade twelve. In addition, there were to be one-year and two-year occupational courses for pupils transferred from elementary schools. The new three-stream programme was to be implemented at the option of school boards, beginning with grade nine in September 1962. The programme would be extended by one grade each year after its initial implementation. The secondary school course would thus be completely revised by 1966.

The revised course represented a major change in the emphasis of the secondary schools – away from the purely academic, university preparatory orientation, and towards a broadly vocational orientation. Preparation for immediate employment and for post-secondary institutions other than universities was to be given at least equal emphasis with preparation for university. The change was made in such a way that all the components of the new course of study, save only the arts and science branch, met the standards of the federal government for inclusion in the terms of the capital grant scheme. Machinery for the detailed planning of the revised programme was not set in motion until after the minister's announcement. Responsibility for this planning was delegated to sixteen committees of secondary school teachers, which began their deliberations in the autumn of 1962.[28]

It is quite clear then, that the course of study was revised in response to the conditions of the federal grant proposal. In order to allow school boards to take maximum advantage of those federal grants, the general nature of the revisions was announced even before the machinery for detailed planning had been established.

The second element in the cabinet's two-fold response to the federal proposal was its decision to assume the full cost of the capital expansion programme (subject, of course, to federal reimbursement of three-quarters of this cost). In announcing this decision, the minister of education stated that this policy would continue for a period of two years only – that is, for the period of the 75 per cent federal grant (1 April 1961 to 31 March 1963).[29] It was not indicated at that time just how capital

* / John P. Robarts was minister of education at the time.

expenditures would be handled when the federal grant reverted to 50 per cent.

This decision had two clear, and presumably intended, results. First, since it relieved school boards of all but the incidental costs[30] of expanding vocational and technical facilities, it provided a compelling incentive for boards to undertake such projects, and to do so immediately. Second, since it rendered the full costs of such projects provincial expenditures, it obliged the federal government to contribute 75 per cent of all approved expenditures, not just that portion which would have been the responsibility of the province under some scheme of proportional grants to school boards.

This decision, however, established a pattern for treating capital expenditures on vocational facilities which had rather far-reaching implications. This pattern is revealed in the procedures established for handling the intergovernmental transfers.[31] School boards were required to submit capital proposals, together with estimated costs, to the technical adviser in the Department of Education (this office was reorganized in 1965 as the school plant approvals section) in the same manner as all other such proposals. Simultaneously with its own assessment of the proposals, the department forwarded copies to the federal Department of Labour. Upon tentative approval being granted at both the provincial and federal levels, the school board was authorized to call for tenders or submit orders for construction, equipment, and machinery. If the tendered cost did not greatly exceed the estimated cost, no further approval was necessary from the federal government, and the school board was given final approval by the province to proceed with the project. From this point on, however, the programme was administered by a special section of the provincial Department of Education, created within the business administration branch, but charged solely with the responsibility of administering the programmes falling under the terms of the federal-provincial technical and vocational training agreement. As expenditures were incurred, school boards were required to submit invoices or architects' certificates to this special section of the department. These statements were then compiled, approved by the provincial auditors, and submitted to the federal Department of Labour for final approval and repayment under the terms of the agreement. For the latter purpose, the federal department seconded two officers to the provincial department, to obviate the necessity of transferring the actual documents from Toronto to Ottawa.

Noticeably absent from this procedure was any involvement by the grants section of the Department of Education. According to department officials,[32] this was a deliberate decision, based on the premise that processing the claims for federal reimbursement was simply an accounting procedure but one which required a clear separation of all expenditures falling under the terms of the agreement. This procedure had some logic so long as the federal and provincial payments were not really grants to the school boards but rather payments for provincial expenditures incurred by the school boards as agents of the province (which was the case for the first two years). At the same time, however, a clear separation was established between capital and operating grants for vocational schools, for the latter were administered by the grants section.

The separation of the federal-provincial capital grant programme from the normal provincial grants to school boards became even sharper with the reorganization of the Department of Education in 1965-6.[33] Under that reorganization, the business administration branch was split into a departmental business administration branch and a school business administration branch. In 1965 the school plant approvals section, and in 1966 the grants section, were placed in the school business administration branch. The federal-provincial programme, however, remained in the departmental business administration branch, along with budgeting, payroll, and personnel. Communication between those responsible for administering the two grant programmes was provided by the involvement in both of the school plant approvals section and by the general supervision of P.H. Cunningham. Cunningham was in charge of business administration and then departmental business administration from 1958 to 1965, as well as being chairman of the departmental grants committee. In 1966, however, he became director of financial administration and relinquished direct responsibility for the federal-provincial section.

In the first fiscal year of the agreement alone (1 April 1961 to 31 March 1962), Ontario's secondary school boards initiated approved projects for the construction of no fewer than 124 new vocational or composite schools,[34] as well as fifty-two additions to existing schools. The new schools represented 90 per cent of all such projects in Canada. The total cost of the projects, plus a few involving trade schools or institutes of technology, amounted to an estimated $229,829,000, over fifteen times the original estimate of the total expenditure for the six-year term of the agreement.[35] With a new course of study and assumption of the full capital cost by the provincial and federal governments, the initial response of the school boards is understandable. In the second fiscal year of the agreement, a further forty-six new schools and six additions were approved at an estimated cost of $90,087,000 (again including a relatively small expenditure on trade schools and institutes of technology).[36]

By 31 March 1963, when the 75 per cent federal grant was due to drop to 50 per cent, Ontario had completed expenditures of $164,319,000 and received grants from the federal government amounting to $128,-017,000.[37] These grants represented 65 per cent of all the capital grants paid by the federal government. Without doubt, Ontario had taken quick and full advantage of the federal conditional grant programme.

Both the federal grant programme and the Ontario response to that programme were changed in very significant ways over the life of the agreement. In February 1963 the federal government agreed to extend the termination date of its 75 per cent grant beyond 31 March 1963. This change was prompted by concerted pressure from the provinces who argued that construction delays and the necessity of developing a response to the federal programme would leave them with large commitments outstanding at 31 March for which they would receive no federal assistance. The federal extension applied only to expenditures incurred up to 30 September 1963 if the contracts had been signed or the orders placed before 1 April 1963.[38]

The general elections of 1963 returned a Liberal government,* and in June of that year it committed itself to an extension and expansion of the terms of the federal provincial agreements.[39] This was done under an amendment to the Technical and Vocational Training Assistance Act, passed in December 1963.[40] The amendment removed the 31 March 1963 deadline altogether and committed the federal government to paying a grant of 75 per cent of provincial expenditures up to 31 March 1967 (the termination date of the whole agreement) or, and herein lay the crux of the amendment, until such time as was fixed by agreement with the provinces.

The revised federal offer was to pay grants at the rate of 75 per cent until each province had claimed a total grant equal to the largest per capita grant paid to any province by 31 March 1963. The largest per capita grant had, in fact, been paid to Newfoundland which had claimed the equivalent of $480 for each person between the ages of fifteen and nineteen inclusive. The federal government therefore offered to pay a 75 per cent grant until each province concerned had also claimed $480 per capita between the ages of fifteen and nineteen. After that point had been reached, the grant would revert to 50 per cent until the termination of the agreement.[41] This offer was accepted by Ontario and the revised agreement signed in May 1964.

* / The Progressive Conservative party formed the government between 1957 and 1963.

The population of Ontario between the ages of fifteen and nineteen (the 1961 census figure was used consistently here) was 436,883. This created a potential claim on the federal government of $209,703,840. By 31 March 1963, when the 75 per cent grant had originally been intended to terminate, Ontario had expended $164,319,000 and drawn a total of $128,017,013 in federal grants. The $480 quota would be reached when the provincial expenditure reached $279,605,000, leaving a total of $115,286,000 in provincial expenditures covered by the federal extension of the terms of the agreement. Some of this amount would have been covered by the earlier extension to 30 September 1963, but the exact amount cannot be determined (no data are available on partial-year expenditures). The total net benefit to Ontario can be estimated, then, at approximately $25 millions if we assume that approximately $100 millions in expenditures had not been made subject to grant at 75 per cent by 30 September 1963. The $25 millions is equal to the difference between a 50 per cent grant and a 75 per cent grant on the expenditure of $100 millions.

By 31 March 1963, however, Ontario had received federal approval on projects the total cost of which was estimated at $319,916,000.[42] Since the quota on the 75 per cent grant would be reached at an expenditure of $279,605,000, then not even all of the projects approved by that early date would receive the higher rate of grant. Ontario reached its quota of $480 per capita in mid-1965.[43] As had been agreed the federal rate of grant dropped to 50 per cent thereafter.

In 1966 the federal programme was changed once again. This time a maximum limitation was placed on the 50 per cent grant as well as on the 75 per cent grant. The 50 per cent would apply only until the total claim of any one province reached $800 per capita (again between the ages of fifteen and nineteen as indicated by the 1961 census), or until 31 March 1967, which ever came sooner.[45] This change created a maximum potential grant for Ontario of $349,506,400 − $209,703,840 at 75 per cent and a further $139,802,560 at 50 per cent. This was the final change in the federal programme prior to the termination of the agreements. The grant plan as it stood in 1966 and 1967 may be summarized as follows: 1) 75 per cent grant to a maximum of $480 per capita; 2) 50 per cent grant on the next $320 per capita; 3) no grant after maximum of $800 per capita.

As was noted in the description of the original response of the provincial cabinet to the federal offer of conditional grants, the assumption by the province of the full cost of capital expenditures on vocational construction and equipment was intended to apply only until 31 March

1963. This decision was adhered to, except that it was applied in a manner most favourable to the school boards. All expenditures given tentative approval by 1 February 1962 were to be financed entirely by the province, subject to federal reimbursement, regardless of when the expenditures were actually incurred. Furthermore, all expenditures incurred before 1 April 1963 were to be financed entirely by the province regardless of when the approval had been given. For all other expenditures, the province would assume responsibility for only 75 per cent, leaving the remaining 25 per cent as a responsibility of the school boards.[45]

This change in policy on the part of Ontario altered the basis upon which the federal grant was paid. That grant applied only to the expenditures incurred by the province and not to expenditures incurred by school boards. When Ontario dropped its support from 100 to 75 per cent, therefore, the federal grant applied only to 75 per cent of the total expenditure. A 75 per cent federal grant then became a 56.25 per cent grant, and a 50 per cent grant became a 37.5 per cent grant, if applied to the total expenditure of the province and school board combined. The sharing ratio established by the combination of changes at the federal and provincial levels, disregarding the period of transition in which previous commitments were being honoured, was 37.5 per cent from the federal government, 37.5 per cent from the provincial government, and 25.0 per cent from the school board.

The effect of requiring school boards to contribute 25 per cent of the capital expenditure was to highlight the basic difference in principle embodied in the vocational grants and the regular provincial or foundation grant plan. As well, this requirement allowed school boards to choose the more advantageous of the two schemes. The vocational grants involved a single grant of 75 per cent at the time an expenditure was incurred. The foundation plan provided a grant of from 35 to 95 per cent, but paid in respect of capital expenditures from current funds and debt charges.

As will be developed at greater length in the following chapter, the effective fiscal treatment of school boards is virtually the same if the same rate of grant is applied under either scheme. The basic difference lies in which level of government is held responsible for any resultant indebtedness. Consequently, except where a school district, or its parallel municipality, had reached or was approaching the maximum allowable indebtedness, it would be to the board's advantage to opt for the grant scheme which entailed the higher rate of grant. Thus, boards eligible for a grant on extraordinary expenditure under the foundation plan of more than 75 per cent were placed in the position of being able to choose which method of capital financing they preferred. The federal-provincial grants entailed a flat rate of grant for all boards. The foundation plan entailed rates which varied inversely with taxing capacity and directly with relative expenditure. The effect of the revised federal-provincial grant scheme, then, was to limit the applicability of the equalizing features of the regular grants to only those boards which opted for inclusion. All other boards received preferred treatment.

Ontario made a second significant change in the nature of its response in 1965. In June of that year, the minister of education announced that the province would assume responsibility for the full cost of vocational facilities, as under the original response, where such facilities were to be used by two or more secondary school boards under an agreement between the boards. The only condition, assuming the project were approved by the school plant approvals section on technical grounds, was that the combined enrolment in the school be at least 1000.[46] This change repeated the original stimulus for school districts which, because of size, had been unable to justify building a vocational school or wing to serve that district alone.

Although the federal-provincial agreements were due to expire on 31 March 1967, provincial leaders appeared to assume that these would be replaced by revised agreements. This had been the tradition developed since the inception of the federal-provincial vocational training agreements in 1942.

It was with some surprise that the provinces learned, at the October 1966 Federal-Provincial Conference, of the federal government's decision to terminate these agreements altogether.[47] That decision was considerably softened for a number of provinces when the federal government agreed to phase out the capital grants after 31 March 1967. All provinces would be allowed to claim the full $800 per capita regardless of how long it took for this level to be reached.

For Ontario the phasing out agreement created a potential post-1967 grant of approximately $72 millions. The maximum grant at $800 per capita was $350 millions, and of this approximately $278 millions had been claimed by 31 March 1967.[48] The federal cabinet limited the amount to be paid to Ontario in 1967–8 to approximately one-half the total potential grant. The federal government did agree, however, to pay interest on the unpaid balance.[49]

Ontario's response to the termination of the federal-provincial agreement was determined during February and March 1967. On 9 February 1967 the minister of education stated in the Legislature that: '[School] boards have not yet been informed of the grant treatment of vocational capital expenditures as the province has not yet developed a policy in the face of the sudden termination of the plan ...'[50] Exactly one month later, however, the minister was able to announce that Ontario was proceeding with its own scheme of grants.[51] Under this scheme, the province agreed to pay 75 per cent of school-board capital expenditures for vocational projects approved before 31 March 1969, regardless of when the expenditures were incurred. This extension of the programme, with limited federal reimbursement, was estimated to cost the province $200 millions.[52]

The impact of the federal-provincial vocational education policy must be viewed in terms of the interaction of two factors: the revised secondary school course of study and the capital grants. The former placed the school boards in a position to take advantage of the latter. Yet without the latter, the former would have been relatively ineffective. These two interdependent policies produced the dramatic shift in secondary enrolment noted in Chapter 5. In 1960, the year before the programmes were launched, the proportion of secondary school pupils in technical-commercial courses had been 23.7 per cent. By 1964 this proportion had increased to 40.5 per cent, and in 1967 had reached 46.4 per cent.[53] Between 1961 and 1966, 278 new vocational or composite schools and fifty-five alterations or additions to existing schools were begun or completed under the terms of the agreement.[54]

To appreciate the dimensions of this enrolment shift and construction boom more fully, it is interesting to examine the impact in relation to the existing stock of secondary school buildings. Between 1961 and 1967, the total secondary school enrolment increased by 200,961 pupils. Yet the total number of new pupil-places constructed during this period was 254,027.[55] Of the latter, then, 53,066 pupil-places were constructed to replace existing accommodation. This replacement represented 21 per cent of all construction. As the following figures show, virtually all of the replaced accommodation must have been in very small school buildings. The additional pupil-places constructed between 1961 and 1967 (254,027) produced an increase in the total number of secondary schools of 105.[56] Yet, between 1961 and 1966 alone, 278 new vocational or composite schools were constructed under the federal-provincial agreement (there were, as well, academic schools built outside the terms of the agreement). The result was an increase in the average enrolment per school from 611 in 1960 to 867 in 1967.

The federal-provincial agreement clearly led to a centralization of secondary school buildings. However, this centralization was not restricted to vocational facilities, for the majority of schools constructed during this period were composite schools – containing both academic and vocational pupils. The programme thus had an important 'spill-over' effect in sparking a construction boom in the academic sphere as well. No special provision was made to assist school boards in financing the latter, however.

The intergovernmental fiscal transfers involved in this programme raise a number of important questions related generally to the political and economic efficacy of conditional grants and specifically to the way in which this particular programme was initiated and implemented. A number of students of intergovernmental relations have challenged the validity of federal conditional grants in areas of provincial responsibility on the grounds that such grants distort the spending priorities developed within the provincial political system.[57] The Ontario Committee on Taxation (the Smith Committee), reporting in 1967, made the following succinct analysis of the effect of the federal-provincial programme:

The federal capital grant for vocational school construction provides an excellent case in point for a debate over the merits and demerits of conditional grants. On the one hand, it can be argued that to the extent that manpower training affects national economic performance, a federally extended incentive for provincial vocational school construction was entirely desirable. At the same time, and precisely inasmuch as the federal incentive proved effective, provincial priorities were distorted and commitments undertaken that may not have been as much in keeping with the provincial interest as those that would have prevailed had the same cash resources been made available in the form of additional tax abatement.[58]

There are three specific areas in which this criticism appears to be most relevant. The first concerns the implementation of the Robarts Plan, the revised secondary school course of study. As was described earlier, this plan was developed under conditions of utmost haste, as a condition of Ontario's acceptance of the federal offer. The haste was a function of the terms of that offer – limiting the 75 per cent grant to expenditures incurred before 31 March 1963. The planning of the new course of study was further constrained by the federal condition that grants would be paid only in respect of facilities constructed for school programmes in which at least 50 per cent of the students' time was devoted to technical or vocational training. While it is impossible to determine what the provincial policy would have been in the absence of the conditional federal incentive, one is probably justified in assuming, as did the Smith Committee, that this policy was distorted by the existence of the incentive. After all, had Ontario not fitted its revised course of study to the federal conditions, it would have waived the largest part of the $350 millions in federal grants that it received. One is led to the assumption, then, that without the federal stimulus, the Ontario secondary school course of study not only would have been developed at a more leisurely pace, but also would have expressed more fully the educational interests of the province. This assumption is further strengthened by the fact that almost immediately upon claiming its full quota of federal grants, the Department of Education began to dismantle the Robarts Plan and institute a secondary school curriculum without the segregation of academic and vocational pupils.

The second area of criticism concerns the relationship between capital expenditures, supported by the federal grants, and normal operating expenditures, virtually unsupported by such grants.[59] The federal incentive was exceptionally effective in stimulating and supporting the construction of vocational facilities. But the full burden of operating and maintaining those facilities, and supporting the programmes for which they were constructed, fell upon the provincial and local governments. The decisions made between the federal and provincial governments placed heavy constraints upon the policy alternatives available at the provincial-local level respecting the financing of current expenditures. Since there was no effective co-ordination of activities in the two areas – that is, between those responsible for vocational capital grants and those responsible for the foundation-plan grants (there was only a modest overlapping of responsibilities) – the latter were left in the position of developing policies to support a programme the creation of which continued to be the responsibility of another group.

This leads directly into the third area of criticism, the inequity in the formula used to determine the vocational capital grants and the contrast between this formula and that used in the regular, foundation-plan grants. During the first years of the programme, when responsibility for vocational construction was completely removed from the school boards, the question of equity was not, of course, relevant (except on an interprovincial basis, which is beyond the scope of this study). When the percentage rate dropped to 75, however, that question became very relevant. Holding all school boards responsible for a fixed proportion of capital expenditures produced a local burden directly proportional to local taxing capacity. The irony in this inequity is that it was in no way a necessary condition of the federal offer. The federal grants were paid in respect of total provincial expenditures. They were not conditional upon any particular method of distribution. Once the federal-provincial grant dropped to 75 per cent, the province could have applied an equalizing formula –

such as was then used under the foundation plan for capital expenditures – so as to pay grants in inverse proportion to taxing capacity.

To have adopted this policy, however, would have implied delegating responsibility to the grants section of the Department of Education – where there was a strong concern for fiscal equity – rather than to a special section – where the concern was with accounting procedures. This situation became particularly anomalous after the termination of the federal-provincial agreement and the assumption of the capital grant programme by the province. With that change even the appearance of a constraint upon the use of an equalizing formula was removed.

It is true, of course, that the use of flat-rate grants creates a stimulus for boards to accept the offer when it imposes an especially light burden. A board which might qualify for a grant of only 35 per cent under an equalizing formula received 75 per cent under the flat-rate formula. This advantage, however, is extended only to the abler districts – others are penalized to the extent that the rate would have been higher under the alternative formula. The latter inequity, but not the former, was corrected in the post-1967 programme. The province continued to extend preferential treatment to the abler districts by holding the grant to a floor of 75 per cent.

The one compelling advantage of the vocational capital grant scheme, over the regular provincial grants, was the payment of the grant at the time an expenditure was incurred rather than over the life of any resultant debt. This relieved the local governments of all debt save that which they would actually have to repay. The normal practice has been for the province to force its local governments to debenture the full cost of a project and then to assist in the repayment of the debt.

Neither system changes the amount of money eventually paid out by each level of government, except insofar as funds can be borrowed at lower rates of interest by the province. The difference lies in the fact that a lump-sum grant transfers the responsibility for borrowing the provincial share of an expenditure from the local to the provincial level of government. This is a question, however, which will be explored at greater length in Chapter 11.

11
The Ontario Education Capital
Aid Corporation

The Ontario Education Capital Aid Corporation stands as the product of a rather unique intergovernmental relationship. It was created by Ontario to resolve a provincial-local problem. Yet the initial stimulus for its creation came from the federal level. Unlike the Technical and Vocational Training Agreement, however, the capital aid corporation was not itself a part of federal policy, but was the unintended offspring of a quite unrelated policy.

While the nature of the federal policy is important in understanding the origin and operation of the capital aid corporation, the process by which that policy was generated is of much less concern. In July 1963 the federal government launched a series of negotiations with the provinces intended to result in a national, portable, contributory pension plan.[1] The original federal proposal was for a plan operating essentially on the 'pay-as-you-go' principle, with the modest surpluses in the initial years being used to finance an increase in the flat-rate, noncontributory pensions. In April 1964, however, the Province of Quebec announced its own plan, designed to produce substantial surpluses for up to twenty years which were to be invested in provincial securities.

The basis of the federal plan was thereupon changed to parallel that of Quebec. Surpluses from the federal scheme would be accumulated in a Canada Pension Plan investment fund and turned over to the other nine provinces in return for provincial securities, in the same proportions as contributions were received from the residents of each province. The federal plan, the Canada Pension Plan, came into effect on 1 January 1966.[2]

At the outset of the arrangement, it was estimated that the pension fund would make available to Ontario approximately $267 millions annually for the first ten years (1966 to 1976), with this amount declining each year for another ten years (until 1986) by which time the fund would have reached its maximum and the pension plan would begin to operate on a 'pay-as-you-go' basis.[3]

The federal pension scheme generated a large source of additional capital financing for Ontario with which the province was virtually free to do as it chose. The cabinet chose to use the funds to support the capital expenditures of school boards and universities.[4] Little can be said about this basic choice, except that it reflected the high priority assigned to education by the cabinet. Other provinces made other choices, presumably reflecting a different set of priorities.[5]

The particular manner in which the cabinet gave effect to this choice is of crucial concern, however. In 1964 the province had created the Ontario Universities Capital Aid Corporation[6] as part of its response to the growing financial problems of the universities. That corporation was authorized to purchase and hold debentures issued by provincially-approved universities for capital projects approved by the minister of university affairs. The corporation was financed by means of advances from the provincial treasury. In March 1966 the cabinet announced its decision to use the proceeds of the Canada Pension Plan investment fund to finance the operations of the universities capital aid corporation and to create a parallel corporation, the Ontario Education Capital Aid Corporation.[7] The latter would use the money remaining after support of the universities capital aid programme ' ... for the purchase of debentures issued by municipalities and school boards for the construction of schools.'[8] The corporation was given authority to borrow money in addition to that advanced by the provincial treasury from pension plan fund receipts. In its first four years of operation, however, its revenue has been restricted to what the province made available from the latter fund.

The corporation was established to resolve a specific set of problems in the financing of capital expenditures for elementary and secondary education in the province. Exactly how the corporation worked to resolve these problems will be examined after a brief summary of the problems themselves.

The basic dimensions of the problems of local school boards and municipalities in financing large capital expenditures were outlined in Chapters 3 and 6. The fundamental problem was the lack of sufficient resources to undertake such expenditures except, in most cases, by recourse to borrowing. Heavy reliance on borrowing itself generated a set of pressing problems. First, a great many school districts and municipalities were so small and isolated from the centres of business and commerce that institutional markets for capital debentures were virtually non-existent. Second, while interest rates on municipal and school board debentures tend to be higher than those of senior governments, this is especially so where the debentures cannot be offered to a competitive market. Finally, the Ontario Municipal Board, the provincial agency charged with policing local indebtedness, imposed ceilings on total debt which further restricted, or, in some cases, even eliminated what access may have existed for expanding total borrowings.

An effective provincial response to this set of problems would appear to have been limited to the pursuit of any or all of three objectives. First, the response could have increased the revenue capacities of local governments by delegating new taxing powers to the local level, by improving the use of the existing tax base, or by increasing the proportion of revenue derived from provincial grants. Secondly, the response could have reduced the fiscal demands placed upon local governments through provincial assumption of greater responsibility either for the initiation of capital expenditures or for the financing of such expenditures (that is, provincial assumption of all or a portion of the school debt). Third, a provincial response could have improved the conditions under which local borrowing was carried out, either by facilitating the access of local governments to the capital market or by interfering with or eliminating the competitive market for school debentures.

As we shall attempt to show in the remainder of this chapter, the capital aid corporation represented the third alternative – a response which removed capital financing for schools from the conditions of the competitive market. The manner in which this was done, however, embodied the second alternative response to a certain extent as well – the reduction of fiscal demands upon local governments.

The detailed procedures in the operation of the corporation are of considerable importance, because it is this detail which provides the evidence necessary to evaluate its role. We shall be concerned here with the development of these procedures up to the year 1968. Reference will be made later to the problems and responses of 1969 and 1970.

One comment on the nature of the capital aid corporation must precede a description of its method of operation. While it was established as a distinct corporate entity, chartered under provincial legislation, the corporation has operated as an integral part of the provincial public service. The corporation is managed by senior officers of the Treasury Department. The day-to-day business administration is handled by the municipal finance branch of the Department of Municipal Affairs. The corporation employs no staff of its own.

The process of capital financing through the capital aid corporation began with the preparation of a project plan by the school board. This plan was then submitted to the school plant approvals section of the Department of Education for approval as to standards of location, design, and construction, and for the establishment of a ceiling on approved expenditure for grant purposes (the department's role will be explained in greater detail shortly). The school board then drafted a budget of its capital requirements for the ensuing fiscal year and an estimate of the proportion of these requirements which were to be financed through the sale of debentures. Public and secondary school boards (and boards of education), but not separate school boards nor, of course, any board in municipally unorganized territory, were then required to submit their capital budgets to the municipal council, or councils, having jurisdiction within the school district. The council might accept or reject all, or any part, of the capital budget. Disputes at this stage were usually settled through negotiation but where this was not possible, judgment was referred to the electors qualified to vote on money by-laws or, more commonly, to the Ontario Municipal Board.

Once the school board capital budget was accepted by the council, it was presented, along with the municipal capital budget, to the Ontario Municipal Board. The Board reviewed the existing indebtedness of the municipality and authorized the council to issue debentures up to a fixed ceiling (the ceiling being determined as the lesser of the budget and a maximum debt-assessment ratio). The municipal board might thus refuse permission to a municipality to carry out its full capital budget, including the school board budget. In such cases the only alternatives were a reduction in proposed spending or a special appeal to the provincial cabinet. School boards not in municipally-organized territory made application to the muncial board on their own behalf. Separate school boards were required to seek such approval only if they intended to borrow from the capital aid corporation. The latter represented a change in provincial policy since, prior to the creation of the corporation, separate school boards were not in any way subject to municipal board regulation.

Once the school board or municipal council had received permission from the municipal board to borrow up to an accepted limit, the process of applying for funds from the corporation began. The treasurer of the municipality or the school board completed a document entitled 'Offer to Sell a Debenture' which outlined the nature of the project or projects being undertaken and the amount and term of the debenture to be offered. This document was then forwarded to the municipal finance branch of the Department of Municipal Affairs.

The municipal finance branch drafted the necessary local by-law, obtained the municipal board's approval of its form, and submitted the draft by-law to the local treasurer for transmission to the municipal council or school board. The council or school board then enacted the by-law and the clerk or secretary-treasurer forwarded a copy to the municipal finance branch. The municipal finance branch submitted the enacted by-law to the municipal board once again, this time obtaining a certificate of validity. This certified that the by-law conformed to the terms of the borrowing approved by the board when the local capital budget was first presented. When the by-law had been validated, the municipal finance branch printed the necessary debenture and forwarded it to the local treasurer. The treasurer then submitted the debenture itself to the municipal board for validation. Again, the board certified that the terms of its original approval were complied with in the borrowing instrument. As the final steps in this process, the board forwarded the validated debenture to the director of the securities branch in the Treasury Department. A cheque in the full amount of the debenture was then issued in the name of the capital aid corporation to the municipality or school board as final settlement of the transaction.

Two additional comments are necessary to complete this picture. First, prior to July 1968 the rate of interest to be charged by the corporation was that in effect on the day the validated debenture was delivered to the Treasury Department. If the rate had changed since the debenture was issued by the municipality or school board, the change was reflected in the purchase price of the debenture (thus, if the interest rate had increased in this interval, the corporation would pay less than the face value of the debenture). In July 1968 the mechanism was changed so that the rate was that in effect on the day the original Offer to Sell a Debenture was received by the municipal finance branch.[9] The rate was thus to be determined at the earliest possible point in the process of borrowing. The effect of this change was also to eliminate the necessity of varying the purchase price of debentures. Since the actual rate of interest was established before the debentures were printed, that rate became the 'coupon' rate printed on the debenture, and the purchase price became the face value of the debenture. This change removed a large element of uncertainty in the cost of borrowing from the corporation.

Second, the final settlement of the corporation's capital loan was not made until the school board project had reached a stage of substantial completion. This meant that most of the expenditures during the construction of a building project had to be incurred by the school board itself, financed from current revenues (usually a short term bank loan). As we shall see, however, the lower rates applying to debentures purchased by the capital aid corporation maintained an advantage over debentures sold on the open market even with the added cost of this short term borrowing.

Although the Department of Education was not directly involved in the operation of the corporation, it played a vital role in the total process of capital financing. Before the process of raising funds began, the school board was required to submit the plans of a proposed building project to the school plant approvals section. Officers of this section then examined the proposal to assure that all departmental standards had been complied with and to establish a maximum approved expenditure for the project for grant purposes under the approvals formula described in Chapter 9. Where problems arose, the department would assist the board in developing or revising its plans and proposals.

Once an approved expenditure figure was determined, the lesser of that amount and the actual expenditure was subject to inclusion in the board's recognized extraordinary expenditure used in the grant programme. If the expenditure were made from borrowed funds – that is, if debentures were sold to the capital aid corporation – then the department calculated the amount of annual debt charges to be included in recognized extraordinary expenditure. If the total expenditure were approved, then so were the total debt charges; if only a percentage of the expenditure were approved, then so were the same proportion of the debt charges.

The annual debt charges which the school board or municipality was required to make to the corporation over the life of a debenture were thus subject to a grant from the Department of Education. The grant would vary from 35 to 95 per cent of the annual debt charges, depending on the taxable capacity of the board and the relative magnitude of its recognized extraordinary expenditure. We shall have cause shortly to comment upon this rather circuitous interdepartmental transfer of provincial funds.

The impact of the capital aid corporation, as the focal agency in the provincial government's response to the problems of local capital financing, lay in two interrelated areas: control of, and assistance in, the process of borrowing funds and interference with the normal operation of the capital money market.

The nature of the province's control and assistance was outlined in the description of the process of capital financing. Building plans were scrutinized and approved by the Department of Education. The capital budget, the debenture by-law, and the debenture itself were all scrutinized and approved by the municipal board. The Department of Education assisted boards in preparing building proposals, and the Department of Municipal Affairs actually drafted the local by-law, printed the debenture, and assumed responsibility for arranging the municipal board approval and the corporation purchase. About the only areas remaining under the exclusive responsibility of local government were the decisions to undertake capital projects and the establishment of priorities among projects. In the second area, the municipal board might intervene when disputes arose between a school board and a municipal council. We shall subsequently examine the context in which the province removed even the first area of local control.

The corporation had two immediate and profound effects upon school board capital financing. First, in its initial three years of operation, it provided a virtual guarantee to purchase all school debentures. In Chapter 16 we shall examine the developments which took place when that guarantee was in effect terminated. Second, the corporation substantially reduced the effective rate of interest on school debentures.

In the fiscal years 1966–7, 1967–8, and 1968–9 the corporation was able, from the pension plan funds advanced by the provincial treasury, to purchase all debentures offered for sale. The net purchase of school debentures amounted to $165,006,000 in 1966–7, $160,535,000 in 1967–8, and $166,132,000 in 1968–9.[10] The ability of the corporation to purchase all debentures depended of course on two factors: the total value of the debentures offered for sale and the proportion of the pension plan funds made available by the province. With respect to the second factor, the corporation was, in effect, in competition with the universities capital aid corporation, the latter assuming responsibility for capital loans to the community colleges as well. In the event that demand for funds should outstrip the supply, the cabinet would be forced either to limit the demand by controlling school board capital spending, or increase the supply by borrowing outside the pension fund. Again, we shall defer to Chapter 16 consideration of just what action was taken when this problem did in fact arise.

The rate of interest charged by the corporation was determined by the rate charged for the use of pension plan funds. The latter rate was prescribed by the federal minister of finance and was equal to the average yield of long-term federal securities, subject to change each month.[11] The corporation attempted to establish a rate as close to the federal rate as possible but without monthly fluctuations and averaging one-quarter to one-eighth of 1 per cent higher (to cover administrative costs).[12]

The practice adopted by the corporation after July 1968, by which the

rate of interest was established before the debenture was actually purchased (allowing the effective rate of interest to be printed on the debenture as the coupon rate), illustrates the marked difference between the
operation of the corporation and the open capital money market. The
coupon rate on debentures sold on the open market bears no necessary
relationship to the effective rate of interest. Purchasers offer a price which,
together with the coupon rate, will yield a satisfactory return. The result
is that the issuing authority has no guarantee that the sale will produce
exactly the necessary revenue – a $1,000,000 debenture might, for
example, be purchased for only $900,000. The policy of the corporation,
then, resulted in a significant stabilization of the procedures involved
in selling school debentures, a stabilization not characteristic of non-
school local capital financing.

From the beginning of its operation until November 1967 the corporation maintained a single rate of interest of 5.5 per cent. In November
1967 the rate was increased to 6.5 per cent, and in March 1968 to 6.75
per cent. These interest rates indicate the magnitude of the preferential
treatment accorded school debentures under the capital aid programme.
Table 31 shows the average yields of a sample of Canadian municipal
and provincial debentures and the yield of debentures purchased by the
corporation with two-month intervals from May 1966 to July 1968.

In the twenty-six month period shown in this table, the advantage of
the interest rate for school debentures over the average rate for general
municipal debentures ranged from .77 to 1.92 percentage points. Local
school debentures had almost as marked an advantage over the average
for provincial debentures – ranging from .60 to 1.46 percentage points.
The median advantage over municipal debentures was 1.075 percentage
points, and over provincial debentures .85 percentage points. In the first
fiscal year of the corporation's operation, the median advantage over
municipal debentures was 0.995 percentage points. Assuming that the
municipal rate would have applied to school debentures as well, in the
absence of the corporation then the total saving in the debt charges
required to service the debt created in that first year alone can be estimated at approximately $24.5 millions ($165 millions repaid over twenty
years at 1.0 per cent interest). Since the province assisted school boards
in meeting their annual debt charges, through the foundation grant programme, over half of the total saving would accrue to the province and
the remainder to the school boards. And, of course, the savings would
continue to grow as new debentures were purchased each year.

The Ontario Committee on Taxation took issue with the basic principles underlying the operation of the capital aid corporation. While

TABLE 31

Comparison of average yields of selected provincial and municipal debentures with OECAC interest rate: bi-monthly, May 1966 to July 1968

Month	Average provincial yield[a]	Average municipal yield[a]	OECAC rate[b]	Advantage of OECAC over province	Advantage of OECAC over municipalities
May 1966	6.10	6.27	5.50	.60	.77
July 1966	6.27	6.48	5.50	.77	.98
September 1966	6.51	6.80	5.50	1.01	1.30
November 1966	6.64	6.74	5.50	1.14	1.24
January 1967	6.25	6.51	5.50	.75	1.01
March 1967	6.18	6.40	5.50	.68	.90
May 1967	6.55	6.75	5.50	1.05	1.25
July 1967	6.70	6.98	5.50	1.20	1.48
September 1967	6.96	7.42	5.50	1.46	1.92
November 1967	7.23	7.54	6.50	.73	1.04
January 1968	7.27	7.58	6.50	.77	1.08
March 1968	7.68	7.82	6.75	.93	1.07
May 1968	7.76	7.93	6.75	1.01	1.18
July 1968	7.48	7.71	6.75	.73	.96

SOURCES: [a]/Taken from *McLeod, Young, Weir Bond Averages*
[b]/J. S. Brown, Department of Municipal Affairs

acknowledging the corporation's contribution in removing the necessity of small school boards cultivating their own capital markets, the committee went on to argue: 'The capital requirements of school boards will gain permanent preference over all remaining capital requirements at the local level. Notwithstanding the importance that is rightly accorded today to public education, the prospect is disturbing.'[13]

The real impact of the corporation is even more important than is suggested by the above statement, for it represented the beginning of a provincial programme designed, in effect, not so much to create a preferred market for school debentures as to eliminate the market concept altogether from the capital financing of schools. The corporation eliminated any relationship between either the fiscal capacity or integrity of the local government and the rate of interest borne by its securities. All debentures were to be purchased at face value and to bear a rate of interest which reflected, not the strength of the local issue, but the long term fiscal strength of the federal government. The system represented a closed intergovernmental transfer of funds in which the spending agency (the school board) was almost completely removed from any market surveillance.

Essentially, the capital aid programme as it operated between 1966 and 1968 represented a half-way step between allowing school boards (or their municipalities) to take their chances on a competitive money market and subjecting school board capital financing to complete provincial control. Largely because it was a half-way step, the programme contained a number of anomalous and even contradictory features. One of the more interesting anomalies in the corporation's operation was its relationship to the Department of Education's grants on debt charges. The provincial Treasury Department borrowed money from the Canada Pension Plan investment fund and lent this to the capital aid corporation. The corporation then lent the money to the school boards (directly or through the municipalities). The school boards then repaid the money (with interest) to the corporation, which repaid the provincial treasury, which in turn repaid the pension plan fund. But interjected in this transfer system were the school grants, under which the provincial treasury (through the Department of Education) assisted the school boards in repaying the corporation's loan. The grant on debt charges thus went from the provincial treasury to the school board, back to the corporation (directly or through the municipality), and thence once again to the provincial treasury.

The circuitous route along which these monies flowed is illustrated in Figure 25. This example is based on a loan of $1,000,000 repaid over

FIGURE 25
Flow-chart showing steps involved in loan of $1,000,000 from pension fund to
school board and repayment over twenty years

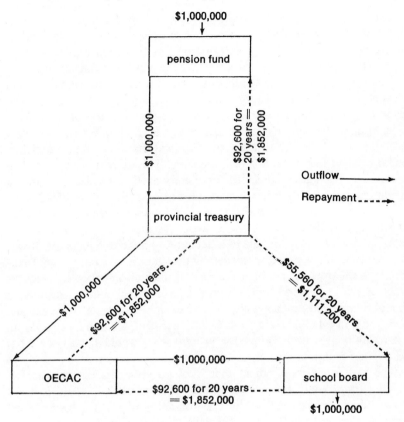

twenty years at an annual cost in principal and interest of $92,600 (using
the corporation's rate of 6.75 per cent effective in 1968). Further, the
school board is assumed to have had a total grant rate of 60 per cent,
meaning that the Department of Education paid 60 per cent of the annual
$92,600 debt charges, or $55,560. The net cost to the school board was
thus 92,600 − 55,560 = $37,040 each year. The school board or munici-
pality was hereby held legally responsible for the full repayment of a
loan 60 per cent of which would actually be repaid by the province itself.
It would seem more reasonable for the province to have paid the school
board the 60 per cent grant at the time the loan was arranged – that is, a
grant of $600,000 in the above example. This would have left the school
board (or municipality) to borrow only $400,000. Such a change would

not necessarily have implied the abolition of the corporation. If it so desired, the province could have advanced $400,000 (the amount remaining from its loan of $1,000,000 from the pension fund) to the corporation to be used to purchase the $400,000 debenture issued by or for the school board. If the same preferred rate of interest were charged, the school board would have repaid the corporation $37,040 each year for twenty years – the same as the net amount under the existing arrangement.

Under this first alternative, then, the two levels of government would have remained in precisely the same fiscal position except that the local level would not have been held legally responsible for an artificially inflated debt. The latter factor could be extremely important, of course, since it was the total debt, and not just the local share, which the municipal board used in fixing the borrowing ceiling. This system is illustrated in Figure 26 which uses the same parameters as Figure 25 except that a single grant of $600,000 is substituted for an annual grant of $55,560.

A second alternative would have involved the abolition of the corporation altogether, leaving the school board (or municipality) to raise the required $400,000 by the sale of a debenture on the open market. It was this policy which was recommended by the Ontario Committee on Taxation.[14] If this were done, then the rate of interest on school debentures would have risen generally and would have varied among the issuing school boards and municipalities. If, for example, the rate rose from the 6.75 per cent established in 1968 to 7.75 per cent, the annual charges on a $400,000 debenture issued for twenty years would have risen from $37,040 to $40,000.

The province's requirement that local governments assume the full liability for capital debts which would subsequently be repaid in large part by the province itself was justified on the grounds that this provided some control over total municipal debt (since the total debt could not exceed a proportion of the local assessment).[15] Again because the capital aid corporation was only a half-way step between local responsibility and provincial control, the provincial cabinet often intervened to prevent this implied control from delaying what were deemed to be essential school projects. In 1967 alone, the cabinet authorized cash capital grants to eight school boards whose parallel municipalities were prevented from increasing their indebtedness sufficiently.[16]

As a final example of confusion in the capital aid programme generally, we need only recall that the Northern Assistance Grants, described in Chapter 9, provided cash capital grants in order to overcome the inadequate borrowing capacity of the small northern school districts and municipalities.

FIGURE 26
Flow-chart showing steps involved in loan of $1,000,000 from pension fund to
school board and repayment over twenty years with grant paid in initial year

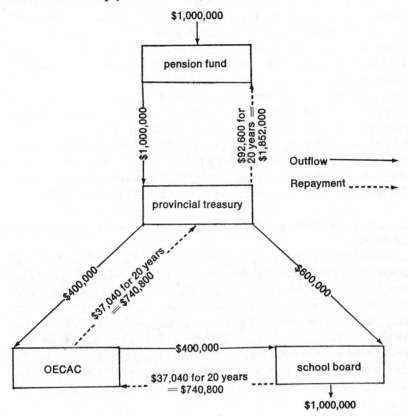

The capital aid corporation did not represent a very adequate response
to the problems of local capital financing. Primarily, it did virtually
nothing to resolve the disparities between local capital needs and fiscal
capacities. The ability of a local government to borrow funds continued
to be a function of its fiscal capacity except when the cabinet chose to
intervene and make funds available regardless of capacity.

The payment of capital grants at the time of an expenditure would
have largely eliminated this weakness. Under such a scheme, the portion
of the total capital requirements to be borrowed by the school board would
have been fully equalized in terms of relative taxing capacity (that is,
the local debt resulting from a given capital expenditure would have
represented the same proportion of taxing capacity for all school dis-

tricts). If the 'growth-need' concept as applied to grants on debt charges had been embodied in such grants, local borrowing would have been equalized in terms of fiscal need as well (that is, the local debt resulting from dissimilar capital expenditures would have represented the same, or a similar, proportion of taxing capacity for all school boards).

The explanation of this somewhat confused and internally contradictory policy would appear to lie in the origin of the capital fund with which it operated. The enactment of the Canada Pension Plan by the federal government created an immediate and unplanned pool of investment capital of some $300 millions annually for Ontario. The Ontario government responded to the federally initiated scheme by devising a programme to make use of the capital fund to purchase school debentures. There was nothing inherent in the federal scheme that prevented Ontario from developing a more consistent and comprehensive response to the problems of financing capital expenditures in education. For example, Ontario could have sold its own securities to the pension plan fund and used the proceeds to pay cash grants to school boards under its regular grant programme.

It would appear from the policy responses examined in this study that comprehensive and consistent policies are developed only when the policy formulation process has access to and makes use of a broad range of the governmental agencies whose responsibilities touch upon the problems being attacked. The case of the capital grants under the Technical and Vocational Training Agreement has provided another example of how policies tend to be isolated and contradictory when devised and administered in isolation. In part IV we shall see a clear example of the opposite: how an effectively integrated response can emerge from an integrated policy-making structure.

In providing a guaranteed source of funds for school boards' capital requirements, and in reducing the cost of those funds, the Ontario Education Capital Aid Corporation certainly had a short-term beneficial effect upon educational finance generally. The long-term role of the programme was intimately related to the organization of local educational governments, however, because the difficulties and high costs of borrowing on the open market were to a considerable extent the results of the inefficient organization of local governments. The corporation replaced the normal market constraints with bureaucratic controls and supports. These could be justified because the units of local government could not gain reasonable access to the competitive market. In the process it removed a large element of local government responsibility for capital financing. Reorganized local governments, in contrast, should have been able to gain access to the capital market themselves and thus re-assume responsibility for their own fiscal decisions. As we shall see, however, the province did not choose between a reform of local government and the capital aid programme; it followed both courses simultaneously. The latter changed the essential nature of the capital aid programme, but a consideration of that development must be deferred until we have examined the province's structural responses.

PART IV

Provincial structural responses

12
Township school areas

In Chapter 2 considerable attention was paid to the history of provincial attempts to enlarge school districts, especially for public elementary schools. Compulsory legislation was passed as early as 1841 (creating township units), only to collapse through lack of acceptance. Compulsion was attempted twice after that, in Ryerson's draft bill of 1868 and in Ferguson's abortive bill of 1925. During the 1930s provincial policy shifted from compulsory measures to the provision of financial and structural incentives to voluntary local consolidation. The three components of the new policy consisted of authorization for the establishment of township school areas by the township (municipal) councils, the payment of a special annual grant for each school section dissolved into a larger unit, and the use of the provincial inspectors to persuade the councils and school boards of the advantages of consolidation.

The combination of these incentives and the problems imposed by inadequate and unequal units of local government resulted in a substantial reduction in the number of such units during the 1940s. As was noted in Chapter 2, however, the movement towards township school areas had lost its momentum by 1950.*

During the fifties provincial policy entered yet another, and extremely interesting, phase. Ostensibly, the cabinet continued its commitment to support voluntary consolidation; at least the stimulation grant was retained and even liberalized. Yet W.J. Dunlop, minister of education from 1951 to 1959, withdrew the most effective of the three components of the provincial policy. According to officials of the Department of Education,[1] Dunlop's instructions to the department, and especially to the provincial inspectors, prohibited any activities which could be construed as encour-

* / See above, p. 16

aging school district consolidation. Information was to be provided upon request, but no initiatives were to be taken by representatives of the department.

Dunlop's position, however, was paralleled by a virtually unanimous consensus within the department that larger units of government for public elementary schools were essential. In some cases inspectors attempted to persuade local groups of the advantages of larger units in spite of the ministerial prohibition. Generally, however, the officials simply bided their time through Dunlop's tenure in office.

In 1959 Dunlop retired and was succeeded by John P. Robarts. While Robarts held the portfolio for only three years, the last concurrently with the prime ministership, he succeeded in revitalizing the department and setting the stage for a number of developments which would bear fruit and be further extended by his successor, William G. Davis. Probably the greatest contribution Robarts made to the department was his assurance of support for his officials and his recognition of the necessity of change in education. In the context of the present policy, this meant he fostered the exploration and development of proposals for the reform of educational government by his departmental officials.

Naturally there was no immediate committment to a policy of legislated consolidation of school districts. Some period of time would invariably have been required to overcome the legacy of Dunlop's discouragement of official intervention in the structure of local educational government over the previous eight years. Furthermore, the long-standing cabinet commitment to voluntary local reorganization was not likely to be altered without some clear and compelling objective which necessitated such a change. It is quite clear, however, that by the time Robarts became minister of education, the policy of encouraging local consolidation had effectively reached the limit of its potential.

By 1963 there were still 1212 rural public school boards with jurisdiction over only a single school section. Of these, 1064 operated schools. At the same time there were 622 township school areas, ranging in size from a union of two sections to an area coterminous with the township. Of these, 601 operated schools (township boards not operating schools tended to be in the suburban areas where pupils could conveniently be transported to schools in the central urban municipality).

When Prime Minister Robarts announced the basic outline of the provincial grant plan in February 1963, he stated specifically that no legislated consolidation of school districts was contemplated.[2] He argued that the British North America Act denied the province power to consolidate separate school districts and therefore no compulsory consolidation could be effective. Yet when the new grant plan was fully developed, by 1964, it proved to be the impetus required to force a re-evaluation of the cabinet's opposition to legislated consolidation.

The relationship between the implementation of a foundation plan and the need for a reorganization of the territorial units of local government in Ontario had been recognized as early as 1936 in Maxwell Cameron's doctoral dissertation.[3] It had been repeated on numerous occasions after that. Both Dr Jackson and Professor Rideout, the key advisers in the development of the new grant programme, had been firmly convinced that a consolidation of the local units was an essential preliminary step in the implementation of an effective foundation plan.

The Ontario variant of the foundation plan was, in fact, designed as it was to forestall the necessity of a radical consolidation of school districts.[4] Ironically, perhaps, its effect was quite the opposite, for it heightened the pressure on the cabinet to accept just such a consolidation. The plan recognized the principle, if not the fact, that all school districts could be treated equitably only if they were subject to the same grant formula. This was the essential difference between the use of a foundation plan formula and the use of distinct schedules of grants for distinct groups of school districts. Having recognized that principle, then, the continued resistance to a policy which would create the local structures capable of supporting such a grant programme became more and more untenable.

While it is not possible to determine the precise time at which the cabinet accepted the necessity of a provincially mandated reform of local government, the decision of when to announce the change was clearly related to the timing of the general election. This was to be the first of two occasions on which the provincial government announced its intention of consolidating school districts shortly after success at the polls (the second occured in 1967 and will be examined in a subsequent chapter). The announcement of the impending legislation was made in February 1964 – five months after the election and just one month after the release of the new grant regulations.

Legal effect was given to the cabinet's decision in a rather terse clause of the Act amending the Public Schools Act: 'On and after the 1st day of January, 1965, every township shall be a township school area.'[5] In that short sentence one of the oldest public institutions in Ontario, the three-member board of trustees of the rural public school section, was eliminated.[6] The provision went slightly further than this, requiring that all urban (village, town, or city) school districts with populations of less than 1000 or average daily attendance of pupils of less than 100 be attached to the adjacent township school area.

As a result of this legislation over 1600 school sections and smaller township school areas ceased to exist, replaced by 255 new township areas. The total number of school boards, both before and after the reorganization, are given in Table 32.

TABLE 32
Total and public elementary school boards
in Ontario

	1964	1965
Public elementary	2419	1037
Total	3472	1933

SOURCE: Minister's Report, 1964 and 1965,
adjusted by estimated number of boards not
operating schools.

While the importance of this reduction in the number of public elementary school districts can not be overlooked, the most important aspect of the legislation was the change in government policy which it represented. As recently as 1950, the 'official line' on larger units could still be expressed as in the following question and answer format of a departmental circular:

Does the organization of a Township School Area result in the organization of a consolidated school or schools?

No. The consolidation of schools is entirely separate from the organization of Township School Areas, and any consolidation will depend entirely upon the wishes of the people concerned..[7]

But in reporting upon the 1964 enactment, the Minister of Education could make the following statement:

Although the legislation of 1964 does not refer to centralization of accommodation, there is every reason to believe that with greater availability of local financial support on a broader basis and with continued provincial legislative grants on a generous scale, the trend towards rural central schools will be accelerated under the township school area boards established by the new legislation.[8]

The intent of the legislation was emphatically to clear away the one- and two-room rural schools and the 'nuts and bolts' school board which was traditionally associated with such schools.* In both of these objectives the legislation met with a high degree of success.

Table 33 shows fairly clearly the impetus given to rural school consolidation by the enforced amalgamations. Whereas 66,245 pupils were still enrolled in schools in single rural school sections in 1964, this number had dropped to only 4831 by 1965 (it dropped further to 4370 in 1966 but increased slightly thereafter to 5783 in 1967 and 5160 in 1968). The growth in the average size of the rural (township area) schools is also quite apparent: the average enrolment per school rose from 95 in 1964 to 121 in 1966 (the stability of the figure in 1965 is due simply to the necessary time lapse between the establishment of the township boards and the construction of central schools. There was an even more dramatic increase in this figure for 1967, with the average enrolment per school increasing to 176. In 1968 the average increased more modestly to 196.

TABLE 33
Total enrolment and enrolment per school in the
public elementary schools of Ontario, 1960–8

	Total enrolment			Enrolment per school		
Year	All schools	Township school areas*	Rural sections	All schools	Township school areas*	Rural sections
1960	843,737	169,856	89,263	148	71	47
1961	861,715	163,434	n/a	156	73	n/a
1962	880,198	164,679	77,277	164	76	46
1963	901,830	172,461	73,743	176	86	47
1964	925,068	182,632	66,245	190	95	49
1965	949,374	250,511	4831	222	95	47
1966	976,720	254,352	4370	257	121	54
1967	1,002,555	268,095	5783	297	176	81
1968	1,021,482	279,135	5160	326	196	83

*/Includes county and district school areas after 1965
SOURCE: Minister's Reports

The changed organization of school government had an impact, as well, on the attitudes of school board members. The creation of boards with jurisdiction over an area large enough to support at least a fully graded school impelled board members to consider the larger economic and educational implications of school government as well as the detailed

* / The term 'nuts and bolts' school board has been a derisory term applied to the type of school board whose members concentrated their attention upon the rudimentary facilities of the school – plumbing, heating, supplies – with little concern for the instructional and ancillary programmes.

administration of a single school. This emergent attitude is expressed fairly clearly in the following excerpts from a paper delivered to a gathering of public school trustees by a member of a newly-enlarged township board.

There was no substantial opposition to the new legislation in our Township and we quickly got on with seeing what we could gain with our newly enlarged area.

Our first move was to hire a full time Secretary-Treasurer who also held the title of Business-Administrator. For the first time in history, we opened a school administration office ... A stenographer was soon employed ...

Meetings were organized between all School Principals for curriculum planning and selection of approved texts ...

For the first time, there was sufficient work ... to allow the employment of one full-time maintenance man ...

By this time, kindergartens had been established, and a more efficient school bus system over the enlarged area had permitted a large reduction in the number of multiple grade classrooms ...

On the combined basis, there are enough students requiring [Opportunity Classes] to arrange Junior and Senior classes of the correct size ...

A very well stocked film library serves the entire area ... [9]

The legislation of 1964 was of crucial importance because of the subtle but very real way in which it broke the bond of control over local school policy by small rural communities. It is true that a number of factors facilitated this move and thus explain the contrast between its success and the failures of 1841, 1868, and 1925. Improvements in transportation rendered centralized education geographically feasible, while the prior or concurrent centralization of shopping, cultural, religious, and secondary school institutions created an air of inevitability about the process.

Unlike any other institution, however, the size of the rural public school district had always been determined by local representatives. Until 1932 that determination had even been ratified by the local citizens directly. The 1964 legislation simply wiped out the small sections by fiat. Once the provincial government had assumed major responsibility for the size of local units of government, the question in many minds became the extent to which this responsibility would be exercised. At first, as we shall see shortly, any further enlargements were to be voluntary once again. But within less than four years the provincial government had grown impatient and again moved to legislate the precise nature of local units. That, however, is the subject of subsequent concern.

The mandatory establishment of larger units of government for public schools had yet another, and an unintentional effect. It heightened the pressure on rural separate schools to reorganize themselves voluntarily. The major obstacle to larger units for separate schools was removed in 1963 when the basis of the prescribed three-mile zone was changed from the school site to an area radiating about a designated point. Because of this change, enlarged districts no longer needed to consist only of unions of previously self-sufficient districts. 'Dummy' zones could be established with no provision for the purchase of a site and could immediately be dissolved into a larger district (known since 1963 as a 'combined zone').

The rapid development of central schools in the public elementary sector – with the resultant increase in the level of educational service provided – impelled the separate school boards towards a parallel move. The result may be gleaned from Tables 34 and 35 which show the growth in the number of combined zones since 1960 and the consequent growth in the number and proportion of central schools. Thus, while there had been a definite movement toward the enlarged separate school district prior to the public school legislation, there was a very marked increase in the proportion of combined zones after 1965.

The shift in average size of the schools is not so dramatic here as in the case of public elementary schools. The reason for that is simply that there had not been as many small, rural separate schools as there were public schools. Even the most sparsely settled areas of the province (except for the far northern regions) are included in public school districts, whereas separate schools exist only where there are concentrations of supporters.

As well as the immediate consolidation of rural school sections, the 1964 legislation was designed with a longer term objective. Machinery was established to facilitate the voluntary enlargement of districts beyond the township. Every county council was henceforth required to establish a 'Public School Consultative Committee.' The committee was to consist of either three or five persons (both the number and personnel to be determined by the council) with one of the public school inspectors, designated by the minister of education, added as secretary. The provision extended also to the territorial districts wherein a public school inspector was authorized to call a meeting of representatives of the munici- palities and public school boards in any area within a high school district. This meeting could, but was not required to, elect a public school con-

TABLE 34

Number and proportion of combined separate school zones[a], 1960–8

Year	No of boards[b]	No of combined boards[b]	Proportion of combined boards
1960	706	106	15%
1961	773	127	16
1962	743	141	19
1963	753	157	21
1964	721	196	27
1965	525	204	39
1966	526	270	51
1967	482	297	62
1968	455	295	65

[a]/Known as union separate school boards prior to 1963
[b]/Includes only boards operating schools
SOURCE: Minister's Reports

TABLE 35

Total enrolment and enrolment per school in the separate elementary schools of Ontario, 1960–8

Year	Enrolment	Enrolment per school
1960	282,651	208
1961	301,338	213
1962	316,831	223
1963	331,334	233
1964	353,405	247
1965	370,669	261
1966	387,971	279
1967	402,497	292
1968	408,914	299

SOURCE: Minister's Reports

sultative committee with terms of membership similar to the county committees.

The purpose of these committees was to report on petitions regarding the formation of county (or district) school areas, and to obtain information and make detailed recommendations regarding the desirability of forming or enlarging county (or district) school areas comprising two or more municipalities, and 'any other matters affecting public school education in the county [district].'[10] The county councils, or local municipalities in the districts, were then authorized to establish units of public school government larger in area than a single township. These units were to be known as county or district school areas.

The legislation essentially shifted responsibility for the organization of local government of the public schools one level closer to the province. Prior to 1964, the school section was the basic unit with township councils having authority to effect enlargements. With the 1964 legislation, the township became the basic unit with the county councils having authority to effect enlargements. As we shall see in a subsequent chapter, legislation of 1968 carried the process to the next logical step – the county became the basic unit with the minister of education having the effective responsibility for enlargements or alterations.

Two significant changes were made in the legislation in 1965.[11] First, the terms of reference of the consultative committees were broadened. They were now to investigate and report on the desirability of establishing or enlarging county school areas, of altering township school areas, or on any other matters affecting public school education in the county.[12] Second, the county (but not the district)[13] school areas which might be established as the result of the work of these committees were to be at least coterminous with, but could be larger than, an existing high school district. The intent of the latter provision was quite clear and had been spelled out by the Minister of Education in a memorandum to the consultative committees in December 1964.

The formation of larger units of administration in which public and secondary schools are under boards of education is a long term objective ...

The minimum desirable size of a county or district school area is considered to be the area capable of supporting a composite secondary school organization.[14]

All counties in the province established consultative committees under the terms of the legislation. The dates of formation, number of members (excluding the provincial inspector and warden if the latter sat as an *ex officio* member), and the distribution of members by office are summarized in Table 36.

The predominance of municipal councillors on the consultative committees is significant. Of the total membership of 175, 89 or 50.9 per cent were councillors. Of these, 85 or 48.6 per cent of the total were also county councillors. This contrasts rather sharply with the membership of public school or secondary school board members. The latter groups made up only 10.9 per cent of the total membership. It is interesting to speculate concerning the effect of this general absence of school board

TABLE 36

Dates of formation and membership composition of
county public school consultation committees

County	Date of formation	No of members	Municipal councillors[a]	Public or high school trustees	Non-office holders
Brant	Dec. 1964	5		3	2
Bruce	Jan. 1966	5	5(5)		
Carleton	Jan. 1965	5	5(5)		
Dufferin	Jan. 1965	5		4	1
Elgin	Jan. 1965	5	5(5)		
Essex	Nov. 1964	5	1	2	2
Frontenac	May 1965	5	5(5)		
Grey	June 1964	5	5(5)		
Haldimand	May 1964	3		1	2
Haliburton	June 1964	5	1	2	2
Halton	Sept. 1965[b]	5			5
Hastings	Jan. 1965	3	3(3)		
Huron	Jan. 1966	3	3(3)		
Kent	Nov. 1964	5			5
Lambton	Dec. 1964	5			5
Lanark	June 1964	5			5
Leeds, Grenville	Dec. 1964	5			5
Lennox & Addington	March 1965	5			5
Lincoln	May 1964	5	1(1)	2	2
Middlesex	Feb. 1965	5	5(5)		
Norfolk	Jan. 1965	5	4(2)	1	
Northumberland, Durham	Jan. 1965	5	5(5)		
Ontario	Apr. 1965	5	1(1)	1	3
Oxford	1966[c]	5	5(5)		
Peel	Apr. 1965	5			5
Perth	Mar. 1965	5	5(5)		
Peterborough	June 1964	5	5(5)		
Prescott, Russell	June 1964	5	3(3)	1	1
Prince Edward	Jan. 1966	5			5
Renfrew	Mar. 1966	5	2(2)		3
Simcoe	Jan. 1965	5	5(5)		
Stormont, Dundas, and Glengarry	Nov. 1964	3	3(3)		
Victoria	Jan. 1965	5	5(5)		
Waterloo	Jan. 1965	5			5
Welland	Oct. 1964	3	1(1)		2
Wellington[d]	June 1964	5	5(5)		
Wentworth	March 1965	5	1(1)	2	2
TOTALS		175	89(85)	19	67
PERCENTAGES[e]		100.0	50.9(48.6)	10.9	38.3

members and whether in particular cases it retarded or accelerated the movement toward voluntary larger units. In at least two counties in which larger units were formed within the first year of the new legislation (Grey and Peterborough counties), it was quite clear that the public school inspector – the non-voting secretary of the consultative committee – had, to a very large extent, controlled the outcome of the deliberative and decision-making processes.[15] The inspector may well have been a more authoritative figure in relations with municipal, as opposed to school board, politicians.

In the first year of the new provisions, a total of twelve county or district school areas were established, taking effect on 1 January 1966. Thirteen additional larger areas were created the following year.[16]

As was mentioned earlier, the legislation of 1964 (with the two significant amendments of 1965) made two fundamental changes in the nature of educational government in Ontario. First, it erected the township as the basic geographical unit of local government for public schools, and in so doing both removed the last vestiges of control over public school district government by the small rural community and added a compelling incentive to the voluntary enlargement of units of separate school government. Second, the legislation established machinery with a strong structural bias (and, in some cases, a strong personnel bias as well) in favour of the creation of still larger units of public school government combined with the existing larger secondary school districts.

In view of the next step taken by the province in the area of structural reorganization of local government, the advice of the Minister of Education to the county and district consultative committees reflects some ambivalence in the specific longer-term objectives of the provincial government.

The consultative committees are composed of people ... who are in a position to determine the best plans [sic] for the amalgamation of township school areas and urban municipalities. It should be recognized by all concerned that

---

a /The figures in brackets indicate municipal councillors who were also county councillors.
b /The date of formation was not given here. The date cited refers to the first meeting of the committee.
c /The exact date was not given here.
d /A subsequent committee was formed in January 1966 composed of three county councillors and two non-office holders
e /Figures may not add due to rounding.
SOURCE: S. W. Semple, 'Matters Relevant to the Establishment of Public School Consultative Committees in Ontario'

some counties are compact and that the whole of the county may form a single unit. Other counties or districts may be very large or irregularly shaped and populations may be sparse in certain portions ...

In order to keep the educational programe within a geographic area which can be administered by a single board, it may be necessary in some instances to establish *more than one unit within an area served by a secondary school* [italics mine].[17]

This essentially voluntaristic approach, based on the assumption that local politicians could decide the best form of government for schools, was abandoned just three years later. In Chapter 13 we shall explore one factor – the reorganization of the provincial Department of Education – which can be seen as having contributed to this abandonment. Perhaps of equal importance, however, was the opposition which reorganization of school districts met in certain areas of the province. One specific example of this opposition will be explored in some depth in Chapter 14.

13
Reorganization of the Department
of Education

The organization of the provincial Department of Education reflects the provincial government's involvement in the formulation and execution of educational policy in the province. From the beginning of government control of schools in 1807 to the union of Upper and Lower Canada in 1840 there was, in fact, no provincial office of education at all, save for a ten-year interlude (1822 to 1832) when an advisory General Board of Education attempted to manage the royal land grant of 1797. What concern the colonial administration had with education was handled by the provincial secretary.

The ill-fated attempt at erecting a uniform system of schools in the united Province of Canada in 1841 called forth the establishment of a central office in that year. There was to be a superintendent of education for the whole province, aided by assistant superintendents responsible for each of the former provinces. The superintendency was held by the provincial secretary, while the duality of the province was reflected in the dominance and autonomy of the respective assistant superintendents. Egerton Ryerson, the great builder of the Ontario school system, was appointed assistant superintendent for Canada West in 1844.[1] Reflecting the collapse of the grand design of a single system for the whole province, Ryerson's title was changed in 1846 to that of chief superintendent of schools for Canada West. He was assisted by an appointed Council of Public Instruction and reported to the government through the provincial secretary.

This organizational pattern remained unchanged until Ryerson retired in 1876. That the Council of Public Instruction had, under Ryerson's leadership, become an effective department of education is evidenced by the reorganization which followed Ryerson's retirement. The office of chief superintendent was given the status of a ministry, Ryerson's assistant superintendent became deputy minister, while the executive of the Council of Public Instruction was reconstituted as the Department of Education. The change in titles did, however, reflect the fact that public education had become an important area of provincial activity and was to be more fully integrated with overall policy decisions.

The increasing importance of education in provincial political decisions was reflected again in the creation of a new senior position in the department in 1906. Day-to-day administration of provincial educational matters continued to be the responsibility of a deputy minister, but the formulation and investigation of new policy directions was assigned to the office of superintendent, assisted by an Advisory Council of Education. This reorganization began a long period of confusion as to which of the offices – deputy minister or superintendent – was superior. Whichever was ascendant at any point in time was largely a function of the individuals occupying the offices. Certainly the first superintendent, John Seath, was the dominant figure in matters of provincial involvement in education during his occupancy of that role.[2]

Upon Seath's death in 1919 the office of superintendent was abolished, administration being co-ordinated with policy formulation once again under a single deputy minister. This structure only lasted for the life of the 'farmers' government,'[3] and in 1923 the dual leadership was re-established, policy this time being the responsibility of a chief director of education. The only formal change between 1923 and 1965 was the appointment of a second deputy minister in 1956 (the division of responsibilities between the two being largely that between elementary and secondary education).

The same confusion over ascendancy recurred with the 1923 reorganization, and perhaps reached its peak in the second of the Hepburn administrations when the offices were shuffled in a manner which approached a game of 'musical chairs.'[4] As Conservative hegemony was re-established in Ontario during and after the Second World War, however, the office of chief director emerged as the dominant sub-ministeral position. The organizational chart published in the 1946 Minister's Report[5] placed the deputy minister beneath the chief director in bureaucratic rank (the 1944 report had pictured the two offices in parallel positions). This situation was never disputed after that.

Educational policy, however, began to assume much greater importance in overall provincial policy in the decade of the 1960s. The problems producing this importance and the policies giving effect to its recognition constitute the substance of this book. One of the fundamental ingredients of the provincial government's re-examination of educational policy, which began with John Robarts' assumption of the ministry, was a very close scrutiny of the organization and style of the Department of Education.

There appear to have been two major areas of concern with respect to departmental organization. First of all, the department had grown – as most institutions do – by a process approximating that of organic cellular reproduction. When a particular function of one of the departmental divisions assumed sufficient prominence, it would be split off from the parent division and established as a divisional entity in its own right. The reverse situation seldom occurred; once established, departmental divisions tended to assume a considerable degree of permanence. This aspect of the department's growth can be grasped fairly quickly from the following three organizational charts (Figures 27, 28, and 29) for the years 1946, 1958, and 1964. While it is recognized that organizational charts seldom depict the reality of bureaucratic responsibility, the charts are informative for the changes they reveal over the course of eighteen years. The number of departmental divisions immediately beneath the deputy minister level rose from five in 1946 to thirteen in 1958, and reached nineteen in 1964.

There was thus a rather obvious need for reorganization, if only to reduce the number of divisional heads reporting to the deputy ministers and chief director. The logical response to this need was either a re-

FIGURE 27
Organization of the Department of Education, 1946

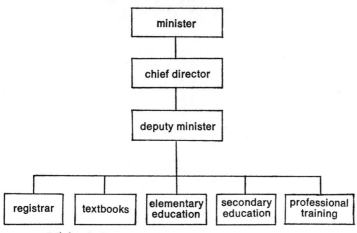

SOURCE: Minister's Report, 1946

FIGURE 28
Organization of the Department of Education, 1958

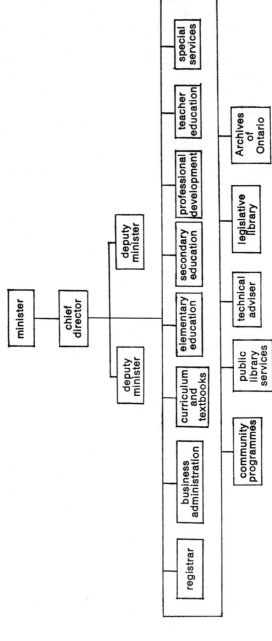

SOURCE: Minister's Report, 1958

FIGURE 29
Organization of the Department of Education, 1964

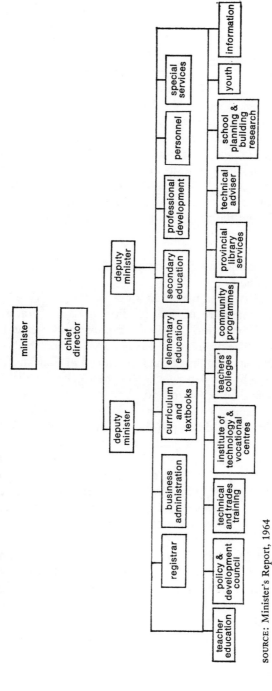

SOURCE: Minister's Report, 1964

grouping of the department's activities into a more manageable number of categories or the creation of a new level of responsibility between that of deputy minister and divisional head, so that co-ordination would be more complete by the time issues reached the level of deputy minister.

The second major area of concern was the relation between departmental organization and overall government policy in education. The kind of department depicted in the 1946 chart (Figure 27) was essentially a regulatory one. The actual provision of educational services was primarily the responsibility of the local school boards. The role of the provincial department was to regulate, control, and stimulate, but only rarely to actively intervene in, the provision of these services. There were a limited number of areas in which the department became actively involved in providing services prior to the Second World War. All of these, however, were clearly beyond the competence of local school boards. Thus, the department offered correspondence courses and sent railway school cars to scattered settlements, produced radio broadcasts in co-operation with the Canadian Broadcasting Corporation, and operated a school for the deaf and for the blind.

Four of the five major departmental divisions shown in Figure 27 reflected the four major areas of regulation. The fifth division – professional training – reflected the single long-standing exception to the general rule of department policy. The training of elementary teachers had, since 1908, been the direct responsibility of the Department of Education. The assumption of this role by the department was the result of the inability of the local boards, as then organized, to perform it to the satisfaction of the provincial government (or the educational establishment).

The inability of local boards to provide adequate service, justifying the assumption of responsibility for teacher education by the department, led to departmental involvement in other areas in subsequent years. Thus, for example, divisions responsible for community programmes, special education services, and planning and building research were created or erected as distinct entities between 1946 and 1964. Each of these bears witness to a greater direct involvement of the department in the provision of services falling into these categories.

There were two conditions necessary for a major reform and reorganization of the Department of Education. First, there had to be created within the department an atmosphere conducive to change; a prevailing attitude which neither feared nor subverted proposals for change but which accepted change as the necessary prerequisite to meeting needs more effectively. Under W.J. Dunlop, minister of education throughout the 1960s (1951 to 1959), this atmosphere had been anything but present. According to one astute observer:

W.J. Dunlop ... made no real effort to defend his officials. They thus drew together and erected barriers to defend themselves ... There was a sense of alienation that was reinforced by certain qualities that made him difficult to approach with anything but reinforcement for his own well solidified ideas.[6]

This necessary change in atmosphere was created by the appointment of John P. Robarts as minister of education in 1959. As the same observer described Robart's tenure:

... he was particularly eager to open lines of communication with non-official educational interests and to encourage the flow of new ideas. In debates in the Legislature, he dealt with the faults of the educational system with the kind of candour that had not been heard from a government spokesman for a long time, and yet managed to ensure that his officials felt supported and encouraged.[7]

After only two years in this portfolio, Robarts was elevated to the prime ministership of the province. He retained the education portfolio for another year and in 1962 passed it to William G. Davis. The appointment of Davis assured that the kind of changes which had begun to develop within the department would not only be continued but would be pushed forward with new vigour and considerable determination.

The second requirement for change and redirection in the department was the injection of an external stimulus. This is not the appropriate place for an excursion into the theory of organizational change, but it can be argued with relative certainty that the Department of Education in the early 1960s was poorly equipped to develop within itself a new concept for its purpose and organizational structure. Interestingly, this external stimulus was provided by the provincial Civil Service Commission. The process by which this stimulus emerged began with a classification and salary problem in 1962. The immediate problem was the department's inability to compete with the larger school districts for highly qualified personnel. The department's requests to the Civil Service Commission for authorization to raise salary levels and alter job classifications led to a preliminary investigation by the commission of the personnel practices in the department.

This preliminary study was undertaken in April 1962 by T.C. Campbell. He found two basic weaknesses in the departmental organization: too little delegation of authority and too much diffusion of functional re-responsibility. Campbell suggested the department be restructured with emphasis upon the responsibilities of a relatively small number (seven or eight) of functional branches with the head of each having sufficient authority to make administrative decisions.[8]

Campbell's initial report led to a series of discussions between officers of the commission and department, and culminated a year later (May 1963) with the Minister of Education requesting a formal study of the '... staffing in relation to organization and administration' of the department by an officer of the commission seconded for that purpose.[9] J.S. Stephen, executive director of the Department of Civil Service, was immediately appointed to undertake this study.

Stephen submitted a preliminary recommendation calling for the immediate creation of a personnel branch within the department to be responsible for the development and administration of a comprehensive personnel policy. This recommendation was accepted and in August 1963 T.C. Campbell, author of the original commission study, was appointed director of personnel. This was undoubtedly a key appointment for it injected a strong-willed and determined 'outsider' into the central policy-making arena of the department. In his new position, Campbell soon joined a small group of departmental officers who comprised the nucleus of what was to become the 'new' department (in 1965 Campbell became executive assistant to the deputy minister and joined C.H. Wescott, executive assistant to the minister, as the 'grey eminences' of the department).

Stephen's formal but confidential report, entitled 'Staffing in Relation to Organization and Administration in the Department of Education,' was submitted to the minister in December 1963. The report was in many ways an extension and amplification of the ideas contained in the initial Campbell study of 1962. Calling for functional integration and delegation of authority, he recommended the abolition of the dichotomy between elementary and secondary education, the consolidation of special subject branches (art, music, physical education, and the like) into the curriculum and supervision sections, and a clear-cut separation of education from general administration, with the implication that educators no longer be employed to perform administrative tasks.

The Stephen Report constituted the basic document in a planning process which preoccupied the minister and his 'inner circle' of officials for the subsequent twelve months. The membership of this 'inner circle' was of course informal, but it clearly centred upon C.H. Westcott and T.C. Campbell. What emerged from this largely extra-bureaucratic policy formulation process was a design for the Department of Education which embodied the administrative concerns of the Stephens Report but also facilitated the realization of a quite new and significantly different role for the department as a whole. In the remainder of this chapter we shall explore each of these aspects separately.

The process which began with a concern in the Civil Service Commission for classification and salaries of departmental officials culminated in January 1965 when the Minister of Education announced the major changes to be made in the organization of his department. According to this announcement, the planned reorganization had four basic purposes:

First, to bring the elementary and secondary school panels closer together; second, to reduce the number of special subjects branches and to integrate them in the main instructional stream; third to decentralize departmental administration ... and fourth, to relieve professional educators of responsibility for school business wherever possible, and to place such business in the hands of senior clerical staff, professional accountants and school business officials.[10]

These four purposes rather closely paralleled the three major recommendations of the Stephens Report.

An organizational chart of the department as established in 1965 is set forth in Figure 30. The basic changes as compared with the 1964 pattern may be summarized in three points. First, the title of chief director was changed to that of deputy minister, but the nature of this office was not altered, as it remained the chief executive office in the department. Second, the title of deputy minister was changed to assistant deputy minister. Of greater importance, the division of responsibilities among the three assistant deputy ministers (there had been only two deputy ministers) was clearly delineated. One was to have responsibility for the entire instructional programme in the elementary and secondary schools – including teacher education, the second for special schools and services and for post-secondary (but not university) education other than teacher education, and the third for all aspects of administration. Stephen's recommendation for a two-fold division between education and administration had thus been amended in the erection of two sections responsible for the educational programme. The separation of education from administration was clearly implemented, however. One of the interesting features of this aspect of the reorganization was that Stephen himself was appointed assistant deputy minister, administration, in January 1965 – a position from which he could preside over the implementation of his own recommendations.

FIGURE 30
Organization of the Department of Education, 1965

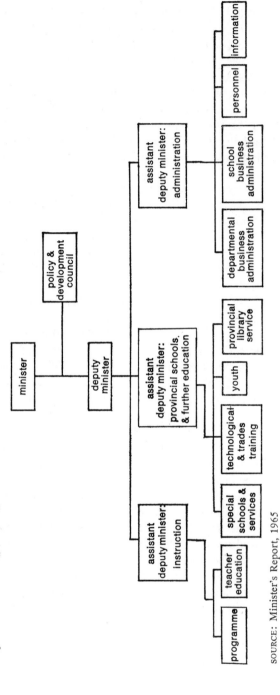

SOURCE: Minister's Report, 1965

The third change involved a regrouping of the major departmental divisions. The nineteen divisions shown in Figure 29 for 1964, all of which had reported directly to the deputy ministers, were divided into primary and secondary categories. The primary category – shown in Figure 30 – were designated 'branches' and were to report to one of the three assistant deputy ministers. The secondary category were designated 'divisions' and were to report to one of the branch directors. Of these nineteen divisions, fifteen continued largely unchanged, seven as branches, seven as divisions, and one as a ministerial staff advisory body (the Policy and Development Council). Two of the former divisions were split, one of these into two branches and one into two divisions. Finally, two of the former divisions were combined into a single division (with some adjustments).

Of more importance than these formal lines of authority and bureaucratic titles were the changes made in the functions assumed by each office and the administrative machinery established to carry out these functions. Three of these areas deserve special comment: the integration of departmental activity into two broad areas or categories, the separation of business administration and instruction, and the reorganization of the department's field activities.

The Department of Education was first established at a time when elementary schools constituted the bulk of the province's concern in the provision of education. High schools were renamed as such only five years prior to the very creation of the department. As secondary education assumed a position of increasing importance in the twentieth century, however, the supervision and control of this sector of the system consumed an increasing proportion of the department's energies. Following the Second World War two additional major areas of concern emerged – post-secondary and 'special'* education. As each of these emerged it tended to become the responsibility of a 'sub-department' – a division of the department whose personnel and objectives were considered to be, if they were not in fact, unique. Policies such as those requiring distinct training experiences and certification procedures for the different areas of educational activities tended to solidify these intra-departmental boundaries.

The reorganization of 1965 upset these established divisions. Ele-

* / 'Special education' is a somewhat euphemistic term used to describe a varied package of educational services falling outside the pale of the regular instructional programme. The content of special education changes rather rapidly over time, as services which are 'special' at one time tend to become 'regular' as their provision becomes more general. By and large, however, 'special' services tend to be those designed for pupils who cannot benefit fully from, or are not admissible to, the regular elementary or secondary or post-secondary schools.

mentary and secondary education were merged as a single area of concern and activity. This was to have fairly rapid and far-reaching implications for the structuring of local school government and particularly of separate school government. The impact in those areas will be taken up in Chapter 14. Also as a function of the 1965 reorganization, all of the activities of the department related to post-secondary and 'special' education were to be grouped together under a single assistant deputy minister who was to be responsible for library services, special schools for the deaf and blind, colleges of applied arts and technology,* and programmes for youth not attending school.

The reorganization thus established but two functional categories in the department's educational activities: elementary and secondary schools on the one hand and post-secondary and special schools on the other.

In providing for the separation of administrative and educational concerns, the departmental reorganization gave belated recognition to a professional distinction which had been implemented for some years in the larger school systems of the province. Most of the larger boards which employed their own supervisory personnel had established two approximately parallel positions, that of superintendent or director of education and that of business administrator.

As is indicated in Figure 30, the assistant deputy minister: administration was to be responsible for four main categories of activity or departmental branches. Of these, three (departmental business administration, personnel, and information) covered the essential 'housekeeping' responsibilities of the department and need no further elaboration here. The really significant development was the creation of the school business administration branch. This branch was to control and co-ordinate all of the multi-faceted fiscal and administrative relationships between the department and the school boards. It did not become fully operative for some time after the official announcement of the reorganization. With the appointment of G.D. Spry as director, however (he had been comptroller of the Toronto Board of Education), it began to emerge as the central provincial agency in planning and controlling the intergovernmental fiscal relationship in relation to elementary and secondary education. We shall return to this more recent development in Chapter 17, however. Of particular importance here is the fact that this branch was staffed with persons

---

* / Under the 'community college' system initiated by legislation of 1965 (13 & 14 Eliz. II, c. 28) most of the provincial post-secondary institutions, other than the universities, are being integrated and expanded into a system of schools, known as Colleges of Applied Arts and Technology.

qualified in the technical aspects of school business administration, especially accountancy, rather than educators who had climbed the bureaucratic hierarchy of the department to the occupancy of an administrative position for which they might well have had no special training or even relevant experience.

The Department of Education had for many years employed a staff of field representatives, responsible for a host of matters in the department-school board relationship, and known uniformly as inspectors. Aside from supervisory personnel employed by the larger school boards (who also assumed the role of departmental inspectors in relation to their employing boards), there had developed four distinct types of provincial inspectors in Ontario. The first type comprised elementary school inspectors who exercised general supervision over, and were located within, a territorial unit known as an inspectorate. These were relatively small units, usually comprising several elementary school districts. The inspectors were responsible to the elementary education section of the department in Toronto.

The second group of inspectors had an equally general supervisory responsibility, but in relation to secondary schools and exercised over a much larger area. This scheme originated in 1951 and was an attempt to decentralize the supervision of secondary schools which had previously been exercised directly from Toronto. The province had been divided into fifteen regions and to each was assigned a secondary school inspector who established his office within the region. The third category consisted of the secondary school subject specialists who worked directly from the Toronto offices but who exercised a supervisory responsibility only in relation to the teaching of a particular subject or subject area (mathematics, English). Finally, several of the special subject branches of the department employed their own field staff, also designated inspectors, who worked from the Toronto offices and supervised the teaching of the special subject (art, music) in both elementary and secondary schools.

This somewhat unwieldy field organization was brought into a co-ordinated scheme by the 1965 reorganization. The province was to be divided into ten administrative regions and all of the field personnel were to be assigned to these regions and located within them.

The first five of the regions were designated in February 1965 to become effective in September. The remainder were designated in April 1966, to become effective in August. The ten regions are depicted in Figure 31. In all cases except the two involving Metropolitan Toronto, the regions comprised groupings of counties in the south and districts in

FIGURE 31
Administrative regions of Department of Education

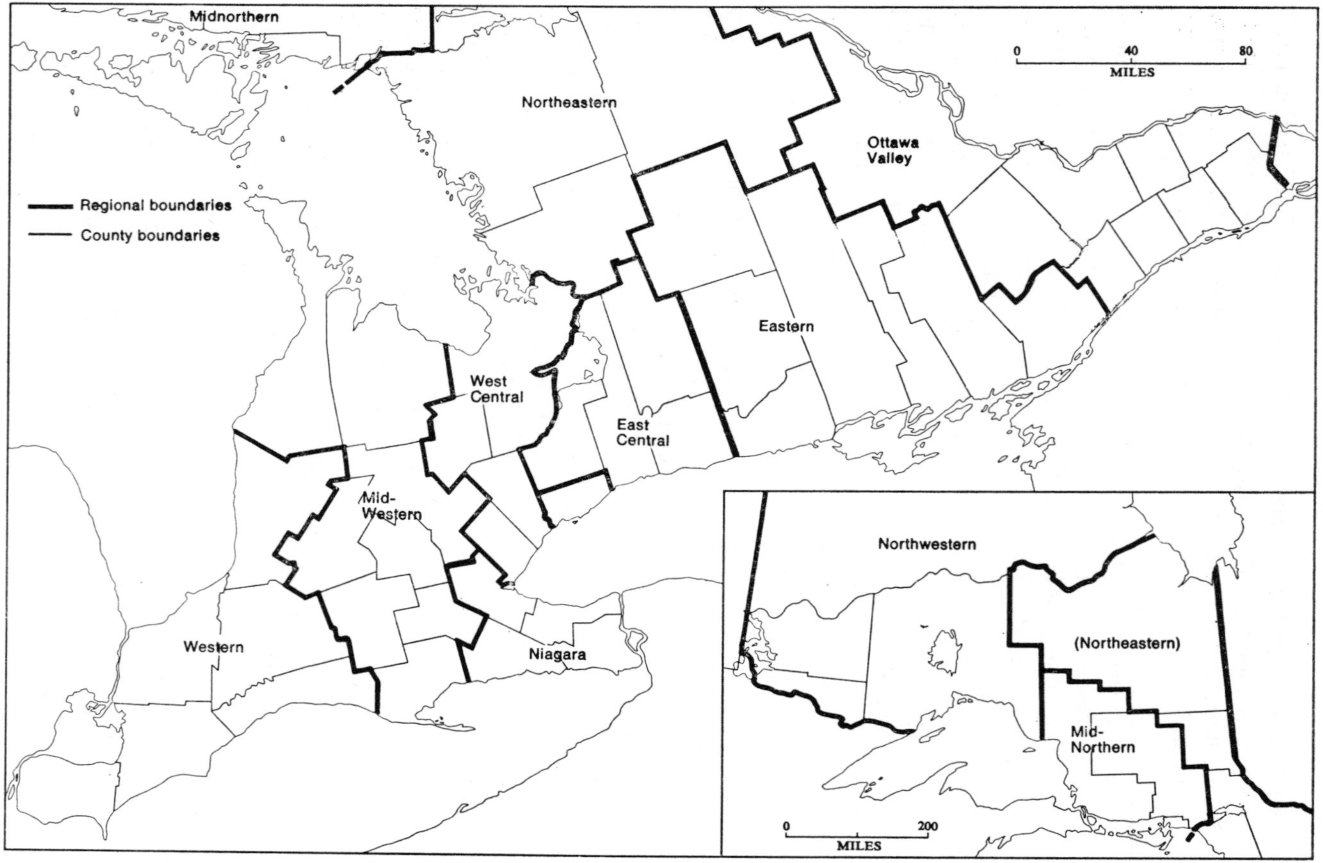

TABLE 37
Administrative regions of the Department of
Education: counties or districts included and
location of office

Region		Counties or districts	Office
1	North-western	Kenora, Rainy River, Thunder Bay	Port Arthur
2	Mid-northern	Algoma, Sudbury, Manitoulin	Sudbury
3	North-eastern	Cochrane, Timiskaming, Nipissing, Parry Sound, Muskoka	North Bay
4	Western	Essex, Kent, Lambton, Elgin, Middlesex, Huron, Bruce	London
5	Mid-western	Grey, Wellington, Brant, Perth, Waterloo, Norfolk, Oxford	Waterloo
6	Niagara	Haldimand, Lincoln, Welland, Wentworth	St Catharines
7	West-central	Dufferin, Halton, Peel, Simcoe, City of Toronto, Metro boroughs west of Yonge St.	Toronto
8	East-central	Durham, Ontario, Victoria, York, Borough of North York and Metro boroughs east of Yonge St.	Don Mills
9	Eastern	Frontenac, Leeds, Hastings, Haliburton, Lennox & Addington, Northumberland, Peterborough, Prince Edward	Kingston
10	Ottawa	Carleton, Dundas, Stormont, Lanark, Glengarry, Prescott, Russell, Grenville, Renfrew	Ottawa

SOURCE: Minister's Report, 1965 and 1966

the north. The counties or districts included in each region, and the location of the regional office are enumerated in Table 37.

There was a good deal of confusion in the initial months of this reorganization of field activities concerning the names and responsibilities of the various officers involved. This was largely clarified after J.R. McCarthy was appointed deputy minister in January 1967 (his predecessor, Z.S. Phimister, died in office during 1966). Under McCarthy's scheme, the four-fold grouping of inspectors gave way to a three-fold functional categorization of field activities. Each regional office was to be responsible for three functions: supervision, programme development, and business administration. Supervision became the concern of the regional superintendent (usually a former assistant superintendent from the Toronto office) and his staff of area superintendents (the former general inspectors). Programme development was assigned to a cadre of 'programme consultants' (in many cases former specialist inspectors) who lost their supervisory duties and were to assist schools only upon the latter's invitation. Finally, the regional offices were staffed with business administrators, recruited by G.D. Spry and his school business administration branch and responsible for much of what had previously been the concern of the general inspectors (advice on and some control over budgeting, planning, determination of building approvals, compilation of grant data).

The establishment of the regional offices was not entirely an exercise in administrative decentralization. In fact, the elementary school inspectors had been decentralized to a much greater extent than became the case with the change to area superintendents responsible to regional superintendents. The system of regional offices was of greater significance for the extent to which it facilitated the co-ordination of the department's field activities and the extension to this area of the kind of functional specialization and expertise which the whole reorganization process was intended to develop within the department.

The reorganization of the Department of Education was of far greater potential significance than has thus far been indicated. There was, in fact, what could almost be described as a 'hidden purpose' behind the reorganization. That purpose was to alter in a basic and even radical manner the division of power and responsibility between the provincial and local governments in education. Such alteration, however, could not proceed without a complementary reorganization of the units of local government. Thus, it was not until after the latter process had been set in motion that the nature of this 'purpose' was revealed.

On 4 June 1968 William Davis, minister of education made the following statement in the legislature:

In all honesty, we must admit that while the tradition of a centralized system of education served the province well, it did lead to an undue emphasis on regimentation and conformity ...

Over the years, the Ontario Department of Education, to its credit, has played an important role in the development of local educational authorities to the point where they have become responsible agents, capable of assuming many of the functions which were hitherto carried by the department. This evolution has required a fundamental re-examination of the role of the department. While it will continue to play a most vital part in Ontario education, the distribution of emphasis on its activities will be radically changed.

At a time when the size of government at all levels seems to be increasing at a tremendous rate, our aim will be to reduce the size of the department while at the same time increasing its effectiveness, measured in terms of service to education ...

It follows that the function of departmental officials is to develop and continuously review a comprehensive philosophy of public education. This educational planning – which must cover an extremely broad spectrum, taking into account the social and economic needs of all citizens – is then expressed as policy in two principal ways: through the medium of the educational laws ... and through the distribution of funds ... Being centrally located, the department is also specially qualified to be a resource centre for new information and a clearing house for worthwhile ideas emanating from within and outside the province.[11]

This changed role is certainly not yet fully effective, and a number of factors to be reviewed in Chapter 16 may even prevent it becoming effective. The Minister's statement spoke of an objective rather than an accomplished fact. But it spoke of an objective which clearly supported the reorganization of the department. The essential element in this objective was the abandonment of the regulatory role of the department and the assumption of a much more service-oriented role. Responsibility for the operation of the elementary and secondary schools was to be delegated much more completely to the school boards supported by competent professional staffs. Chapter 14 will explore the latter aspect of the change. The department was to be responsible, not for the regulation of this system, but for overall planning and co-ordination, and for providing expert advice and technical and financial support to the local school organizations.

The new concept of the department's role represented a recognition of the growing professionalism and technical sophistication of the educational enterprise. In such an enterprise, technical and entrepreneurial competence are of greater consequence in the control of policy than legal authority or fiscal capacity. It was precisely for the development of this kind of competence that the Department of Education was reorganized.

This change can perhaps be seen most clearly in the creation of the regional offices and the new position of programme consultant. The regional offices were in fact designed to act in large part as service centres to their constituent school districts. In conformity with that role, the programme consultants were to offer advisory assistance (service) in their respective areas of specialized competence when such was requested by the administrative or instructional personnel of the local school systems. They were to lose completely their former role as inspectors of the quality of teaching within those schools.

One of the interesting aspects of the changed departmental role was the extent to which it was constrained by bureaucratic organization. In fact, two of the major components of the new provincial orientation were forced wholly or partly outside of the departmental organization. In 1965 the Minister of Education, in collaboration with Dr Jackson and others involved in educational research established the Ontario Institute for Studies in Education,[12] intended to be a large-scale research, development, and teaching centre for education in Ontario. The Institute, with Jackson as director, has been almost entirely financed by, but is in no way a part of, the provincial Department of Education.[13] Another key element in the province's new educational role was the provision of educational television programming for school boards wishing to make use of such. Educational television was established as a small unit within the expanded curriculum division of the department when the original reorganization was begun in 1965. In 1966 it emerged as a distinct branch. While there is a good deal of uncertainty about future developments in this whole area (including not only the role of educational television itself but the respective roles of the federal and provincial governments), recent provincial government policy statements have indicated the intention to transfer educational television from the Department of Education to an Educational Communications Authority.[14] The latter would be a crown corporation, reporting to the Legislature through the Minister of Education, but autonomous – like the Institute – in its internal policy and daily operations.

The reason these activities were forced outside the departmental organization has been the perceived conflict between their objectives and those of a bureaucracy. In the case of the Institute, the decision to adopt the model of the university rather than of a government department was a function of the decision to attempt to attract as staff members academics rather than civil servants. In the case of ETV, some of the same constraints came into play – as, for example, the need to employ artistic personnel (actors, producers) and the inability of the provincial Civil Service Commission to classify them.[15] As well, however, ETV was envisaged as becoming involved directly in the creation and broadcasting of television programmes, in the ownership of facilities, and in the purchase and sale of programmes from and to other broadcasting authorities. The necessity of dealing through the Department of Public Works would serve only to restrain the flexibility and productivity ⸱f the ETV enterprise.

The reorganization of the Department of Education involved a stream-lining of the lines of communication and responsibility, a decentralization and co-ordination of administrative activity, and a delineation of areas of professional competence. It involved a transfer of regulatory control to the local school systems themselves, and an assumption by the province of responsibility for research, planning, dissemination, and support. Where major efforts were made in the latter directions, it became clear that the nature of a provincial government department militated against the effective performance of this role in certain areas. In such cases, extra-departmental organizations were established or contemplated.

If this change in the emphasis of provincial involvement in education should fully materialize, it will lead to far-reaching consequences in a number of areas. It very quickly necessitated a radical change in the nature of the provincial programme of grants to school boards. The existence of stimulation grants, for example, represented a contradiction of the policy of delegating to school boards the responsibility for operating and regulating the school programme. We shall outline the nature of this change in Chapter 16. One of the most immediate and obvious impacts of the change, however, was in the organization of local government in education. Virtually no mention was made of this impact in the early years of the departmental reorganization, and it was not until the legislation creating large school districts was well advanced in the legislative process that the Minister of Education, in June 1968, spelled out clearly what had been implied.

With the decentralization of many of the traditional departmental functions to local authorities which are situated more closely to the public they serve, departmental officials will be better able to concentrate on those responsibilities which they are best equipped to perform.

The main condition needed to bring about this ideal situation is that local educational authorities should be large enough to be able to provide a full range of programme plus the highly specialized staff of psychologists, reading consultants, speech therapists, and others that are required if all children are to be given the opportunity to achieve their maximum potential.[16]

The following chapter will take up the policy which established these large school districts in 1969.

14
County school districts

On 14 November 1967 Prime Minister John Robarts made the following statement in the course of an address officially opening a secondary school addition in Galt:

We believe that ... our objective should be to reduce the number of administrative units to approximately 100 boards of education. Each of these boards will be responsible for education in the public, elementary and secondary schools.

It is the intent of the Government of Ontario that these boards of education be established on a county-wide basis in Southern Ontario. These units will include the cities and separated towns within the county. However, there will be a few exceptions. For example, this development will not affect the existing system in Metropolitan Toronto. A few other large cities will have their own boards of education.

In Northern Ontario it is feasible and necessary to establish larger school units and these will be designated.

The possibility of establishing larger units for separate schools is also contemplated.

Legislation is in preparation to be presented to the next session of the Ontario Legislature so that this reorganization of school units can become effective on January 1st., 1969.[1]

In that statement the government brought to a climax the series of responses to the problems of education in Ontario which has been the subject of discussion and analysis in this book.

Three factors seem capable of explaining the rather dramatic shift which occurred in provincial policy regarding local units of government between the reluctant adoption of compulsory legislation in 1964 and the announcement of a radical reorganization in 1967.

First, and probably most important, the kind of intergovernmental relationship envisaged in the reorganization of the Department of Education could be effective only if the provincial bureaucracy were paralleled by large local units with resources and enrolments sufficient to support highly competent professional staffs and diversified programmes. There would be little use, for example, in the department erecting television broadcasting facilities and preparing elaborate programming if most of the school boards lacked the potential to use, or even receive, the programmes. Similarly, the departmental regional offices of superintendent, programme consultant, and business administrator were designed as counterparts to parallel offices at the local level. A board with one school and a very small total enrolment could not be expected to employ professional staff of this nature.

Second, the experience of the township school area reorganization almost certainly emboldened the government to move in the direction of mandatory legislation once again. The 1964 legislation climaxed over one hundred years of provincial frustrations in attempting to erect township-sized units. In 1841, 1868, and 1925, compulsory legislation had been considered and found impractical because of the strength of local opposition. Yet in 1964 the legislation was received with very little opposition from any source. It is undoubtedly true, and certainly the leading figures in the department recognized this, that the township was too small a unit, even in 1964, if judged on either educational or economic grounds. But what was crucial about the 1964 provisions was not so much the specific units prescribed as the assertion by the provincial government of its right to prescribe local units. Having successfully made that assertion in 1964, and thus breaking the 150 year old tradition of local responsibility in this area, the province had established a position from which a subsequent reorganization could be effected with little chance of effective opposition. The preliminary legislation of 1964 had thus removed the basis of local strength for any potential resistance to subsequent legislation.

The third reason for the rapid provincial response was the slowness of the process of voluntary reorganization under the 1964 legislation (there were but twenty-five county or district school areas established by 1967) and the complete collapse of this process in one area – the county of York. The York County council had appointed its public school consultative committee as required by the 1964 legislation. The committee undertook an exhaustive study of educational government in the county, and in November 1966 submitted its report to the county council. The report called for a two-tier system of government – a regional board for the whole county and three local boards for the northern, central, and southern sections of the county respectively. This recommendation was not fully in accord with the policy favoured by the Department of Education at that time – single-level governments, preferably covering whole counties. The department never had a chance to rule on the advisability of the York County proposal, however, for when the council finally considered the report in June 1967, it voted to reject the plan by a margin of nineteen to six. Serious local jealousies were exhibited in the discussions of this proposal, and the unguarded position taken by a number of councillors appeared to be that if the province wanted county units it should assume the political responsibility for creating them.[2]

In a fairly extensive analysis of the behaviour of those involved in the proposed voluntary reorganization of York County, Sondra Thorson discovered an interesting phenomenon. She was able to distinguish a clear difference in the value-orientations of those favouring and those opposing the consolidation of school districts.

Those trustees, officials, and teachers who favored the reorganization proposal were attuned to the scientific culture. By virtue of their education, occupation, age, relative mobility, their identification was with the scientific establishment, their orientation was universal, and they found an argument made in universal, scientific terms convincing.

Not so those who opposed the proposal. Their community was the local community, their values particularistic. An argument justified in terms of scientific reason was not convincing to them because their values and style of thought were not those of the scientific establishment. Their roots in their local communities were deep. Their education, occupation, age, stability, oriented them not to the scientific establishment but away from what they perceived as a cold, impersonal bureaucracy of experts. What they sought was the warm, personal solidarity of the community.[3]

Thorson's analysis strikes at the heart of the issues involved in the whole reorientation of education in Ontario. It is abundantly clear that both the reorganization of the Department of Education and the consolidation of local school districts were designed to orient education towards what Thorson termed the 'scientific establishment,' with its emphasis on efficiency and its reliance on technical expertise. That the values underlying this reorientation are not shared by a significant portion of the population may well create serious consequences as the impact of the 1968 change becomes clearer.

Public elementary and secondary schools

The process from which the radical consolidation of school districts emerged involved a complex interaction between the cabinet, several levels of officials in the Department of Education, and, in the case of separate school districts, an association of local governments (the development of the policy respecting separate schools will be treated separately in a subsequent section).

The intimate relationship between the reorganization of the Department of Education and the consolidation of school districts was recognized from the beginning in the policy-making structure from which the school district plan emerged. When the second half of the regional offices of the department were designated in April 1966, one of the regional superintendents, J.F. Kinlin (who was seconded to the latter position from the department's policy and development council), was commissioned to undertake a study of the administration of the regional offices, particularly in relation to the organization of local school districts.[4] He proceeded to examine the possibility of consolidating local school districts into units based on the existing high school districts. He soon concluded, however, that these lacked any rational justification and in the first phase of his report requested that one of the department's assistant superintendents be seconded to undertake a continuation of the study.

Gordon Duffin, assistant deputy minister for instruction, responded to Kinlin's suggestion in November 1966 by creating a formal 'larger unit committee' within the supervision division of his programme branch.[5] The committee consisted of five people: Kinlin himself, G.H. Waldrum, T.H. Houghton, H.K. Fisher, and J.R. Thomson. The latter four members were all assistant superintendents of supervision. This membership is especially interesting because of the interlocking relationships which Thomson's participation created. Thomson was, as we saw in Chapters 8 and 9, a long-standing member of the grants committee. He was also a member of the department's legislation committee. The other member of the latter committee, aside from the legal counsel, was W.G. Chatterton, also a member of the grants committee. The net result of this overlapping membership was that the larger unit committee had direct access to the two committees which would be most crucial to the success of any proposed school district consolidation. The legislation committee would have to resolve the host of legal problems encumbent upon any legislated consolidation, while the grants committee would need to amend the grant programme to conform to the new demands and constraints which such legislation would create. Conversely, the effectiveness of the larger unit committee's planning would be dependent upon the extent to which it appreciated the effect alternative forms of consolidation would have upon the two other areas. The speed with which the consolidation planning proceeded, and the remarkable success of the plan eventually developed were both undoubtedly a product of the intentional interrelation of these three crucial areas of responsibility.

The larger unit committee faced an arduous task and in the early months of its planning a good deal of time was spent in examining alternative criteria for the consolidation of school districts.[6] The committee considered the creation of districts relatively uniform in size (and determined from a review of research in the area that 20,000 pupils would be the optimum size) but rejected this scheme because it would necessarily disregard existing municipal and public elementary school boundaries and thus create tremendous problems during the transitional period. They considered the results of local government reviews sponsored by the Department of Municipal Affairs but found in them no formula of general applicability for the whole province. They likewise considered and rejected the concept of a two-tier system, such as had been proposed for York County and as already existed in Metropolitan Toronto, on the grounds that it was unnecessarily complex. Finally, they concluded that the nature of contemporary education demanded the integration of public elementary and secondary school boards into boards of education.

In this preliminary phase of its work, the committee restricted its terms of reference to public elementary and secondary schools in southern Ontario, deferring for subsequent consideration the separate elementary schools and the vast but sparsely populated area of northern Ontario. By its process of eliminating alternatives, the committee reached the conclusion that the only reasonable basis for consolidating school districts in the south would be the creation of boards of education for the thirty-eight counties. Virtually no public school districts and few high school districts crossed county boundaries so that the transitional problems of transferring pupils and physical assets from one board to another would be minimized. Furthermore, the counties had existed as municipal entities for well over a century and they could therefore be considered to define self-conscious communities to some extent at least. The committee did recognize, however, that the largest cities would likely have to be continued as distinct school districts or they would overwhelm the political process in the counties in which they were situated.

During the months from the formation of the committee until the autumn of 1967, the members undertook what were often gruelling schedules of speaking engagements and less formal meetings throughout the province. The objective in doing this was twofold: to anticipate the attitudes of local politicians and educators prior to the formulation of a consolidation plan, and to prepare the ground for general acceptance of such consolidation when it would be announced.

By the autumn of 1967, then, the committee had not only determined the basic outlines of its recommended policy for school district consolidation in southern Ontario, but had, through its interlocking membership with the legislation committee, prepared draft legislation to bring this policy into effect.

The timing of the announcement and implementation of this scheme, however, was not determined by the departmental committee. The Prime Minister's speech of 14 November, 1967, apparently written by the Deputy Minister of Education,[7] was delivered without the knowledge of the members of the committee.[8] And while the real reason for the decision to implement the new policy at this relatively early date are hidden from view, the recency of the general election has generally been recognized as the primary factor. Just as the township consolidation followed shortly after the election of 1963, the announcement of the impending county consolidation followed just a month after the government was re-elected in October 1967.

It was not until after the initial announcement that the departmental committee was instructed to develop a set of school districts for northern Ontario. Since there were no established county boundaries in the north (the existing territorial districts had no municipal status and were used only for purposes of provincial administration) and since the centres of population were so scattered, it was taken for granted that consolidated school districts in the north would have to be determined by the committee itself. In doing so the committee placed heavy reliance upon the advice of the regional and area superintendents and business administrators located in the northern regions. Draft proposals were drawn up by the committee, submitted to these officials, and subsequently amended on the basis of the latter's criticisms and suggestions.

Eventually, the committee developed a set of districts based largely on a grouping of public school sections into units accessible to existing secondary schools. The component areas contained within these units were not always geographically contiguous, parcels of territory being joined into single school districts with the unpopulated areas between the parcels remaining outside the district altogether. It followed from this that a great deal of territory was not included in school districts at all, either because it was unpopulated or because it was too remote from centres of population.

The details of the new policy were revealed in two major steps. In

February 1968 the Department of Education issued two 'white papers'[9] setting forth the proposed school districts, the general method of election of school board members, and the steps to be taken by existing boards prior to consolidation in 1969. Then in March 1968 the key legislation to implement this programme was introduced by the Minister.[10]

The legislation set forth the reorganized territorial units of government for the public elementary and secondary schools in three categories, to take effect 1 January 1969. First, all boards in southern Ontario, with the exception of five urban areas, were to be combined into thirty-eight county boards of education.

Second, the cities of Hamilton, London, Windsor, and the Municipality of Metropolitan Toronto were to continue with the boards of education existing in 1968. Hamilton, London, and Windsor each had single boards of education. Metropolitan Toronto had a two-tier system, with six boards of education for the city and five boroughs respectively and a metropolitan board of education responsible for the entire area. Separate legislation in 1968[11] created a modified form of metropolitan government for the greater Ottawa area. The sixteen existing area municipalities were retained intact but a second-tier, or metropolitan, municipal government was created for the whole region. The legislation consolidating school districts, however, rejected this scheme. Instead of the two-tier system, the latter legislation created two single-level boards of education, one for the cities of Ottawa and Eastview and the village of Rockcliffe Park, and the other for the remainder of the regional area (the Ottawa regional area was coterminous with Carleton County except for the inclusion of one township in Russell County). The consolidation in Ottawa and Carleton County was to be delayed for one year, taking effect 1 January, 1970.

Third, northern Ontario was to be reorganized into boards of education responsible for territorial units prescribed by regulation. These units had been tentatively set forth in the February white paper. With only two modest changes (two of the tentative units were incorporated into larger districts), the same units were set forth in the official regulation. As was noted previously, the northern districts were developed on the basis of combinations of existing public school sections which were accessible to secondary schools. This produced two anomalies in the organization of school government: large areas of the province were not included in school districts at all, while some forty-eight existing public school sections were retained as distinct units because of their isolation from secondary school facilities.[12]

For public elementary and secondary schools, then, the legislation and subsequent regulation established a total of seventy-seven boards of education and retained forty-eight public school boards. On 1 January, 1969 (excepting the Ottawa-Carleton area) these 125 boards replaced the 1010 which had existed in 1968. A further consolidation of educational governments was provided in separate legislation which transferred control to the enlarged boards over the ninety-four schools formerly operated by retarded children's authorities.[13] There was no similar consolidation of other special areas, however, and so the forty-two provincially-appointed school boards continued to function on Canadian Forces bases (16), hospitals and related institutions (19), Indian settlements (2), and Ontario Hydro installations (5).

Considering the magnitude of the policy, the school district consolidation met very little initial opposition. What opposition did develop appeared to centre upon the choice of the county as the basic unit for school government in the south. As early as January 1968 the leader of the opposition, Robert Nixon, argued that in many cases the county was not a rational unit. 'Here we have the county spelled out as the basis of the school district reorganization in southern Ontario, without any commitment that these boundaries will be revised where they are obviously no longer appropriate on educational, geographic, economic or sociological grounds.'

The school districts were not only anomalous in shape in the north, but were far from uniform in size throughout the province. The following maps and tables show the enlarged districts and their populations in southern and northern Ontario respectively. In the south, the population ranged from 7973 in Haliburton to 667,571 in Toronto, or to 219,273 in Waterloo if the segregated urban areas are excluded from the comparison. In the north, the smallest district was to have a population of only 1739 (Hornepayne), with five districts having populations under 5000, while the largest district (Sudbury) was to have a population of 140,001.

Separate elementary schools
Both the process by which larger school districts were established and the nature of the districts themselves differed significantly for the separate elementary school system. The differences stemmed from the government's interpretation of the constitutionally entrenched guarantees to separate school supporters and reveal an interesting dimension of intergovernmental relations in Ontario.

During the time that the larger unit committee of the department was considering alternative bases for the consolidation of school districts in

FIGURE 32
School districts in southern Ontario: Boards of Education

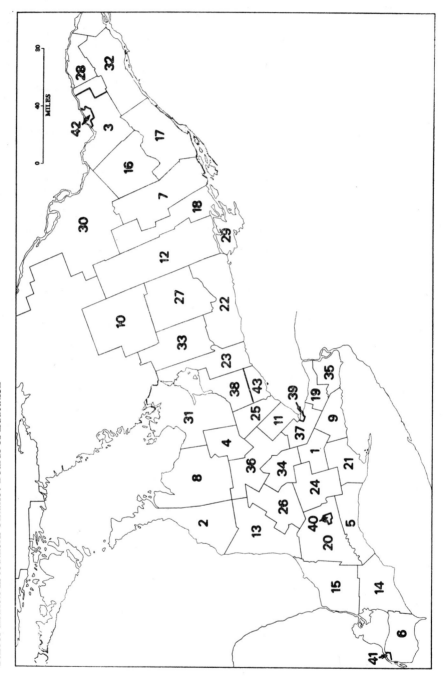

FIGURE 33
School districts in northern Ontario: Boards of Education

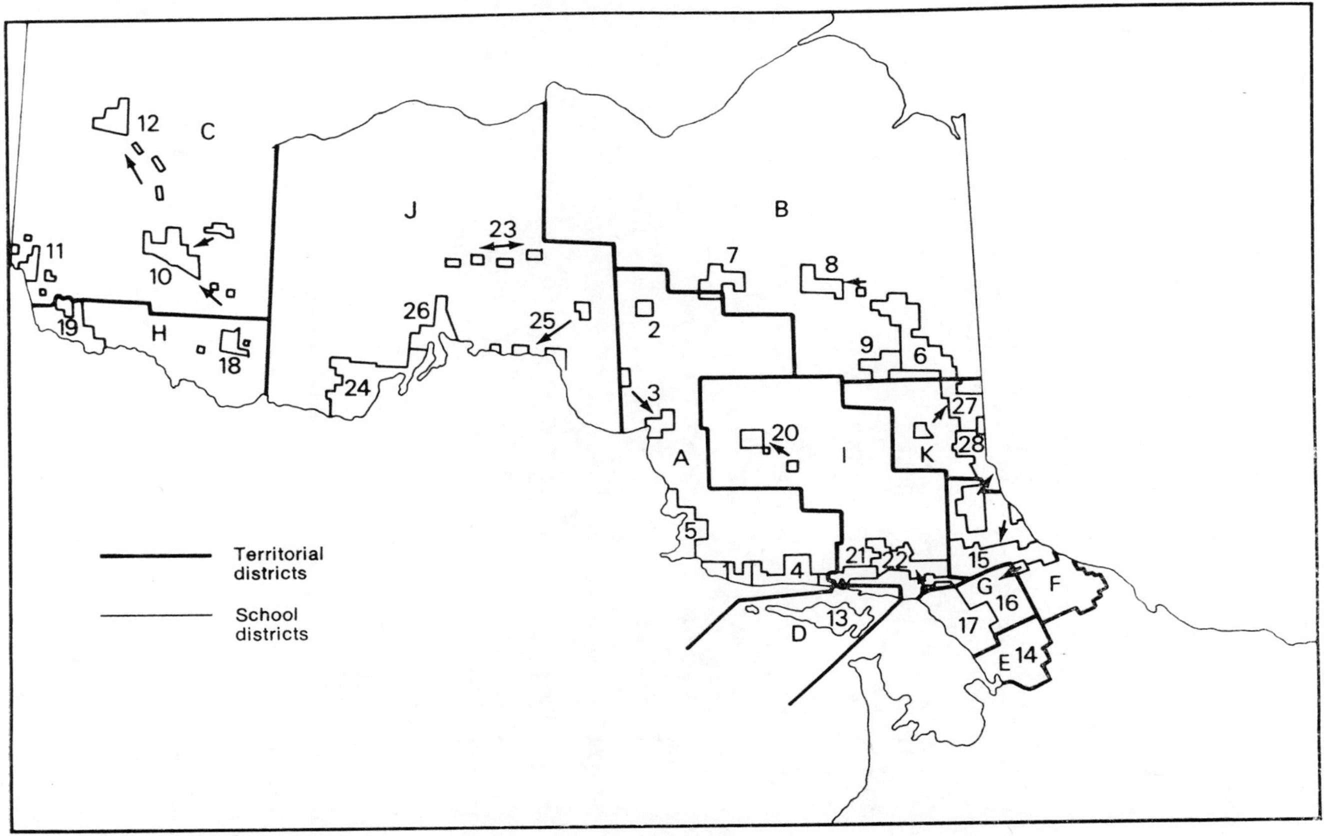

Territorial
districts

School
districts

TABLE 38
Populations of county and urban school districts
in southern Ontario for public and secondary schools

Counties	Population*	Counties	Population*
1 Brant	86,528	29 Prince Edward	19,152
2 Bruce	41,054	30 Renfrew	76,217
3 Carleton	94,927	31 Simcoe	137,886
4 Dufferin	17,284	32 Stormont, Dundas	
5 Elgin	55,542	& Glengarry†	92,725
6 Essex	87,450	33 Victoria	29,818
7 Frontenac	86,490	34 Waterloo	219,273
8 Grey	63,215	35 Welland	177,823
9 Haldimand	29,306	36 Wellington	94,641
10 Haliburton	7,973	37 Wentworth	86,910
11 Halton	160,256	38 York	143,642
12 Hastings	87,516		
13 Huron	49,500	CITIES	
14 Kent	94,248		
15 Lambton	105,954	39 Hamilton	288,993
16 Lanark	38,779	40 London	196,420
17 Leeds &		41 Windsor	191,762
Grenville†	71,069		
18 Lennox &		URBAN AREAS	
Addington	25,187		
19 Lincoln	147,019	42 Ottawa§	315,883
20 Middlesex	53,044	43 Metro Toronto	1,847,359
21 Norfolk	50,936	East York	96,569
22 Northumberland &		Etobicoke	263,743
Durham†	87,977	North York	405,153
23 Ontario	172,374	Scarborough	273,992
24 Oxford	75,417	Toronto	667,571
25 Peel	188,566	York	140,331
26 Perth	60,256		
27 Peterborough	79,684		
28 Prescott &			
Russell†	49,111		

*/1967 population
†/United county
§/Includes Ottawa, Eastview, and Rockcliffe Park
SOURCE: Ontario, Department of Municipal Affairs, *1968 Municipal Directory*

southern Ontario (largely during 1967) it became clear that separate
school trustees were anxious to have their system included in any proposed reorganization. According to members of the committee,[14] this
desire was impressed upon them repeatedly, both in their trips throughout the province and in their discussions with separate school representatives in Toronto. Through a highly informal process of discussion and
negotiation, the committee had even resolved the difficult problem of

TABLE 39
Populations of enlarged school districts in northern
Ontario for public and secondary schools

Territorial district		School district		Population*
A	Algoma	1	Central Algoma	7144
		2	Hornepayne	1739
		3	Michipicoten	4724
		4	North Shore	11,654
		5	Sault Ste Marie	75,390
B	Cochrane	6	Cochrane-Iroquois Falls	8073
		7	Hearst	2972
		8	Kapuskasing	14,858
		9	Timmins	51,634
C	Kenora	10	Dryden	12,128
		11	Kenora	15,658
		12	Red Lake	4260
D	Manitoulin	13	Manitoulin	6339
E	Muskoka	14	Muskoka	24,497
F	Nipissing	15	Nipissing	65,403
G	Parry Sound	16	East Parry Sound	11,721
		17	West Parry Sound	11,397
H	Rainy River	18	Atikokan	6586
		19	Fort Frances-Rainy River	15,847
I	Sudbury	20	Chapleau	3599
		21	Espanola	9145
		22	Sudbury	140,001
J	Thunder Bay	23	Geraldton	5547
		24	Lakehead	109,184
		25	Lake Superior	9902
		26	Nipigon-Red Rock	5083
K	Timiskaming	27	Kirkland Lake	18,858
		28	Timiskaming	22,578

*/1967 population of incorporated municipalities.
SOURCES: Ontario, Department of Education, *Index of School
Boards of the Province of Ontario on and after
January 1, 1969.* Ontario, Department of Municipal Affairs, *1968
Municipal Directory.*

how separate school consolidation might be accomplished by the time
the public and secondary school consolidation was announced. The committee could proceed no further, however, for the question of provincial
interference in the structure of separate school government was caught
up in a century-old tradition of constitutional interpretation.

As recently as February 1963 the prime minister, John Robarts, had
presented the province's position regarding separate school organization
in the following terms:

While either a municipal council or the Minister of Education may amalgamate several public school sections, no such power exists with regard to separate schools. This right runs to any number of persons, not less than five, being the heads of families and freeholders or householders resident in any municipality, and being Roman Catholics, who may form a separate school board. The rights to amalgamate separate school areas, or to dissolve the same, rest with them in the local community, and with no one else.[15]

It might be pointed out that in some of the western Canadian provinces, as well as in certain American states, the government has arbitrarily imposed larger school units. In other words, they have wiped out the smaller school boards. I point out that in Ontario, aside from every other consideration, as already indicated, The Separate Schools Act of 1863 would preclude any such possibility for separate schools.[16]

Section 93(1) of the British North America Act declares *ultra vires* of a provincial legislature any statute which would 'prejudically affect any Right or Privilege with respect to Denominational Schools which any Class of Persons have by Law in the Province at the Union.'[17] Two kinds of interpretations can be placed upon this constitutional provision. The traditional interpretation advanced by the provincial government was that employed by Robarts in 1963, that 'the provisions of the Separate Schools Act of 1863 became unalterable.'[18] The second is that advanced by Mr Justice Meredith in 1915, that 'it was never meant that the separate schools or any other schools should be left forever in the educational wilderness of the enactments in force in 1867.'[19]

In 1967 the provincial government moved away from its long-standing acceptance of the first interpretation and towards acceptance of the second. It was not prepared to make this shift in a single step, however, and simply dictate the terms of a reorganized system of separate school governments. In his speech of 14 November 1967, announcing the government's intention to legislate a consolidation of public and secondary school districts, Robarts went only so far as to say that 'the possibility of establishing larger units for separate schools is also contemplated.'[20] That statement was clearly intended and received as more than a political 'kite' flown to test the acceptability of a possible future policy shift. It was, in fact, a clear indication that the province had abandoned its traditional literal interpretation of the British North America Act. At the same time it represented an invitation to the representatives of separate school trustees to assist the province in giving effect to a new policy. The tacit position of the government was that if the acknowledged spokesmen of the separate schools could agree amongst themselves on the outlines of a reorganization scheme, and if this scheme were reasonably similar to that for public and secondary schools, then the government would translate the proposal into provincial legislation.

The separate school spokesmen lost little time in responding to this invitation. A special committee of the executive of the Ontario Separate School Trustees' Association was established and drafted a set of specific proposals. The separate school brief[21] was submitted to the cabinet in March 1968, just over four months after the Prime Minister's announcement and less than two weeks after the public and secondary school legislation had been introduced. The trustees' brief proposed the consolidation of all separate school zones in southern Ontario into thirty-one county units and three urban units. Two of the urban centres isolated from their counties for public and secondary purposes – Hamilton and London – would be included with the county for separate school purposes. The Windsor and Metropolitan Toronto boards would remain unchanged,[22] while the consolidation of Ottawa, Eastview, and Rockcliffe Park would be similar to that in the public and secondary panel.

The brief proposed a major realignment of counties for separate school government. Seventeen of the thirty-eight counties would be established as territorial units, nineteen counties would be amalgamated into nine units, and two united counties would be split into four units for separate schools. This would result in the three urban units and thirty-one county units. In addition, the brief recommended the consolidation of separate school zones in northern Ontario into twenty-three units, with seventeen isolated zones remaining unchanged. The proposal, then, called for a grand total of seventy-four separate school districts.

The provincial government responded almost immediately to the separate school brief. Legislation was introduced in June 1968,[23] differing from the trustees' proposals only in that four counties were combined into a single unit instead of two units, the two united counties were not split, and eighteen somewhat larger units were prescribed for the north, leaving only twelve isolated zones. The legislation thus provided for only sixty-one separate school districts in the province, as compared with the seventy-four proposed by the trustees, to replace the 499 existing in 1968.

Both the trustees' brief and the government legislation contained a rather curious feature. The prescribed districts did not necessarily contain all of the territory within their borders, but only that portion which had been organized into separate school zones (areas radiating three miles about a designated point). Thus, only existing separate school organizations were affected by the change. The legislation provided as well, however, that any separate school zone established in the future, the centre of which would be located within one of the prescribed larger units, would immediately be dissolved into the larger unit. This feature was developed in the informal negotiations between the larger unit committee and the separate school spokesmen.[24] It was deemed to be the least offensive basis for asserting provincial control over separate school boundaries and contained certain clear advantages for both the government and the separate school trustees. For the government, it avoided the potential danger of having appeared to have extended the privileges of separate school supporters by eliminating the three-mile limit. For the trustees, it avoided the necessity of separate school boards being held responsible for the education of children whose parents might opt for support of the separate school system but who lived considerable distances from any concentrations of supporters. At the same time, however, the feature retained the anomaly of separate school organizations outlined in Chapter 2 whereby the legal right to support a separate school is a function of the concentration of supporters rather than simply the proximity to a school.

Furthermore, the legislation, in accepting the trustees' proposals, established units of separate school government which in the majority of cases were not co-terminous with the public and secondary school units. Under present circumstances this creates no particular problem, but it may well develop into a constraint upon any future extension of co-operation between the two systems and would certainly render any amalgamation much more difficult. These considerations do not appear to have been involved in the consolidation programme, however.

A composite picture of the effect of the 1968 legislation, for public, separate, and secondary schools, is shown in the following table. There were to be a total of 230 school boards. Excluding the isolated and special schools, the province had been reorganized into just 126 school districts – seventy-seven for public elementary and secondary school purposes, and forty-nine for separate school purposes. It was indeed a far-reaching reorganization.

Other changes
As was noted above, virtually all public and secondary school boards were amalgamated into boards of education by the legislation of 1968. This integration represented a long-avowed objective of the provincial government and followed logically from the integration of elementary and secondary education within the provincial department. This integration created a special problem with regard to separate schools. The separate

TABLE 40
Number and type of school boards in
Ontario, 1969

Boards of Education	County	38
	District	28
	City	10
	Metropolitan	1
		77
Combined Roman Catholic Separate School boards	County	28
	District	18
	City	3
		49
Isolated boards	Public	48
	Separate	12
Protestant Separate School boards		2
Special boards (appointed)	Canadian Forces	16
	Ontario Hydro	5
	Hospitals	19
	Indian schools	2
		42
GRAND TOTAL		230

SOURCE: *Index of School Boards of the Province of Ontario*

school trustees did not miss the opportunity, and in their brief proposing large units argued that, 'the logical corollary ... is that ... the jurisdiction of the separate school boards be extended to include all grades from Kindergarten to Grade 13.'[25] Thus far the government has resisted the pressure to extend the separate school system, but the resistance will be difficult so long as the argument is that elementary and secondary education should be integrated except when a child attends a separate elementary school.

The legislation made three other basic changes in the organization of school government. First, in establishing boards of education, the province made all school boards, with the exception of the few special cases, elective (high school boards had previously been appointed). School board members were to be elected by general votes in each municipality or combination of smaller municipalities comprising the school district. The total number of members would vary from fourteen to twenty* and be determined by the total population of the district. The number of members to represent each municipality, or the number of municipalities to be combined to form one electoral constituency, would be determined

* / Provision is made for a smaller number in the smallest districts of the north.

by the proportion of the total equalized residential and farm property assessment in each of the municipalities. Using relative assessments rather than population as the basis of apportioning school board constituencies runs counter to the tradition of representation by population in the Canadian political system generally. Assessment, however, had always been used and would continue to be used as the basis for apportioning the school board's tax requisition amongst the constituent municipalities. Some justification, admittedly weak, could therefore be found in the argument that representation was by municipality and each municipality would be represented in proportion to its fiscal contribution to the school board.

The legislation also provided, for the first time, for the direct election of the separate school supporters on the boards of education. Previously two such supporters were appointed by the largest separate school board in the district. Under the new system, the number of separate school members will be based on the proportion of residential and farm assessment held by separate school supporters, and the members will be elected in the same manner as public school supporting members. As a consequence of this change, it is quite possible for the separate school supporters to form a majority of the board of education, a board which has no jurisdiction over separate schools. Trustees elected by separate school supporters are to continue to vote only on matters affecting secondary schools. If elementary and secondary education are really to be integrated, this situation may create some uncertainty and confusion in the future.

Second, the legislation changed the system of capital, but not current, financing. Specifically, it authorized school boards to issue their own capital debentures, rather than requiring the municipality to do so on behalf of the board. The practice of requisitioning current funds from the municipal councils was continued, however.

Third, the province transferred virtually all responsibility for the inspection of schools to the enlarged boards. Beginning in 1969, all boards with at least 2000 pupils were to be required to appoint a 'director of education' or a 'superintendent of separate schools,' such officer to be the chief education officer of the board.[26] Boards with fewer than 2000 pupils were authorized to appoint such supervisory personnel as would be approved by the Minister.[27] This provision gave effect to one of the basic objectives of the reorganization of the Department of Education. The underlying objective of the latter had been to shift the department's role from one of supervision and regulation to one of support and service. Such a shift could not be effective without shifting the primary responsibility for supervising school personnel to the school boards themselves.

Yet accomplishing that required school boards large enough to employ sufficiently qualified supervisory personnel. This again demonstrates the intimate relationship between the reorganization of the department and the consolidation of school districts.

Not unexpectedly, the enlarged school boards found their supervisory personnel largely by employing departmental inspectors who had recently become area or regional superintendents. Immediately following the consolidation, the number of departmental superintendents was reduced from 147 to forty, and that number is expected to decline even further, levelling off at approximately twenty.[28] The department will continue its direct involvement in supervision only in relation to the small and isolated boards and in meeting special problems which can be expected to develop from time to time.

The consolidation of school districts represents the last of the provincial policy responses to be examined in this study. As the last of a number of interrelated responses, it contained the potential for effecting a radical change in the nature of intergovernmental relations in education. After a brief examination of the interdependence of these policy responses, we shall consider a set of circumstances which raise some doubts as to whether the above-mentioned change will, in fact, be allowed to develop.

PART V

Conclusions

15
The matrix of responses

The preceding chapters have been devoted to the examination of a set of interrelated problems in the governing and financing of elementary and secondary education in Ontario, and to the policies developed by the provincial government, with limited involvement by the federal government, in response to those problems. It is now appropriate to re-examine the set of policy responses in order to ascertain their effect upon the problems and upon each other. The present chapter will attempt to do this by focusing attention upon each of the problem areas in turn, with the purpose of determining the combined effect of the policy responses.

Local government
The acceptance of the federal conditional grants for vocational school construction and the consequent reorganization of the secondary school course of study – the earliest of the provincial responses examined here – was possible on a large scale only because the problems of inadequate and unequal units of local government were least severe in the case of secondary school districts. At the same time, however, the implementation of this policy highlighted the areas in which voluntary consolidation remained inadequate. A number of districts could not support the differentiated 'Robarts Plan' and therefore could not qualify for the full benefits of the federal-provincial grants. This situation led to a modification of provincial policy, encouraging the joint operation of single schools by two or more school boards. The logical extension of that policy, however, was the reorganization of school districts so that every district would at least be capable of supporting the basic secondary school programme.

One of the major products of inadequate and unequal territorial units of local government was the constraint placed upon the development of an equitable, general system of financing education. By introducing a foundation-type scheme of grants in 1964, the provincial government made the dimensions of this problem even clearer. The foundation plan carried with it a far-reaching commitment on the part of the provincial cabinet to the principles of fiscal and educational equalization. It was the pre-eminence of equalization in the plan which denoted its basic difference from earlier schemes. The cabinet thus committed itself to a policy the effectiveness of which largely depended upon the reversal of another, and long-standing, policy – that which opposed any compulsory reorganization of the units of local government.

This second policy was indeed reversed by the introduction of legislation consolidating all rural public school districts (as well as the very small urban districts) into township school areas. That legislation was introduced in the very first year of the operation of the foundation plan. The township school area reorganization was effective in eliminating many of the most inadequate units of local government and in reducing the range of inequality among these districts. The effectiveness of the grant plan continued to be constrained, however, by the inadequacies and inequalities which remained. The greatest significance of the township reorganization lay in its elimination of the basic contradiction in provincial policy. Having once adopted a policy of compulsory reorganization of local units, the cabinet was in a position to extend that policy by means of a more basic and more effective reorganization. The necessity of such an extension was subsequently highlighted when the structure and responsibilities of the Department of Education were changed. The organization of the units of local government became constraints upon the realization of the objectives of that policy as well as the policy embodied in the foundation grant plan.

While the vocational capital grant scheme, the foundation plan, and the reorganization of the Department of Education all added to the pressures for a legislated reorganization of local units, the institution of the capital aid corporation ran counter to this development. The corporation resolved the basic difficulties in capital borrowing by small units of government with limited access to the major capital lending agencies. In resolving one of the more visible consequences of inadequate local units, the corporation thereby reduced the pressure for reorganization. This reduction of pressure, however, was not sufficient to counteract the pressure resulting from the conflict between the organization of local government on the one hand, and the objectives of the provincial grant scheme and of the educational bureaucracy on the other.

The latter conflict was finally resolved by the radical reorganization of local government (for school purposes) undertaken in 1968. The establishment of county-sized units of government for public, separate, and secondary schools in the southern portion of the province (involving the amalgamation of several counties for separate school purposes) and the designation of larger districts in the north represented a basic resolution of the problems of local units of government. Some of these enlarged units will almost certainly continue to prove inadequate to the demands placed upon them (that is, they will be too small to offer programmes and services comparable to those offered in the larger districts) and at the same time substantial inequalities have been retained in the size of these units. Provision was made for the subsequent resolution of the remaining inadequacies,[1] while the inequalities will be within such a relatively small range that few constraints will be imposed upon the realization of the objectives embodied in either the grant plan or the reorganized Department of Education.

One of the more interesting implications of both the township and departmental reorganizations was the pressure they placed upon the organization of local units of government for separate schools. The leaders of the separate school bloc were well aware of the tremendously disadvantageous position in which their system would be placed if it were not included in the changes occasioned and envisaged by the two policies. In one area – the integration of elementary and secondary education – separate school leaders were not in a position to control the development of the system. In response to this situation they tried to rouse public support for the extension of the separate school programme to include the secondary grades.

A vigorous campaign of voluntary school district consolidation followed quickly upon the compulsory establishment of township units for public schools, however. When the Prime Minister announced the government's intention of legislating county-sized units for public schools, the separate school leaders cast aside any concern over constitutional difficulties and pressed for a legislated consolidation of separate school districts as well. In this unprecedented move, the separate schools were brought fully into the mainstream of public education in the province, an accomplishment which may finally have ended the struggle for existence which was so much a part of the history of separate schools in Ontario.

Local fiscal resources
The original vocational capital grant scheme removed virtually the full

252

cost of an area of educational need from the local tax base. It is important to note, however, that the need itself was identified by the federal government and was then located within the secondary school system by the provincial government. The vocational grants thus relieved local governments of responsibility for assuming the capital costs involved in implementing a response which had itself been imposed upon them.

Implementing this response, however, entailed other costs than those subsumed under the federal-provincial agreement. First, and most important, the grant scheme did not cover the cost of operating the vocational programmes. The per-pupil cost of operating vocational programmes averaged $106 more than the per-pupil cost of academic programmes between 1961 and 1966.[2] As a result of the exansion of vocational facilities, the proportion of secondary school pupils enrolled in vocational programmes increased from 23.7 per cent in 1960 to 46.4 per cent in 1967.[3] Of the 463,736 secondary school pupils enrolled in September 1967, 215,174 were in vocational programmes, whereas the 1960 distribution would have placed only 109,905 in that category. With a cost differential of $106 per pupil, the added burden imposed by the shift to vocational education amounted to approximately $11.2 millions in 1967 alone.

An accurate estimate of the additional costs involved in accepting the capital grant programme would also have to include the effect this programme had upon the holding power of the secondary schools. The expansion of vocational facilities undoubtedly increased the total enrolment in the secondary schools as well as the proportion opting for vocational courses. There is no way of determining the exact nature of this effect, however, since the programme was clearly complementary to strong market forces. The estimate of additional costs used above did assume that the capital grant programme was entirely responsible for the relative shift to vocational courses. Doubtless some of that shift would have occurred in the absence of the programme, and therefore these factors may be taken as balancing each other to some extent.

Second, many high school boards found it most economical to establish vocational facilities as integral components of a single school building (that is, a 'composite' school). In many cases, this involved the erection of new facilities for the academic programmes as well as the vocational. The special capital grants, however, covered only the vocational components. Thus, while the 100 per cent capital grants placed no additional burden on local fiscal resources for the construction of vocational facilities, they generated other capital needs and operating expenditures which were not met by the grant programme.

This weakness became even more crucial when the combined federal-provincial grant dropped from 100 to 75 per cent. With that change, even a substantial portion of the vocational capital costs became a charge upon local resources. Furthermore, this additional charge bore no relation to local fiscal capacity unless the school board opted out of the federal-provincial grant scheme and chose instead to receive grants under the foundation plan. In choosing that alternative, however, the board was forced to assume responsibility for debenturing the full cost of the project and subsequently receiving provincial grants in respect of the annual debt charges.

Resolution of the problems of inadequate and unequal local fiscal resources, as heightened by the vocational capital grant programme, was the primary objective of the Ontario Foundation Tax Plan. As was noted above, however, the plan was severely constrained in this by the government's refusal to legislate a consolidation of school districts. The foundation plan did succeed in establishing a basic equalization of fiscal resources. In the secondary school system this equalization encompassed most of the school districts and pupils. In the elementary school system, however, equalization was established only among the smaller, less able districts. Of necessity (because the needs of the small and large districts were not comparable), the grant scheme contained sufficient flexibility to enable the larger, abler school districts to meet a greater fiscal need with a 'standard' rate of local taxation. This flexibility, while it enabled the grant plan to circumvent the constraints imposed by the problems of local units of government, represented an inability to effect a complete resolution of the problems of inadequate and unequal local fiscal resources. The fiscal resources of school boards were equalized up to arbitrary levels of local capacity and expenditure (different levels for elementary and secondary school boards). Beyond these levels, provincial grants ceased to vary inversely with local fiscal capacity and thus served only to augment the unequal revenues obtained from local taxation.

The problems of local fiscal resources were somewhat alleviated as a result of the capital aid corporation. The cost of capital borrowing was reduced for all school boards, but since this cost no longer bore any relation to the fiscal strength of the local governments the benefits were greatest for those governments which were previously in the weakest positions. Thus, even the smallest and poorest school district was given access to capital funds at the same cost as applied to the largest, wealthiest district. This contribution of the corporation was constrained by the continuation of the policy of requiring local governments to assume responsibility for all school debt, even though assistance was provided in meeting the subsequent debt charges. The ceiling placed on total borrowing capacity by the Ontario Municipal Board varied directly with local fiscal capacity (the maximum debt was a proportion of taxable assessment). Thus, while both the capital aid corporation and foundation plan were successful in substantially equalizing the capacity to service a capital debt, neither did anything to equalize the capacity to incur such a debt.

Because the problems of local fiscal resources were so intimately related to the problems of local units of government, the three structural responses of the provincial government affected the former in much the way they affected the latter. That is to say, the township reorganization eliminated some of the extremes of inadequate and unequal resources. In contrast, the departmental reorganization highlighted the inadequacies and inequalities which remained. The establishment of county sized school districts, while it did nothing to increase the total fiscal capacity of local government in the province, did succeed in bringing the inequalities within a manageable range. As a consequence, it will require only a relatively simple provincial grant structure to augment and equalize the fiscal resources of all school districts.

Separate schools

One of the most noteworthy departures of the foundation plan from all previous grant plans was the recognition it accorded to the revenue deficiency of the separate school system. The separate schools were, in fact, the major beneficiaries of the scheme. Because of the limited equalization provided in the plan, however, the attempt at resolving the revenue problem of separate schools was only partially developed within the basic formula. In setting the original foundation level of expenditure $32 per pupil above the actual average level of expenditure in the separate school system, the plan involved a major commitment of provincial resources to bridge the gap between the two systems under a general formula.

This was quite insufficient, however, to resolve the problem in a number of particular instances, most noticeably in those local areas which had substantial amounts of corporately held property assessment (which was disproportionately taxed for the support of public schools). The corporation tax adjustment grant – an integral component of the foundation plan – was designed to alleviate this specific aspect of the problem. Under a formula which became more liberal each year, the corporation tax adjustment grant represented only the second attempt ever made by a provincial government in Ontario to correct either the causes or the consequences of the unequal access of public and separate school boards to revenue from the taxation of corporate property. It was the first attempt which achieved any substantial success.

Even with these two measures, however, there continued to be a substantial differential in the per-pupil revenue available to the public and separate elementary school systems.

Enrolment

In essence, the problem of rapidly increasing enrolments was the general strain this expansion placed upon the administrative and fiscal resources of the educational governments and, especially, the unequal distribution of this strain throughout the school system. The three most important elements in the unequal distribution of enrolment increases were the disproportionate burdens placed on suburban schools, separate schools, and the vocational panels of secondary schools.

We have already noted, both earlier in this chapter and in Chapter 5, the crucial role played in the shift to vocational education by provincial policy – namely, the adoption of the federal capital grants and the introduction of the Robarts Plan. We have also noted that for a short period of time the federal-provincial agreement relieved school boards of the capital costs involved in supporting this enrolment shift. Not only were the federal-provincial capital grants subsequently reduced to a rate of 75 per cent, but at no time was any special assistance provided under the agreement to meet the added burdens of replacing academic facilities or of operating the new secondary school programmes.

The resolution of these problems, as well as those occasioned by the rural-urban and public-separate shifts, thus fell upon other areas of provincial policy. The primary provincial response to these problems was embodied in the foundation grant plan.

The foundation plan contained two elements which were directed towards the fiscal needs of school boards experiencing rapid growth. The first of these was the growth-need grant for recognized extraordinary expenditures, carried over from the earlier plan of 1958. The essence of the growth-need provision was that a school board's grant would increase at progressive rates as the approved per-pupil expenditure on extraordinary items (capital and transportation) increased. Thus, the faster the rate of expansion was for a school board, the greater was the proportion of expenditures met by provincial grants. This provision did not eliminate the additional burdens imposed by a rapidly increasing enrolment even in the area of extraordinary expenditures (not all expenditures were approved for grant purposes, and even so, an increase in

approved expenditure normally involved an increase in the local contribution). Furthermore, the growth-need provision did nothing to reduce
the burdens of increasing operating expenditures.

One of the basic weaknesses in the foundation plan was its use of the
preceding year's enrolment and expenditure data in calculating the
minimum and equalization grants. Any board experiencing a disproportionate rate of growth was thus forced to assume the cost of each year's
increase in pupils from local taxation. Even when this need was recognized in 1966 and the attendance (later enrolment) growth grant was
introduced, the special formula took no account of local fiscal capacity
but provided flat-rate grants to all qualifying boards.

The capital aid corporation was also directed in part towards a resolution of the problems of enrolment. One of the major factors responsible
for the increasing borrowing for schools was, of course, the need to
expand school facilities. In substantially improving the availability of
capital funds, and in reducing their cost, the corporation reduced both
the administrative and fiscal burdens imposed by increasing enrolments.
As has been noted previously, however, the corporation did not reduce
the necessity of local borrowing (which would have been the case had
capital grants beens paid at the time of the initial expenditure) but rather
effected a relative reduction in the cost of servicing the increasing debt.

One of the consequences of the establishment of county-sized school
districts was the consolidation of many rapidly growing areas with more
slowly growing, or even declining, areas. The suburban school districts –
those most burdened by the geographic inequalities in enrolment growth
– have in many cases ceased to be isolated from their urban centres (the
exceptions occurred with respect to the largest urban centres which remained distinct) where growth has been much less rapid, or from their
rural hinterlands where growth has been very slow if it occurred at all.
Having thus eliminated the small school district, the reorganization of
1969 eliminated the basic need for the capital aid corporation. Virtually
all school districts assumed positions from which they could gain access
to the regular sources of capital loans. They no longer required the kind
of preferential treatment embodied in the corporation's programme.

It is quite clear that the provincial responses to the problems of enrolment were slow in being developed and, until 1968, did not represent a
comprehensive resolution of the problems. The peak year in the postwar
growth of total enrolment occurred in 1952 (when total enrolment increased by 8.4 per cent). It was six years later that the first response, the
growth-need grant, was introduced, and it was more a response to the

creation of larger high school districts than to the growth in enrolment *per se*.

Expenditure

Despite a declining rate of growth in total enrolment,[4] expenditures on education continued to increase dramatically throughout the 1960s. In 1967, total school board expenditure increased by 19.3 per cent over 1966.[5]

The impact of the federal-provincial vocational capital grants on local expenditures has been described earlier. In prompting a dramatic shift to the more expensive vocational programmes, the grants prompted a substantial increase in the operating expenditures of school boards.

The impact of the foundation plan upon expenditure patterns was a complex one. The plan did establish a somewhat higher proportional contribution from the province to total school board expenditure, rising from 39 per cent in 1963 to 45 per cent in 1967. But the level of expenditure nominally supported under the plan – the foundation level of expenditure – was decreased in relation to actual expenditures for elementary, secondary academic, and secondary vocational pupils, although the elementary level had risen between 1965 and 1967 and then dropped back sharply in 1968. The foundation plan was not designed to control or reduce expenditures. Rather, its purpose was to equalize both expenditures and fiscal burdens among the school districts, as well as to provide a general level of support to all districts. The plan was severely constrained in its pursuit of the first purpose, and as a result expenditures continued to vary proportionately with local fiscal capacity.

One of the important elements in the overall rise in expenditures was the increasing rate of interest on school debentures. The institution of the capital aid corporation in 1966 resulted in a dramatic reduction of nearly a full percentage point in the average rate. The programme embodied in this corporation was thus the only one of the provincial policies designed to reduce the expenditures of school boards (the vocational capital grants can not be considered to have had this effect because they generated a series of expenditures and then relieved school boards of only a portion).

All three of the province's structural responses will undoubtedly lead to a general increase in total expenditure on elementary and secondary education. The local reorganizations created jurisdictions almost all of which will be capable of offering educational programmes and services which could have been offered previously in only the larger (usually urban) systems. As well, the orientation of the reorganized Department of Education – emphasizing planning, research, and the provision of technical services – will create new demands upon the school boards which will lead to new expenditures.

The combined impact of the structural responses will likely be a levelling up of expenditures within and among the school districts. To a certain extent this was made compulsory in that all school boards (except the very small ones) were required to establish a professional administration such as had been established in only the large systems before 1969. As well, there will most certainly be tremendous pressures from within school districts to establish a basic equality of service between the various areas, especially rural and urban, within the district.

The establishment of regional school districts on 1 January 1969 brought the series of provincial (and federal-provincial) policy responses into a markedly different context. The Technical and Vocational Training Agreement had been terminated, the twin aspects of the province's structural policy had been implemented, the foundation grant plan was clearly in need of major revision if not complete change, leaving only the capital aid programme as a continuing policy. This is therefore a logical point at which to terminate the study. Yet the immediate post-1968 period has provided some interesting insights into the legacy of the policies developed up to that time, and before attempting to draw conclusions about the nature of intergovernmental relations in Ontario, some reference to this legacy will be useful. The fact that the short-term impact was the generation of a minor political crisis only adds to the usefulness of this examination.

16
The legacy of provincial responses

Were we to limit the focus of our attention to the development of provincial policy prior to 1969, we would probably be justified in concluding that beginning in the latter year Ontario was to enter a 'brave new world' of intergovernmental relations in education. Hundreds of school jurisdictions, some of them tiny, were nearly all replaced by a small number of regional units. Paralleling this local structure was to be a provincial Department of Education shorn of its concern with inspection and supervision and dedicated instead to providing resources, advice, and technical services to the responsible boards of education.

We are still too near in time to these changes to determine what their long term impact will be. At this point we are justified in being neither cynical – dismissing the changes as only superficial – nor naïve – believing implicitly that everything has changed. There have been changes, some of them dramatic, as a result of the matrix of provincial responses to the problems of education in the 1960s. At the same time, however, there are impressive signs that the extent of change will itself be controlled, and there are factors within the current environment of provincial-local relations in education which may force some retreat from the bold positions advanced on the occasions of the departmental and school district reorganizations. Certainly in the short term there has already been some retreat.

It will be useful, therefore, to examine the developments in the provincial-local governing and financing of schools in the initial months after the consolidation of school districts. We shall do this by looking at three provincial fiscal responses in the 1969–70 period: the grant plan introduced in 1969 to replace the foundation plan, the special local tax rate subsidy of 1969, and the changes in the capital aid programme. On the basis of this examination, we should be in a position to reach some informative conclusions about the nature of intergovernmental relations in Ontario, both as evidenced during the 1960s and as they appear to be developing in the 1970s.

The 1969 grant plan

The joint membership of J.R. Thomson on the grants and larger unit committees and of W.G. Chatterton on the grants and legislation committees placed the departmental grants committee in an excellent position to develop an effective fiscal response to the changed conditions which the consolidation of school districts would create in 1969. At the same time, however, the committee suffered from a lack of policy direction as to just what objectives the province wished to pursue by means of its fiscal transfers to the enlarged school boards. As a consequence, the committee was left to develop a grant programme largely on its own, and this isolation created a near political crisis when its consequences became apparent. We shall return to that point later, however.

As was described in Part II, formulation of policy by the grants committee was a cyclical process, changes in each year's grant programme being developed mostly in the summer and autumn of the preceding year. This process worked well within the context of a continuing programme, but allowed very little time to consider the adoption of a completely new programme. Yet the timing of the announcement of the impending school district consolidation left the committee no more than a year to develop such a programme if it were to take effect simultaneously with the reorganization of local government. There were, of course, rather pressing and obvious reasons why the two responses should take effect at the same time.

The two consultants to the grants committee (the author and Professor E.B. Rideout) set to work in the summer of 1968 to devise the outlines of a new grant scheme to be discussed with the committee. In the absence of a clear statement of provincial policy objectives, it was assumed that a new grant plan should pursue three objectives as compared with the existing foundation plan. First, it should extend the principle of fiscal and educational equalization wherever possible. Second, it should eliminate the countless protective features of the foundation plan, many of which would become unnecessary with the consolidation of school districts. Third, the new plan should embody the principle of decentralization in decision-making which was so much a part of the departmental and school district reorganization. It is clear that to a large extent these objectives represented the values of the two consultants. But at the same time, those values had themselves been shaped by participation in the deliberations of the grants committee and similarly were conditioned by the consultants' knowledge of government policy directions as indicated by the nature of related programmes.

The consultants toyed with a number of alternative schemes, beginning with only limited modifications to the foundation plan but quickly turning to consideration of a major departure as more and more of the foundation plan's provisions appeared unsuited to the changed situation.

It was primarily the consultants' acceptance of the objective of decentralized decision making which led them away from continued use of the foundation plan model. If the new school boards were really to be delegated responsibility for determining the educational programmes to be offered in their districts, then this contradicted a fiscal transfer scheme based on the notion that all boards should be offering a standard, or foundation, level of service. And if local discretion extended only to augmenting the foundation programme, then the varying fiscal capacities of the local boards severely constrained the extent to which provincial grants could achieve the objective of equalization. Under a foundation plan, then, the effective decision making authority of school boards would continue to be a function of their taxing capacities. And while these capacities would be equalized to a considerable extent by the consolidation of school districts, there would still remain large discrepancies.

The consultants therefore proposed the adoption of a scheme whereby provincial grants would be a function of the school board's expenditure. The essence of the proposal was that the levels of expenditure, and the services to be provided with such expenditures, would be determined by the school boards themselves. Provincial grants would then be employed to equalize the capacity of each board to incur whatever expenditures it determined as appropriate. This did not imply that boards could spend as much as they pleased with equal consequences in terms of local taxes, but that the tax rate required to support a given level of expenditure would be the same for all boards. Conversely, the tax rate would vary directly with the expenditure level so that the more a board decided to spend, the higher would be the rate of taxation it would be forced to levy.

The essence of this scheme can be illustrated in the following equation: $G = \{1.0 - (x)[(BETA/WP)/(PETA/WP)]\}\{Y\}$, where G = provincial grant, x = proportion of total school board expenditure to be raised through local taxation, $BETA/WP$ = school board equalized taxable assessment per weighted pupil, $PETA/WP$ = provincial average equalized taxable assessment per weighted pupil, and Y = expenditure of school board. By substituting specific values for these factors it can easily be demon-

262

SCHOOLS FOR ONTARIO

strated that the formula would both allow all boards to spend at a given level with precisely the same rate of local taxation and at the same time entail a higher rate of taxation for a higher level of expenditure.

For the purpose of illustration, we can assume that the average provincial assessment per pupil is $50,000 and that the province has decided to assume 55 per cent of all school board expenditures, leaving the boards themselves to support the remaining 45 per cent. If, under these conditions, a board with a taxing capacity of $30,000 per pupil were to spend $300 per pupil, its grant would be: $G = \{1.0 - (.45) \ (30,000/50,000)\} \ \{300\}, = (1.0 - .27) \ (300), = (.73) \ (300), = \$219$. This would leave $300 - 219 = \$81$ to be raised locally, entailing a tax rate of $(81/30,000) \ (1000) = 2.7$ mills.

If another board, with a taxing capacity of $60,000 per pupil were to spend at the same level, its grant would be: $G = \{1.0 - (.45) \ (60,000/50,000)\} \ \{300\}, = (1.0 - .54) \ (300), = (.46) \ (300), = \$138$. This would leave $300 - 138 = \$162$ to be raised locally, again entailing a tax rate of $(162/60,000) \ (1000) = 2.7$ mills.

If either or both of these boards were to increase the expenditure level to $400 per pupil, the resultant tax rate would be 3.6 mills. Using this hypothetical illustration, then, the tax rate levied by every board in the province would be equal to 0.009 mills for each dollar of expenditure per pupil. The consultants argued that such a scheme represented the most effective technique for pursuing both equalization and decentralized decision making.

The consultants concluded as well that this formula would completely obviate the need for the corporation tax adjustment grant. The latter had been designed to compensate for the revenue disparity between public and separate elementary schools and had been necessary because the foundation level of expenditure had been set below that required for complete fiscal equalization. Had the provision been retained under the formula proposed by the consultants, it would have destroyed the equalization possible under such a formula by giving separate schools a disproportionate fiscal advantage.

Two additional suggestions completed the set of proposals advanced by the consultants. First, it was argued that the essential provisions of the growth-equalization grant in respect of recognized extraordinary expenditures (capital expenditures from current funds and current expenditures on debt charges and transportation) should be retained, having only been introduced in 1967. The only suggested changes were elimination of the minimum grant of 35 per cent and transformation of the formula for determining the local tax rate from per-classroom to per-pupil data.

Secondly, in line with the objectives of simplifying the grant structure and facilitating local decision-making autonomy, it was argued that as many as possible of the special and stimulation grants should be eliminated, replaced where necessary by a more sophisticated system of weighting pupils.

This 'package' of proposals was presented to the grants committee in the autumn of 1968. The consultants were surprised not only by the speed with which the proposals were accepted by the committee but especially by the extent to which members of the committee sought to extend the basic principles when developing the details of the new grant plan. The consultants had, for example, recommended elimination of the corporation tax adjustment grant but had been quite prepared to see the provision retained under a modification of the basic grant formula in order not to create the appearance of having removed a hard-won concession to separate schools. The committee, however, quickly say the logic of the grant's superfluity and forcefully presented the argument to the Deputy Minister and Treasury Board. Similarly, where the consultants suggested a reduction in the number of special and stimulation grants, the committee proposed their complete elimination.

Two other factors must be mentioned before proceeding to a discussion of the development of the details of the grant plan. First, the Minister and Deputy Minister had decided that the consolidation of school districts should be used as an opportunity to begin paying grants in the same year in which the expenditures subject to grant were incurred. Previously, grants had always been calculated on the basis of the previous year's expenditures. The grants committee was thus in effect instructed to incorporate this feature in whatever new programme it should recommend. Doing so, however, required creating a mechanism for estimating school board expenditures, since the actual figures could not be known until at least the end of the year. Second, the Minister had assured representatives of both the retarded childrens' associations and the school boards that when the latter assumed responsibility for these schools, the province would guarantee at least the same level of support provided in 1968. Honouring this commitment necessitated isolating the grants for retarded children in order that the level of support could, in fact, be easily determined.

The grants committee adopted the basic formula proposed by the consultants but split it in two. In the first step, a percentage rate of grant would be determined and in the second this rate would be applied to the board's approved expenditure. Thus in place of the equation illustrated above, the grant would be calculated as follow: (1) Grant per cent $= 100 - (x) (\text{BETA/WP})/(\text{PETA/WP})$, where $x =$ proportion of total school board expenditure to be raised through local taxation, BETA/WP = school board equalized taxable assessment per weighted pupil, and PETA/WP = provincial average equalized taxable assessment per weighted pupil. (2) G = (grant per cent) (Y)/100, where G = provincial grant, and Y = approved expenditure of school board. This approach was preferred largely because it involved the calculation of the rate of provincial grant to each board, making the level of support more apparent than under a single formula.

Using this scheme, then, it was necessary first to determine the proportion of all school board expenditures that the province was prepared to support by grants. The difference between this and 100 per cent would then be substituted for the factor x in the grant formula. This, of course, had to be a political decision, and we shall return to the way in which the decision was made. Second, it was necessary to determine what expenditures were to be made subject to grant. As was noted previously, the committee had already decided to continue the separate grant on recognized extraordinary expenditures, necessarily implying that the new formula would apply to ordinary expenditures at the most. But the question still remained as to whether or not all ordinary expenditures would be included and if not, what device would be used to determine approved and unapproved expenditures. Third, while no policy decisions were required, it was necessary to determine both the average assessment per pupil in the province and the assessment per pupil of each consolidated board in the province. The second of these calculations presented considerable technical problems for the committee but their resolution need not be explored here. Finally, it was necessary to determine the manner in which pupils were to be weighted in calculating the assessment per weighted pupil.

The committee decided to terminate the complex system of weighting pupils receiving special instruction. This was done for two reason. First, these special services were expected to be provided by virtually all of the enlarged school boards, thus removing much of the disparity in need which their unequal provision had previously entailed. Second, specific reference to specific special services required that the department determine which of these it wished to recognize and this was seen as conflicting with the objective of decentralization.

The committee also decided to abandon the calculation of separate grants for vocational pupils in secondary schools. In part this was designed to anticipate the movement away from the Robarts Plan with its clearly defined 'streams' in the secondary school curriculum (the current thinking called for students to select individual programmes from an array of optional courses). Primarily, however, it flowed from the desire to simplify the grant structure which would result from the calculation of a single grant for all secondary school pupils.

In place of the weighting scheme used in the foundation plan, the committee developed two weighting factors. The first, known as a 'location weighting factor' was designed to recognize the special needs of two classes of school boards: those in the territorial districts of the north, and those in the largest urban centres. School boards in the north had long maintained that the costs of goods and services there were higher than in the province generally. This argument had been recognized in the capital approvals formula introduced in 1967 which divided the province into zones and provided for higher unit expenditures in the two northern zones. For want of an objective measure of cost differentials, the committee decided to weight all pupils in the territorial districts by a factor of 1.1. This had the effect of providing a 10 per cent cost differential between these and southern pupils.

The second component of the location weighting factor was designed to recognize the additional costs of educating pupils in the central areas of the province's largest cities. Again this represented belated recognition of a need which the affected school boards had long maintained was justified. And again because real measures of the precise nature of this need were completely missing, the committee provided a weighting factor arbitrarily set at 1.2 for elementary pupils and 1.1 for secondary pupils residing in urban municipalities with populations of 190,000 or more.

Both of these were arbitrary and crude devices to recognize differences in the needs of differently situated school districts. They represented attempts to extend the equity of the grant plan but were severely constrained in doing so by the lack of reliable measures of the real differences in need.

The 'course weighting factor,' introduced in place of the separate calculation of grants for academic and vocational pupils, was based on the provincial average cost differentials in the three streams of the Robarts Plan. Using the academic pupil as the 'standard unit,' pupils in the business and commerce stream were to be weighted by a factor of 1.05, and pupils in the science, technology, and trades stream by a factor of 1.6. Finally, the scheme was extended to recognize the special costs involved in teaching in the French language (primarily a result of lower pupil-teacher ratios) in a provision for weighting such pupils by a factor of 1.05, to be multiplied by whichever of the other course weighting factors applied to the pupil in question.

In determining the provincial average assessment per weighted pupil, the committee had, of course, to determine both the total value of taxable assessment in the province and the total number of pupils which the above weighting scheme would produce. The committee decided that the calculation of grants would be too complex and uncertain if the percentage rate of grant were determined from estimated data and then revised when the actual data were available. Since the rate of grant depended upon the relationship between the assessment per weighted pupil in a school district and in the province as a whole, there would be little distortion so long as both factors in the relationship were determined from comparable data. It was therefore decided to calculate the factors on the basis of 1967 assessment data (this was the assessment upon which taxes were levied in 1968) and the enrolment on the last school day of September 1968.

This base resulted in the calculation of an average assessment per weighted pupil of $34,000 for elementary schools and $83,000 for secondary schools. The figures were rounded to the nearest $1000 in order to simplify subsequent calculations.

The committee, and subsequently the Treasury Board, had three choices in defining the ordinary expenditures in relation to which the provincial grant would be paid: approve all expenditures not defined as extraordinary, approve expenditures on a prescribed list of programmes and services only, or approve all ordinary expenditures up to a specific maximum. The first alternative was rejected because it retained insufficient control over the magnitude of provincial grants (we shall return to this point later) and the second because it interfered too severely with local decision-making autonomy. This left only the third alternative: specification of a maximum unit expenditure.

The maximum amount actually used in the grant programme was determined in a manner which, if nothing else, was somewhat lacking in logic. In developing their original proposal to the grants committee, the consultants had used the figure of $450 per pupil for elementary schools as a reasonable upper limit to expenditures qualifying for grants. This figure was determined simply as 150 per cent of the foundation level which it was assumed would apply in 1969 if the existing scheme were retained (the 1968 foundation level was $280 and a normal increase would have raised this to $300, 150 per cent of which was $450). As the discussions proceeded in the grants committee, no more sensible figure was suggested and so the $450 remained almost by default. The amount was not unreasonable since it was considerably in excess of the average expenditure and thus allowed some room for boards to determine their own expenditure levels without exceeding the maximum. The amount was, however, selected arbitrarily and not according to an objective measure of essential educational expenditures (in this it was set by a process not unlike that which determined the foundation level in the 1964 grant plan).

The secondary school maximum was set at $700. This figure was determined by the grants committee and was considerably lower than the comparable elementary maximum in relation to average actual expenditures. The effect of the course weighting factors for secondary pupils was to increase the $700 to $735 for business and commerce students, and to $1120 for science, technology and trades students. In the latter case, the effective maximum (after weighting) was considerably higher than average expenditures. The secondary school maximum would be still higher if a board qualified for either of the location weighting factors. The maximum for a science, technology, and trades student in northern Ontario, for example, would be increased to $1232.

In summary, then, the grant percentage determined under the new formula was to be applied to all ordinary expenditures of a school board up to a maximum expenditure of $450 or $700 per weighted pupil.

In order to provide grants in the same year in which expenditures were incurred, school boards were to be required to submit estimates of their current operating expenditures. The grant percentage would be applied to these estimated figures and the resultant grant paid in instalments accordingly. In the subsequent year the grant would be recalculated on the basis of actual expenditures and any adjustment added to or subtracted from the subsequent year's grant. The maximum per-pupil expenditure would be applied to both the estimated and actual data.

Once the basic formula for the new grant plan was accepted, the most crucial decision became that establishing the proportion of total approved expenditures to be supported by provincial grants and local taxes respectively: it had the greatest and most obvious effect upon both the total provincial commitment of funds in support of elementary and secondary education and the commitment of funds to each school board. Once the province determined what proportion of all approved expenditures it would support, the difference between this proportion and 100 per cent would be inserted in the basic grant formula (if the province decided to meet 60 per cent of all approved expenditures, 40 would be used in the formula). This produced the situation in which the relationship of a school board's rate of grant to the rate used in the formula was the inverse of the relationship between the board's assessment per pupil and the provincial average assessment per pupil. Thus, for example, if a board had exactly half the average assessment per pupil, its rate of grant would be exactly double the '40' in the above illustration, or 80 per cent. Conversely, if a board had double the average assessment per pupil, its rate of grant would be half the proportion used in the formula, or 20 per cent in this hypothetical case.

Setting the overall provincial grant rate was clearly beyond the competence of the departmental grants committee and this the committee recognized from the outset. The rate would have to be set by the Treasury Board acting for the cabinet, either directly or indirectly as a consequence of the funds apportioned in support of the grant programme. The rate was not determined by the Treasury Board alone, however, for Professor Rideout and the senior members of the grants committee carried on relatively lengthy discussions with the board in this regard. The purpose of these discussions was to impress upon the board the consequences of setting the overall rate at various levels. Theoretically, there was no maximum level at which this rate could be set as this was constrained only by the total resources made available. But it was argued that the lower the rate was set, the more the effect of the new grant formula would have to be constrained by limitations upon the grant paid to individual school boards.

The new formula was more equitable than the old, and entailed the elimination of several special and protective features of the former plan (such as elimination of the corporation tax adjustment grant and the special calculations for rural school boards). This being the case, the overall rate of grant used in the 1969 plan would have to be significantly higher than the effective rate applying in 1968 to prevent the grant from declining to those boards no longer qualifying for special assistance. Some of these adjustments would be lost in the consolidation of school districts but provincial officials knew that the new boards would be quick to identify any reduction in grant, however theoretical, as compared with the previous year. The committee suggested, therefore, that the province allocate some $150 millions to the grant programme over and above what would have been required to accommodate a normal annual increase. This, they calculated, would permit setting the overall rate of grant at approximately 52 per cent.

It was not until February 1969 that the grants committee finally learned of the Treasury Board's decision. And when it did, the news came as something of a shock. The board decided not to allocate any new funds to the grant programme over what was necessitated by normal increases in enrolment and costs. It reduced the allocation requested by the committee by the full $150 millions.

The effect of this decision was very nearly to destroy any opportunity of implementing the new formula for 1969, and the grants committee did consider the possibility of simply revising the foundation plan, even at such a late date. However, it was decided that the plan would be instituted even though it would have almost no effect because most boards would receive their grants under either minimum or maximum provisions. The reasoning was that if adequate funds were forthcoming for 1970, the limitations could then be relaxed or removed.

The modest funds made available by the Treasury Board (acting, of course, for the whole cabinet) had several important effects upon the grant programme. First, they forced the committee to set the provincial sharing ratio at only 42 per cent, ten percentage points lower than the suggested level. Second, they necessitated the imposition of stringent limitations upon the grants to individual boards, the effect of which was that few boards received the grant calculated under the normal formula. Finally, within a short time they necessitated the provision of a special supplementary grant provision which had the effect of restoring a good part of the funds originally requested but in a manner which paid little attention to equity.

The grant to be paid to an individual school board had already been limited by the imposition of the per-pupil maximums on approved operating expenditure. The allocation of resources approved by the Treasury Board required much greater limitations than this, however. Just as when the foundation plan had replaced the grant schedules in 1964, it was assumed that the new grants for 1969 would have to guarantee every board at least the same level of support from the province it had received in the previous year. This created some administrative complications in 1969 since it meant the grants to the consolidated boards would have to be held to at least the level of the sum of the grants paid to all of the constituent boards in 1968.

In determining the minimum and maximum to be applied to the grants which would keep the total provincial grant within the limits set by the Treasury Board, the committee adopted the device of comparing the grant per pupil received in 1969 with the grant per pupil received by the boards in 1968 which comprised the enlarged school district of the 1969 board. This was to be determined without any weighting of pupils in order to make the measurements comparable. The grant per pupil to any board in 1969 would then be limited to a minimum of 104 per cent and a maximum of 110 per cent of the grants per pupil in 1968. The minimum of 104 per cent was set so as to allow boards some room to accommodate unavoidable increases in the cost of goods and services, while the maximum of 110 per cent was the most that the available funds would allow.

The result of these limitations was that for most boards the new grant formula devised by the committee became irrelevant. The formula applied only if it provided for a grant of between 104 and 110 per cent of the previous year's grants per pupil. Most boards received their grant at either of the extremes.

As was indicated earlier, the 1969 grant plan continued the essential provisions of the 'growth-equalization grant' first introduced in 1967. There was only one significant change in the grant, although several of its provisions were changed in detail or appearance. In the latter regard, the name of the grant was dropped in place of the simpler 'grant for extraordinary expenditure' and the calculation amended to use data on a perpupil rather than a per-classroom basis. As well, fixed sums were substituted for the arbitrary imputed extraordinary element in fees paid by one school board to another (20 per cent of such fees had been considered to be in respect of extraordinary expenditures).

The one major change in the provision was the elimination of the guaranteed minimum grant of 35 per cent of approved expenditure. This change was a product of the committee's concern for an extension of equity and would have allowed the grant rate to find its appropriate level, based entirely on the twin considerations of need (measured as approved expenditure per pupil) and taxing capacity (measured as assessment per pupil). The effect of the removal of the minimum was constrained, however, by the imposition of the overall minimum of 104 per cent of the previous year's grant per pupil, since the grant on extraordinary expenditure was included in the calculation of the latter minimum.

The provision of special grants in respect of what were defined as 'trainable retarded children' simply represented the institution of a guarantee by the minister of education that such grants would be at least as high as in 1968 (responsibility for retarded children was transferred from special authorities to the enlarged school boards in 1969). The special grant provided that in respect of expenditures for the education of retarded children, a school board would receive the higher of the percentage rates calculated under the regular grant formulas or 80 per cent for ordinary expenditures and 50 per cent for extraordinary expenditures (these had been the general rates under the previous arrangement).

As a transitional measure, special provision was made for those areas which had not previously been in a secondary school district but were to become part of a consolidated school district in 1969. This applied only in the territorial districts of the north. Where no secondary school district existed, the province had paid the full cost of providing secondary education in the nearest school (the province paid the equivalent of a tuition fee to the educating school board on behalf of such pupils). There had thus been no local taxation for secondary schools in such areas. In order to prevent taxpayers in these areas from facing a normal tax bill where previously they had paid nothing (for secondary schools), the grant provided two-thirds (67 per cent) of the tax levy which would otherwise have been levied. The school board or municipality was then required to reduce the actual tax levy by the same proportion. The intention was to reduce this grant by half in 1970 and eliminate it in 1971.

The 1969 grant plan provided for the calculation of a percentage rate of grant on the basis of the relationship of a school board's taxing capacity (assessment per pupil) to the average capacity of all boards in the province. This rate was then applied to the estimated ordinary expenditure of the board for the current year, up to a maximum expenditure of $450 per weighted elementary pupil and $700 per weighted secondary pupil. A separate grant was paid in respect of extraordinary expenditures, based on the same principles as under the 1967 and 1968 grant plans but without the minimum grant of 35 per cent. The combination of the above two grants to any board was then limited to a minimum of 104 per cent and a maximum of 110 per cent of the grant per pupil to the comparable school boards in 1968. Finally, two special features were added in respect of retarded children and areas newly established as part of a secondary school district.

The plan suffered from two fundamental and related weaknesses. First, there had been no statement of basic provincial objectives from which the details of the plan could have been deduced. This resulted in the grants committee and its two consultants developing a plan which largely represented their own policy preferences or their own interpretations of what general provincial policy implied in the domain of grants to school boards. Second, the Treasury Board imposed fiscal constraints which effectively prevented the objectives of the committee-developed scheme from being realized. As we shall observe shortly, the remarkable reversal of both these situations changed the grant plan significantly in 1970.

The new plan was to cover the fiscal operations of the school boards during the calendar year 1969. It was not introduced until mid-March of that year, however.[1] This undoubtedly caused some difficulties in the budgetary process at the local level (the revenue available to a board could not be estimated without the grant regulation) but was the result of the delay in the final commitment of funds by the Treasury Board. The grant plan had hardly been released when a flood of protest began to swell. The cause of that and the province's response to it will be examined in the following section.

The mill rate subsidy

A number of factors combined to produce a near crisis in provincial-local relations in 1969. The immediate cause of the problem was the dramatic increase in the tax rates which some municipalities would have had to levy in order to raise their shares of the requisition of funds by the enlarged school boards. As the school board budgets were finalized, it appeared that some municipalities would face tax increases of up to 300 and 400 per cent, as compared with the unequalized rates levied in 1968.

Essentially, the problem was due to the effects of a redistribution of local tax levies consequent upon the consolidation of school districts. Many municipalities (mostly rural) had previously maintained relatively low rates of taxation through a combination of low expenditures on education and special protective features in the provincial grant plan (such as the extra grants for township school areas). Consolidation, of course, meant that they would be faced with a tax rate based on expenditure in an entire county, often with one or more cities included, and the new grant plan removed virtually all of the protective provisions formerly available from the province.

The legislation committee, in developing the details of the consolidation, had anticipated this problem and had provided, so it was believed, for its resolution.[2] In 1969 the apportionment of the public school tax requisition among the constituent municipalities of an enlarged school district was to be calculated in two stages. First, each municipality would be required to raise the funds produced by the tax rate levied in 1968, adjusted to discount any surpluses, deficits, or non-recurring capital expenditures from current funds in that year. Second, the revenue still required after completion of this calculation was to be apportioned in the same proportions as each municipality's equalized assessment was of the total in the school district. Increases in tax rates between 1968 and 1969, then, would be due only to increases in total revenue required, and such increases could result solely from increases in expenditure or reductions in provincial grants.

There were basically three reasons why this legislative provision did not achieve its intended purpose adequately. In the first place, total school board expenditures increased substantially in 1969 and very little of this increase was supported by provincial grants. This meant that tax levies were increased generally throughout the province. Second, apportioning the additional revenue requirements on the basis of relative equalized assessments produced some shocked reactions when the apportionments were translated into local, unequalized tax rates. For example, if property in a municipality were assessed at 20 per cent of its full value, a tax increase of two mills on equalized assessment would be equal to an increase of ten mills on the local assessment. Finally, the special apportionment arrangement applied only to revenue for public schools. The reason for this was simply that high school revenue had always been apportioned in relation to equalized assessments. However, the consolidation of several high school districts into a single county district, again combining rural and urban areas, often had the effect of sharply increasing the amount to be raised by one or more of the constituent areas.

Had the general level of provincial support been high enough to meet most of the increases in school board expenditures there would have been few repercussions when apportionment of local taxes took place. But because that level of support was not adequate to meet this demand, serious political repercussions did, in fact, develop.

Because of the magnitude of the protests from local politicians and taxpayers, the province was forced to develop an additional response which would at least limit the abnormal increases in local tax rates. The result was the special mill rate subsidy, developed in considerable haste by the Department of Education grants committee and introduced by means of an amendment to the 1969 grant regulation in July 1969[3] (just four months after release of the basic regulation).

The mill rate subsidy was designed to achieve a simple objective: to pay a grant to school boards the effect of which would hold any increases in local taxes between 1968 and 1969 to a maximum of one mill (on equalized assessment), except where school board expenditures in 1969 increased by more than 115 per cent of the per-pupil expenditure in 1968. That is, if a school board's expenditures did not increase by more than 115 per cent (on a per-pupil basis) then the local tax rate could not increase by more than one mill over the rate applying in 1968. If the expenditures increased by more than 115 per cent, the local tax rate would increase by one mill plus the amount required to support the excess expenditure. The subsidy became exceedingly complex in appearance because a host of provisions were required to ensure that the tax rates for 1968 and 1969 were, in fact, comparable. The rates actually levied had to be adjusted whenever the municipality had reassessed property to a higher ratio of full value. These provisions were entirely technical and need not be considered here.

The mill rate subsidy worked essentially as follows. First, approved expenditure (for this purpose only) was defined as the total estimated current expenditure of the school board for 1969 up to a maximum of

115 per cent of the per-pupil expenditure of 1968 and reduced by the estimate of provincial grants to be received in 1969.* The approved expenditure thus equalled the total net expenditure to be financed by local taxation. Second, this expenditure was divided between the municipalities comprising the school district on the same basis as funds were to be requisitioned from such municipalities. Essentially, this meant that a municipality would be apportioned the same proportion of revenue as it had of the equalized assessment in the district. Third, what was known as the '1969 presubsidy mill rate' was determined as the rate which a municipality would have to levy in order to raise its share of the school board's approved expenditure. Fourth, the equivalent of one equalized mill was added to the municipality's 1968 tax rate.† Fifth, where the '1969 presubsidy mill rate' exceeded the adjusted 1968 mill rate, the municipality qualified for a subsidy equal to the excess multiplied by its local assessment. Finally, the subsidies calculated for all the municipalities in a school district were totalled, the amount paid to the school board, and the latter required to use the grant to reduce its requisition from each municipality by the appropriate amount.

The grant applied to all municipalities in the province (and to areas not municipally organized but within an enlarged school district) with the exception of the cities of London, Windsor, Hamilton, and Ottawa, and all of Metropolitan Toronto. These urban municipalities were, of course, not affected by the consolidation of school districts in 1969 and therefore increases in tax rates could not be the result of the apportionment of tax levies within the school district. The grants committee had originally proposed that the subsidy be given only to municipalities with populations of less than 60,000, on the assumption that the intention was primarily to help the smaller areas. When it was realized that in some cases the tax rates would increase more rapidly in urban centres than in rural areas, the subsidy was made generally applicable to all qualifying municipalities.

The mill rate subsidy had the effect of restoring a significant portion of the funds originally requested from the Treasury Board for the regular grants but eliminated at the last moment. The subsidy was estimated to cost $50 millions or one-third of the amount cut from the original request.[4] The funds were distributed in a manner which bore virtually no relationship to the principle of equity, however. Where municipalities had been unduly favoured under the foundation plan (due to the minimum and

---

* / Monies transferred to reserve funds or used to accumulate a surplus or retire a deficit were also excluded from approved expenditure.
† / The 1967 mill rate was used if higher than the 1968 rate.

protective features or a relatively high taxing capacity), equity demanded that the tax rate in 1969 should increase in relation to the remainder of the enlarged school district. The subsidy, however, prevented all tax rates from rising by more than the equivalent of one equalized mill, regardless of whether or not the municipality had previously been in a favoured position. Some kind of special tax relief became politically essential, however, when the Treasury Board in effect forced a substantial increase in the general rate of local taxation by failing to make adequate funds available for the new grant plan. The mill rate subsidy was probably as effective a device of tax relief as could have been developed on such short notice.

The 1970 grant plan

As was the case in 1964 with the foundation grant plan, the new plan of 1969 was designed as a long-term provincial programme with revisions to be made each year as deemed appropriate. The changes made in 1970 did not alter the basic principles of the plan, but because they developed out of an overall provincial policy which had been lacking a year earlier, they did considerably alter the impact of the plan. Before outlining the detailed changes for 1970, we shall note some changes in the personnel and operation of the departmental grants committee – changes which may prove to be significant over the long run.

In 1968 the grants committee had consisted of eight people, six officials of the Department of Education and two consultants from the Ontario Institute for Studies in Education. In 1969 several changes were made in this membership. First, P.H. Cunningham, long-time chairman of the committee, retired from the provincial public service at the end of February. The chairmanship was assumed by G.D. Spry, director of the school business administration branch and a member of the committee since 1967. Second, W.G. Chatterton was replaced by L.E. Maki as one of the two representatives of the supervision section (J.R. Thomson remained as the second representative). Finally, in leaving the Institute, the author relinquished his position as consultant to the committee. This left a committee of five civil servants (Spry, Thomson, Maki, F.S. Wilson, and R.K. Fletcher) and one consultant (Professor E.B. Rideout).

There was also a change in the operation of the committee during 1969 which may have more significant long-term effects on provincial policy than the change in personnel. This change was largely a consequence of G.D. Spry's assumption of the chairmanship. Spry felt that the department should itself assume the primary responsibility for the development and administration of grant programmes and should not continue the extensive reliance formerly placed upon the academic consultants. The consultant's role was gradually changed, therefore, to involve advice on general policy alternatives but not participation in the detailed calculation of proposals nor in the discussions and negotiations with the Treasury Board. The logic behind this change is rather compelling and reflected the growing sophistication and confidence of the provincial public service generally and key officials like Spry particularly. It was the kind of growth which the reorganization of the department had, in part, been designed to facilitate.

The important differences between the grant plans of 1969 and 1970 can almost all be explained by the development for 1970 of a fairly clear policy with respect to grants by the provincial cabinet, and the commitment of sufficient funds to implement this policy by the Treasury Board. In 1970 the province undertook to commit itself to two basic objectives: to hold the level of local taxation for education to the approximate level required in 1969 and to increase provincial grants as a proportion of school board expenditures over a period of three years until they reached 60 per cent in 1972–3.[5] This was a major departure in provincial policy, a departure which had obvious short-run implications for increased provincial expenditures but may have even more significant long-run implications for provincial-local relations (the latter will be explored in the following chapter).

The commitment to hold 1970 local taxes to their 1969 average level and to increase provincial grants generally provided the statement of objectives which had been lacking in 1969. It allowed the grants committee to proceed with changes in the grant plan with the knowledge that these changes would be supported by the cabinet and, especially, the Treasury Board.

There were two changes[6] of a somewhat technical nature which yet had a significant impact on the grant structure. First, the general level of assessment, and therefore assessment per pupil, was increased by an improvement in the calculation of equalized assessment data. Specifically, commercial and industrial assessment was to be increased by a factor of 1.111 (the inverse of 0.9) in order to compensate for the differential tax rates levied on the two basic categories of assessment (provincial law required that the rate levied on residential and farm assessment be 90 per cent of the rate on commercial and industrial assessment). Second, the course weighting factors for secondary school pupils were eliminated with the exception of that for students receiving instruction in the French language. This change was necessitated by the rapid movement away from the highly structured Robarts Plan, a movement actively supported by the Department of Education. Various adjustments were made in the grant calculations to compensate for these two changes, the most noteworthy being the increase in the average assessment per weighted pupil from $34,000 to $40,500 in the case of elementary schools, and from $83,000 to $108,000 in the case of secondary schools.

Ordinary expenditures subject to grant in 1969 had been held to a maximum of $450 or $700 per weighted pupil (elementary or secondary). In 1970 this control was changed to a more sophisticated technique which limited both increases in expenditure and total expenditure. It also allowed the greatest increases to boards previously spending the least. The absolute maximum expenditures in 1970 were raised to $500 per weighted pupil for elementary schools and to $1000 per weighted pupil for secondary schools.* Further, however, the elementary expenditure could not increase by more than $50 per pupil over the 1969 level or by 50 per cent of the difference between the 1969 expenditure and $500 per pupil (whichever was greater). The net effect of this was that elementary boards (or boards of education in respect of their elementary schools) which had spent $450 or more in 1969 were limited to $500 in 1970, those which had spent between $400 and $450 were limited to an increase of $50, while those which had spent less than $400 were limited to an increase of $50 plus fifty cents for every dollar by which their expenditure had been below $400. In the secondary panel, boards which had spent the equivalent of $875 or more per pupil in 1969 were limited to $1000 in 1970, those which had spent between $791 and $875 were limited to an increase of $125, and those which had spent less than $791 were limited to an increase of sixty cents for every dollar by which their expenditure had been below $791.

The committment undertaken by the province to hold the average local tax rate to its 1969 level and to increase provincial support to 60 per cent of school board expenditure by 1972–3 was mostly incorporated in a dramatic reduction in the local sharing ratio used in the grant formula for ordinary expenditures. From the 58 per cent used in 1969, this proportion was lowered by a full twelve percentage points to 46 per cent for 1970. This meant that the province would meet 54 per cent instead of 42 per cent of the approved ordinary expenditure of a board with average taxing capacity, and the same proportion of the total approved ordinary expenditure of all boards in the province. This was indeed a major commitment of provincial resources.

Except for the previously noted maxima placed on approved ordi-

* / The sharp increase in the secondary maximum from $700 to $1000 was largely a reflection of the elimination of the weighting factors.

nary expenditure, the 1970 grant plan completely removed any ceiling on the total grant payable to a school board. The 1969 limit of 110 per cent of the 1968 grant had, of course, been necessitated by the limited funds available, and the substantial increase in the Treasury Board appropriation for 1970 removed this need. The 1969 minimum of 104 per cent of the 1968 grant was also removed but was replaced by a minimum provision in the grant on ordinary expenditures, rather than on the total grant.

Under the latter provision, a board's ordinary grant would be at least equal to the ordinary grant paid in 1969 unless its assessment per pupil had increased more rapidly or slowly than the provincial average. If either of these situations applied, then the minimum grant for 1970 was raised or lowered in relation to the grant paid in 1969 in inverse proportion to the increase or decrease in the board's assessment per pupil as compared with the provincial average. Thus, if a board had a relatively higher taxing capacity in 1970 than in 1969, its guaranteed minimum grant would be lower in 1970 than the grant actually paid in 1969. The reverse would apply if a board's relative taxing capacity decreased. A more equitable floating minimum had thus been substituted for the arbitrary minimum and maximum used in 1969.

The formula used in calculating the grant on recognized extraordinary expenditures was again unchanged in 1970. The factors used to determine the actual amount of grant were liberalized, however. The detailed changes need not be described here, but their effect was to pay a higher proportion of the expected 1970 level of expenditure than had been the case in 1969.

Because of the cabinet's commitment to avoid a general increase in the rates of local taxation for education, it would have been inexpedient to have discontinued the special mill rate subsidy in 1970. Three significant changes were made, however, in the apportionment of school board requisitions and in the provincial subsidy in respect of such requisitions.

The method to be employed in apportioning school board requisitions was removed from legislation and instituted instead by regulation.[7] In 1970, 70 per cent of the school boards' net requirements were to be apportioned among the constituent municipalities essentially in the same ratio as had the 1968 requisitions. The remaining 30 per cent were then to be apportioned on the basis of each municipality's share of the total equalized assessment in the school district. If the method of equalizing assessments were to prove reasonably adequate (the province assumed responsibility for assessing property in 1970), the intention was to alter the seventy-thirty proportions until eventually all requisitions would be apportioned on the basis of equalized assessment.

Once the school board requisition had been apportioned, the province undertook, through the mill rate subsidy, to hold local tax rates to a maximum of one-half mill above the 1969 level, so long as the total school board expenditure did not exceed a specified maximum. The maximum was also changed. In 1969 it had been a simple 115 per cent of the per-pupil expenditure in 1968. In 1970 the maximum was calculated under a formula similar to that used for the maximum approved ordinary expenditure (the amount of increase permitted in expenditure being a function of the level in the previous year) but with higher maximum levels because total expenditure, and not just ordinary, was included. The important provision, however, was that limiting increases in local tax rates to a maximum of one-half mill.

The grants committee had argued in 1968 that since the new grant scheme was designed to meet the needs of the enlarged school boards, special provision ought to be made for the remaining, isolated, public and separate elementary boards. The Deputy Minister of Education had vetoed the proposed scheme and it did not appear in the 1969 regulation. The fact that the new grant plan did not meet the needs of these boards became more apparent to officials of the department, but no special provisions were approved during 1969.

With the much greater resources made available in 1970, it was finally accepted that these districts should be given special consideration and so the scheme originally proposed by the committee was incorporated in the 1970 plan. But because this would have highlighted the lack of such a provision in 1969, the scheme was made retroactive to that year, a decision which necessitated reinstituting the 1969 grant regulation in 1970 in order that the 1969 grants to these boards could be recalculated.[8]

The special provision simply provided that isolated school boards would receive the greater of the regular grants or the difference between their total expenditure (all approved extraordinary expenditure plus ordinary expenditure up to a maximum of $550 per weighted pupil) and the yield of seven mills on equalized assessment.

The development of provincial policy in response to the problems of local capital financing for schools up to 1968 was outlined in Chapter 11. This policy changed sufficiently in 1969 and 1970 to warrant further attention at this point.

The federal-provincial Technical and Vocational Training Agreement had terminated in 1967 and the province's limited extension of the capital grant programme lasted only until 1969. Beginning in the latter year, then, virtually all local capital requirements for schools were to be channelled through the basic provincial programme, embodied in pro-

vincial purchase of local debentures through the Ontario Education
Capital Aid Corporation.

Coinciding with this elimination of alternative programmes of capital
aid was a severe shortage of capital funds in the open market, a shortage
which not only made the sale of bonds or debentures extremely difficult,
but pushed the cost (interest rates) to unprecedented heights (even the
capital aid corporation's interest rate reached 8.5 per cent in 1970).

As a result of these factors, it became clear to officials in both the
treasury and education departments that the demand for capital funds by
school boards in 1969 and 1970 would substantially exceed the supply
available through the pension fund and the capital aid corporation. There
were only two responses open to the province: increase the supply of
funds either by borrowing outside the pension fund itself or allow school
boards* to borrow outside the capital aid corporation, or control the
demand for funds by the school boards. The province was especially
reluctant to allow school boards to sell debentures on the open market
because, given the existing tight conditions, this would have rendered the
problems of municipalities even more difficult. The province was thus
forced into adoption of the first alternative.

The province chose, then, to control school board capital expenditures
and to do so by means of the Department of Education's system of building approvals. Previously, such approval had been used only to ensure
adequate standards of construction and to determine the approved cost
of the project for the purpose of subsequent grants. Now, however, it
would be used to assign provincial priorities to local projects, to limit
expenditures to approved levels, and to allow only those projects to proceed whose combined cost would not exceed the funds available from the
capital aid corporation. Whereas the capital aid programme in the period
from 1966 to 1968 had been described as a half-way step between local
autonomy and provincial control, the changes in 1969 and 1970 brought
it almost fully into a programme of provincial control. In effect, school
boards were rendered agents of the province in the expansion or replacement of capital facilities, subject to provincial control in all of the key
areas of designing, constructing, and financing such facilities.

Having changed the nature of capital financing to this extent, it would
no longer make any real difference whether the province paid capital
grants in lump sums or in annual instalments as a proportion of debt
charges. Local debt incurred through the capital aid corporation is 'local'
in name only. In effect it is provincial debt, both the level of which and

---

* / School boards were authorized to sell debentures themselves (rather than
through the municipalities) in 1969.

the projects for which it is incurred being directly controlled by the province. Effective local participation extends only to two areas: negotiating with the province over the assignment of priorities among competing capital projects and contribution of an equalized share of the cost of retiring the debt.

If the development of the province's capital aid programme between 1966 and 1970 represented stages in a continuous process, the logical next stage would appear to be complete provincial assumption of school debt, in appearance as well as in effect.

Between 1965 and 1969 both the Department of Education and the local school districts had been reorganized in such a manner as to facilitate a much greater delegation of authority over elementary and secondary education from the provincial to the local level. Yet we have just noted a situation in the area of capital expansion and financing wherein the province asserted a much more thorough and effective control than had ever been attempted prior to these complementary reorganizations. And while at the time of writing the assertion of provincial control over educational policy and finance has extended only to the capital area, there are impressive signs that further controls are under serious consideration within the provincial government. Two recent pronouncements should suffice to indicate the nature of possible future provincial controls.

In setting forth the province's commitment to assume 60 per cent of total school board expenditures between 1970-1 and 1972-3, the provincial treasurer, Charles MacNaughton, made it clear that this was not intended as an open-ended provincial policy. The 1969 budget statement contained the following pronouncement:

The primary purpose of the Province in assuming this increased share of education financing is to permit some compensating reduction in school board levies. In other words, the increase in provincial taxation for school support is expected to be offset substantially by reduced local taxation for school financing ...

In the past, increased provincial grants have been translated almost entirely into higher total expenditures on schools. This need not be the end result in future, however, because enrolments will level off over the next few years. If school boards do not exercise voluntary restraint in spending, this Government will consider establishing machinery, such as a budget review board, to ensure that increased financial aid from the province is passed on to the local taxpayers.[9]

The intent of this warning requires little amplification. The province was

simply serving notice that if school board expenditures were not constrained by the boards (within limits the province chose not to stipulate),
the province would move to create a mechanism for imposing such constraint through direct controls.

With no fanfare and very little attention, the province did, in fact, create
the legislative framework for just the budgetary control the Treasurer had
warned of. In a brief amendment to the Department of Education Act,
the minister's powers to make regulations were extended to cover regulations 'governing estimates that a board is required to prepare and adopt
and expenditures that may be made by a board for any purpose.'[10] The
minister of education was thus empowered both to specify what expenditures a school board might and might not make, but also to set forth the
procedure to be followed in gaining approval for such expenditures. This
power could, in effect, be exercised at any time by a simple decree, embodied in a departmental regulation.

Asked to explain the intent of this extensive grant of power, the minister of education, William Davis, replied it was nothing more than a
reserve power, to be used in the event that school boards were unwilling
or unable – as a result of policy or salary negotiations – to contain total
expenditures within reasonable (again undefined) limits.[11]

It is quite impossible to determine the long-term implications of these
rather forceful warnings to school boards. The case of capital financing
showed clearly that the province was prepared to impose direct controls
on school board spending. Whether such control will eventually be extended to operating expenditures as well is simply a matter of conjecture
at this point in time. What is abundantly clear from these developments,
however, is a very significant change in the direction of provincial-school
board relations. The nature of this change will be explored in Chapter 17.

17

Provincial policy and the political system

In attempting to formulate conclusions about the nature of the inter-governmental political system in Ontario, it is essential that the limitations of the present study be borne in mind. While the formulation, content, and impact of provincial and federal-provincial policies have been explored in some detail, this has been restricted to a defined area of provincial-local relations within a specific time period. It seems appropriate at this point, however, to broaden the scope somewhat to encompass a more general examination of intergovernmental relations. In order to do this we must draw upon what other studies are available in other areas of the inter-governmental system. And while this field of enquiry is not characterized by an abundance of literature, there are three studies which allow us to extend some of the conclusions suggested in the course of the preceding chapters.

In 1960, Eric Hardy[1] developed a three-point argument which suc-cinctly described the general dimensions of provincial-local relations in Ontario. First, he observed that most provincial departments dealt directly with local governments in the area of the department's concern. Second, each department developed fiscal sharing programmes, usually in the form of conditional grants, to finance the particular function with which the department was concerned. Third, this functional isolation at the pro-vincial level was paralleled at the local level through the creation and maintenance of special purpose governments such as school boards, health authorities, and conservation authorities. He described the situation at the provincial level in the following terms: 'Indeed, virtually every depart-ment of the provincial government has direct dealings with local gov-ernments. And with few exceptions the individual departments also have direct financial relationships with the local authorities.'[2]

A recent study of the whole educational system in Ontario (including post-secondary education) by Robin Harris concluded with an analysis supporting that of Hardy. 'Is the educational system of Ontario so structured,' Harris asked, 'that its various parts function effectively as individual units but also in co-ordination with each other?' To at least the second part of this question the answer unquestionably is no. While it is probably true to say that on the whole the individual units do function effectively as units, there is a good deal of evidence that they operate as units rather than as organic parts of a larger complex.[3]

Finally, in a comprehensive overview of provincial-local fiscal relations in Ontario, J.S. Dupré defined the relationship between the province and its local governments as 'a pattern of hyper-fractionalized quasi-subordination.'[4] In this poetic phrase, he effectively capsulized the conclusions reached by both Hardy and Harris. The local level of government is clearly subordinate to the provincial level, Dupré argued, and yet this subordination is constrained by historical precedent and group interests which protect the existing division of power. Thus the 'quasi-subordinate' dimension in the relationship. At the same time, a highly decentralized provincial bureaucracy, involving a large number of functional departments, deals with a bewildering array of functional local governments (education, health, conservation, recreation, library). Thus the 'hyper-fractionalized' dimension in the relationship.

The present analysis of policy in relation to the governing and financing of elementary and secondary schools adds considerable support to this consensus about the nature of the intergovernmental political system in Ontario. At the same time, however, the analysis contains clear indications that in some respects at least the general description may have to be modified. We shall examine each of these aspects in turn.

One could hardly find a better example of the historically quasi-subordinate status of local government in education than the series of provincial attempts to reorganize the territorial extent of school districts. While constitutionally free to restructure local government as it saw fit (certainly in respect of public elementary and secondary schools, and apparently also in respect of separate elementary schools), the province was effectively constrained in doing just that for over one hundred years. The provincial response to this paradoxical situation was the development of various policies designed to provide financial incentives to local reorganization in place of legislative coercion.

The quasi-subordinate role of local government was also revealed in our examination of the process of change involved in the foundation grant plan (Chapter 9). It was clear that local governments (school boards) did not participate in the process from which programmes of intergovernmental transfer payments resulted. Yet school boards, and especially their delegated spokesmen, were accorded access to this process and were on occasion quite effective in influencing the outcomes. Thus, while there was no commitment to the kind of intergovernmental consultation that is embodied in a mechanism like the federal-provincial conference, the subordinate level of government was able to constrain the policy alternatives of the senior level.

The present study has also provided a wealth of evidence in support of the hyper-fractionalized dimension of intergovernmental relations. The equalization of local property assessments was an essential ingredient of any effective provincial grant plan based on the principle of fiscal equalization. This ingredient was provided in the equalizing factors developed by the Department of Municipal Affairs. When these factors were first introduced in 1958, the education grants committee of the cabinet, in which the minister of municipal affairs was often included, provided a mechanism through which the needs of the Department of Education, which would use the factors, could be communicated to the Department of Municipal Affairs, which would produce them.

After the introduction of the foundation grant plan, however, the cabinet committee ceased to function and the two departments went their separate ways. When the Department of Municipal Affairs changed the basis of assessment equalization in 1966 (from 1940 value to current-year value), it did so without consultation with the Department of Education. The grants committee of the latter department was forced to react by altering its grant formulas. In 1968 the Department of Municipal Affairs undertook a revision of these factors but did not do so for all municipalities in the province. The relative fiscal capacities of school districts were changed dramatically by this partial revision and the Department of Education was forced to permit the use of either the 1967 or 1968 factors, in order to protect those districts whose equalized assessment had been changed for 1968. There was no provision for communication between the two departments even though one was providing a measure which was basic to a policy administered by the other.

The response of the provincial government to the problems of capital financing in education provides another convincing example of hyper-fractionalism. Both the foundation plan and the vocational capital grant scheme involved the payment of provincial grants to school boards in respect of expenditures for capital expansion. Furthermore, the vocational grants generated operating expenditures which were covered under the provisions of the foundation plan. Yet despite this, the two grant formulas were based on contradictory principles and were administered by two entirely separate sections of the Department of Education. Once the vocational grants were reduced from 100 to 75 per cent, school boards were placed in the position of choosing between the two schemes, and even receiving assistance from both for a single building project (if the project involved both academic and vocational facilities).

This situation was further complicated by the introduction of the capital aid corporation. Instead of using the available funds to bring the principles of the foundation plan and vocational capital grants into line, the cabinet superimposed a programme which brought another department (municipal affairs) into direct contact with school boards – thus further fractionalizing the intergovernmental relationships – and created a situation in which the foundation plan grants provided provincial assistance to school boards in repaying provincial capital loans.

Further examples of the hyper-fractionalized nature of provincial-local policy abound. For instance, school districts were consolidated in 1969 on a regional (county) basis with no consideration of the appropriateness of complementary municipal consolidation. Yet the Department of Municipal Affairs was actively engaged in the planning of regional governments through its sponsorship of a series of local government reviews.[5] Both the school district consolidation and the earlier reorganization of the Department of Education were premised on a significant delegation of power to the local level – a delegation which was clearly not a part of any general reorientation of provincial-local relations. Clearly, education and general municipal government were destined to proceed in spendid isolation.

There are some respects in which the term hyper-fractionalized quasi-subordination appears to be inappropriate in describing provincial-local relations in the governing and financing of schools. As has been described in this study, the province did, in fact, overcome the century-old constraints inhibiting a legislated consolidation of school districts. Having accomplished this as early as 1964, it proceeded to extend its newly established authority in a two-pronged reorganization of both the central department and the local governments. No sooner had these twin policies been implemented when the province imposed far-reaching controls upon school board capital spending and issued clear warnings that similar controls would be used for current spending if deemed necessary.* All of this raises doubts about the adequacy of the term 'quasi-subordination' in describing provincial-school board relations. While the future development of such relations is far from clear, it might be more accurate in the present context to refer to school boards as simply subordinate to the provincial government.

* / Such controls were indeed applied in 1971.

The effective subordination of school boards occurred, ironically, at the same time as they assumed greater political responsibilities and fiscal resources than had ever been the case since the provincial government began concerning itself with public education early in the nineteenth century. The Department of Education relinquished the control of the operation of schools it had previously exercised through the cadre of inspectors, while school boards gained jurisdiction over the supervision of their own schools and governing responsibility for large territorial units, giving them extensive potential resources.

The explanation of this apparent paradox would appear to lie in two factors. On the one hand, in giving up its concern with the minutiae of school board operations, the Department of Education assumed a much greater competence to oversee – and therefore control – the broad directions of school board organization and policy. For example, the imposition of controls on school board capital spending was made possible by the development wtihin the department of expertise in the areas of school building research, design, and financing. Such expertise was the direct consequence of the shift to research and service as the primary role of the department, as opposed to direct regulation and control.

On the other hand, the increased resources and responsibilities of school boards were bought at the price of a severance of the identification of those boards with small, self-contained communities. It is not suggested here either that the small school districts were always coterminous with definable communities or that where such did exist it justified the maintenance of inadequate units of government (inadequate in meeting the needs of modern education). What is suggested is that the community orientation of small school boards lay at the heart of the *quasi*-subordinate status of such boards. Removal of the basis of community support through consolidation of school districts also removed the barrier to the assertion of greater provincial control. In short, a much more competent and sophisticated provincial department faced a group of school boards with impressive resources and responsibilities but without the political base to resist provincial direction and control.

It is not yet clear whether this type of subordination will extend to local governments generally. Thus, while quasi-subordination may no longer describe the state of provincial-school board relations, it probably remains adequate when applied to relations between the province and general-purpose municipal governments.

There has clearly been some diminishing of the hyper-fractionalized dimension of provincial-school board relations as well. The consolidation of school districts in 1969 replaced the dual system of elected public elementary and appointed secondary school boards with a relatively uniform system of elected boards of education. The segregation of public and separate school boards remained, however. Furthermore, in eliminating the great divergencies between the sizes and resources of school districts, the consolidation created a situation in which the province will deal with a group of local educational governments relatively equal in both their needs and policy objectives. The complementary reorganization of the Department of Education also removed the basis of much of the former fractionalized relationship with school boards. Elementary and secondary education were co-ordinated while the system of regional offices replaced a host of contacts between the department and the local school systems.

The termination of the federal-provincial vocational school capital grant scheme also tended to reduce fractionalized relations. All provincial grants to school boards would henceforth be channeled through the single, comprehensive grant programme. Furthermore, the new grant plan of 1969 and 1970 removed a host of complex provisions designed to treat different kinds of school boards differently. This, of course, was largely a function of the consolidation of school districts.

Employing a broader perspective, however, provincial-local relations undoubtedly remain as hyper-fractionalized as ever. Rather than moving toward an integration of local governments (educational and municipal), the consolidation of school districts considerably widened the gulf between the two. Even within the educational domain, the creation of semi-autonomous governing boards for the colleges of applied arts and technology in 1965 established an additional set of local governments in education and further fractionalized the government of education. Thus, Harris' description of educational government as a system of units co-ordinated within but not between themselves is as accurate in the 1970s as it was in the 1960s.

This study has examined a set of problems in the governing and financing of elementary and secondary education in Ontario, and the provincial government's policy responses to those problems. In this it has followed the development of provincial policy from a series of largely unrelated responses to interrelated problems to a relatively comprehensive policy response.

We have been forced to modify the descriptive analysis offered by Dupré and refer to contemporary provincial-school board relations as exhibiting a pattern of co-ordinated subordination. As part of the complex of provincial-local relations in general, however, this relationship clearly exists within a context of continuing hyper-fractionalized quasi-subordination.

References

CHAPTER 1

1 / J.S. Dupré, *Intergovernmental Finance in Ontario: A Provincial-Local Perspective*, Toronto, Queen's Printer, 1968, prepared for the Ontario Committee on Taxation, p. 5
2 / Ibid., p. 1
3 / Robin S. Harris, *Quiet Evolution*, Toronto, University of Toronto Press, 1967

CHAPTER 2

1 / Figures taken from principal's processed attendance reports
2 / 47 Geo. III, c. 6, SUC
3 / 56 Geo. III, c. 36, SUC
4 / J.G. Hodgins, *Documentary History of Education in Upper Canada*, Toronto, Warwick Bros. & Rutter, 28 vols., 1894–1910, I, 245
5 / 4 & 5 Vic., c. 18, SPC
6 / 7 Vic., c. 29, SPC
7 / 10 & 11 Vic., c. 19, SPC
8 / 13 & 14 Vic., c. 48, SPC
9 / 34 Vic., c. 33, SO. It was this Act which first designated the non-sectarian common schools as 'public' schools.
10 / 59 Vic., c. 70, SO
11 / 11 Geo. V, c. 89, SO
12 / 'A Bill to Provide for Township Boards of Public School Trustees.'
13 / Ontario, Department of Education, *A Letter from the Hon. G.H. Ferguson, Minister of Education, to those interested in Rural Education*, Toronto, King's Printer, 1925
14 / Ontario, Royal Commission on Education in Ontario, *Report*, Toronto, King's Printer, 1950, p. 328. Hereinafter referred to as Hope Report.
15 / Public school boards in cities were authorized to employ their own inspectors, known as superintendents, in 1847 (10 & 11 Vic., c. 19, SPC).
16 / Ontario, Department of Education, *A History of Professional Certificates*, Toronto 1935, mimeographed, p. 65
17 / 20 Geo. V, c. 63, SO
18 / Department of Education, *History of Professional Certificates*, pp. 65–7
19 / 22 Geo. V, c. 41, SO

20 / Ontario, Department of Education, *Annual Report of the Minister of Education for 1938*, Toronto, King's Printer, 1939, Appendix A, p. ii. Hereinafter referred to as Minister's Report for appropriate year.

21 / J.G. Hodgins, *Legislation and History of Separate Schools in Upper Canada*, Toronto, Wm. Briggs, 1897, p. 22

22 / Cited in ibid., p. 45

23 / 4 & 5 Vic., c. 18, SPC, s. 11

24 / Cited in F.A. Walker, *Catholic Education and Politics in Upper Canada*, Toronto and Vancouver, J.M. Dent & Sons, 1955, p. 142

25 / 12 & 13 Eliz. II, c. 108, SO

26 / 10 & 11 Vic., c. 19, SPC

27 / 13 & 14 Vic., c. 48, SPC, s. 19

28 / 14 & 15 Vic., c. 111, SPC

29 / 26 Vic., c. 5, SPC

30 / 13 & 14 Vic., c. 48, SPC

31 / 62 Vic., c. 37, SO

32 / 3 Ed. VII, c. 34, SO

33 / 5 Geo. VI, c. 82, SO

34 / 2 Eliz. II, c. 119, SO

35 / 34 Vic., c. 33, SO

36 / 9 Ed. VII, c. 90, SO

37 / 3 & 4 Geo. V, c. 72, SO

38 / Ontario, Department of Education, *County High School Districts in Ontario*, Toronto 1946, p. 8

39 / Harris, *Quiet Evolution*, pp. 115–16

40 / 1 Geo. VI, c. 68, SO

41 / 16 Vic., c. 186, SPC

42 / 3 Eliz. II, c. 87, SO

43 / 3 Ed. VII, c. 31, SO

44 / 4 Ed. VII, c. 33, SO

45 / 9 Ed. VII, c. 94, SO

46 / 7 Geo. VI, c. 26, SO

47 / 1 Geo. V, c. 17, SO

48 / 12 Geo. VI, c. 8, SO

49 / 13 Geo. VI, c. 8, SO

50 / For example, see Ontario Regulation 24/67

51 / Taken from principals' processed attendance reports

52 / 30 & 31 Vic., c. 3, SUK

53 / *Ottawa Separate School Trustees* v *City of Ottawa* and *Ottawa Separate School Trustees* v *Quebec Bank*. Supreme Court of Ontario (1915), 34 OLR 624. Cited in F.G. Carter, *Judicial Decisions on Denominational Schools*, Toronto, Ontario Separate School Trustees' Association, 1962, p. 62

54 / *Trustees of the Roman Catholic Separate Schools for Ottawa* v *Ottawa Corporation* (1917), AC 76. Cited in ibid., p. 78

55 / 11 & 12 Eliz. II, c. 132, SO

CHAPTER 3

1 / Assessments have been equalized by application of the Department of Municipal Affairs factors which standardized assessments to the equivalent of full value in 1940. This system was changed in 1966 in order to bring standardized assessments up to full current value. Note will be made whenever the 1940 base is not used.

2 / 4 & 5 Vic., c. 10, SPC

3 / 7 Vic., c. 29 SPC

4 / 10 & 11 Vic., c. 19, SPC

5 / 13 & 14 Vic., c. 48, SPC

6 / 34 Vic., c. 33, so
7 / 10 & 11 Vic., c. 19, spc
8 / Hope Report, p. 690
9 / 13 & 14 Vic., c. 48, spc
10 / 16 Vic., c. 86, spc
11 / 22 Vic., c. 64, spc
12 / 48 Vic., c. 49, so
13 / In areas without municipal organization school boards retained, of necessity, the right to levy and collect taxes.
14 / 4 & 5 Vic., c. 10, spc
15 / 7 Vic., c. 20, spc
16 / Hope Report, p. 689
17 / 10 & 11 Vic., c. 19, spc
18 / 13 & 14 Vic., c. 48, spc
19 / 42 Vic., c. 34, so
20 / 22 Geo. v, c. 26, so
21 / The Ontario Municipal Board, a product of the financial difficulties experienced by local governments in the depression, was the successor to two earlier
boards: the Railway and Municipal Board created in 1906 and the Bureau of Municipal Affairs created in 1917.
22 / Ontario, The Ontario Committee on Taxation, *Report*, Toronto, Queen's
Printer, 1967, 3 vols., II, 29. Hereinafter referred to as Smith Report.
23 / 13 & 14 Vic., c. 67, spc
24 / 16 Vic., c. 86, spc
25 / Cited in Smith Report, II, 33
26 / 53 Vic., c. 55, so
27 / 4 Ed. VII, c. 23, so
28 / 1 Ed. VIII, c. 1, so
29 / 6 Geo. VI, c. 1, so
30 / Smith Report, II, 47
31 / 16 Vic., c. 186, spc
32 / 34 Vic., c. 33, so
33 / In 1872 tuition fees accounted for 11 per cent of the total revenue of
Ontario high schools. See Hope Report, p. 697
34 / 11 Geo. v, c. 89, so
35 / 42 Vic., c. 34, so
36 / 7 Vic., c. 29, spc
37 / 10 & 11 Vic., c. 19, spc
38 / 13 & 14 Vic., c. 48, spc
39 / Walker, *Catholic Education and Politics in Upper Canada*, p. 114
40 / 16 Vic., c. 185, spc
41 / 18 Vic., c. 131, spc
42 / 26 Vic., c. 5, spc
43 / 22 Vic., c. 64, spc
44 / Hope Report, pp. 695–6
45 / 40 Vic., c. 16, so
46 / 42 Vic., c. 34, so
47 / RSO 1960, c. 274, s. 64(5). Under the terms of the Ontario Education Capital
Aid Corporation, created in 1966, separate school boards are required to obtain
the Municipal Board's approval only if they wish to borrow from that corporation.
48 / Hope Report, p. 697
49 / 13 Vic., c. 48, spc
50 / 22 Vic., c. 64, spc
51 / 37 Vic., c. 27, so
52 / According to the 1875 legislation:
'1 This examination will be instituted at a point about midway between the begin-

ning and the end of the High School Course, for promotion from the lower to the upper forms.
2 Candidates ... will be examined in English Grammar and Etymology, Reading, Dictation, Composition, Writing, Arithmetic, Euclid, Algebra, English and Canadian History, Geography and in one of the following branches or groups:
(a) Latin; (b) French; (c) German; (d) Natural Philosophy, Chemistry and Bookkeeping.'

53 / From a total high school grant of $72,000 in 1875, $14,600 was to be distributed on the basis of the examination results, $5000 was paid on the basis of $1 per pupil, $10,000 was based on the inspector's evaluation of the school facilities, and the remaining $42,400 amounted to an unconditional grant of $400 per school.

54 / Hope Report, p. 16

55 / Cited in Minister's Report, 1884, p. 74

56 / M.A. Cameron, *The Financing of Education in Ontario*, Department of Educational Research, University of Toronto, 1936, p. 67

57 / Cited in Minister's Report, 1907, pp. 112–19

58 / Cited in ibid., 1908, pp. 273–84

59 / Cameron, *The Financing of Education in Ontario*, pp. 67–9

60 / Ontario Regulation 49/58

61 / There were six categories for elementary school boards, five based on municipal status and population and one for boards not operating schools. There was a separate category for continuation school boards. There were four categories for high school boards operating academic schools, three for those operating vocational schools, and a final category for those not operating any schools.

62 / See E.B. Rideout, "A New Dimension in the Measurement of Educational Need and Ability to Pay," *Ontario Journal of Educational Research*, I, 2, 1958–9.

63 / Cited in Toronto *Globe and Mail*, 9 July 1943

64 / Ibid., 1 March 1944

65 / Ontario, Parliament, Legislative Assembly, *Debates and Proceedings*, 9 March 1967, p. 1232. (Hereinafter referred to as *Debates*.)

66 / Ontario, Department of Education, *Circular Grants General 12*, 1945

67 / Ibid., 1946, p. 8

68 / K.G. Crawford, *Provincial Grants to Canadian Schools*, Toronto, Canadian Tax Foundation, Tax Paper No 26, 1962, p. 85

69 / 9 & 10 Eliz. II, c. 90, so

70 / 11 & 12 Eliz. II, c. 105, so

71 / Minister's Report, 1966, p. 206

72 / Adjusted to current value by use of Department of Municipal Affairs factors for 1966.

73 / Ontario, Department of Municipal Affairs, *Annual Report of Municipal Statistics*, Toronto, Queen's Printer, 1966

74 / The foundation tax rates were 11 mills for elementary school purposes and 7 mills for secondary school purposes, or a total of 18 mills. These rates applied to the assessments equalized to 1940 value, however, and on 1965 value the combined rate would have been approximately 5.1 mills.

75 / Assessment figures taken from school boards' Financial Reports; expenditure figures taken from Ministers' Reports.

CHAPTER 4

1 / Loyal Orange Association of British America, *Ontario Segregation is Wrong*, Brief presented to the Premier and Members of the Legislature, 1963

2 / This interpretation is invariably proffered by spokesmen for and observers of separate school boards. Serious disadvantages are perceived to arise either when the separate school tax rate is significantly above or below the public school rate.

3 / 26 Vic., c. 5, SPC

4 / 49 Vic., c. 38, so

5 / 3 & 4 Geo. v, c. 71, so

6 / In the Quebec scheme, corporate property has been placed in one of three 'panels.' Where the corporation is tightly controlled and the school support of the owners is known, the property is taxed under either the Catholic or Protestant panel. Where the school support is not known, the property is assigned to the neutral panel, taxed by the larger school board, and the revenue divided between the two boards on the basis of their relative enrolments.

7 / F.A. Walker, *Catholic Education and Politics in Ontario*, Thomas Nelson & Sons, 1964, p. 433

8 / 1 Ed. VIII, c. 4, so

9 / Walker, *Catholic Education and Politics in Ontario*, p. 440

10 / For accounts of the factors involved in the repeal, see ibid., and R.M.H. Alway, 'Mitchell Hepburn, Separate School Taxation, and the Ontario Election of 1937,' *Ontario Journal of Educational Research*, x, 1, autumn 1967.

11 / Cited in F.G. Carter, *Judicial Decisions on Denominational Schools*, pp. 361–8

12 / Walker, *Catholic Education and Politics in Ontario*, p. 479

13 / Cameron, *The Financing of Education in Ontario*, p. 167

CHAPTER 5

1 / Minister's Report, 1946, p. 120

CHAPTER 6

1 / Figures here represent both current and capital account expenditures. This was necessary to make the data comparable. These figures are inflated, of course, if compared with the current account figures used earlier for school board expenditure.

2 / Education is in a somewhat preferred position at the local level insofar as revenue is simply requisitioned from the taxing authority.

CHAPTER 8

1 / W.G. Fleming, 'Ontario's Educative Society,' draft manuscript of eight-volume study of the development of the educational system of Ontario. The author wishes to acknowledge the considerable assistance provided by his access to this manuscript.

2 / E.B. Rideout and R.W.B. Jackson, discussions with the author

3 / E.P. Cubberley, *State School Funds and Their Apportionment*, New York, Bureau of Publications, Teachers College, Columbia University, 1905

4 / G.D. Strayer and R.M. Haig, *The Financing of Education in the State of New York*, New York, Macmillan, 1923, pp. 173–5

5 / P.R. Mort, *The Measuring of Educational Need*, New York, Bureau of Publications, Teachers College, Columbia University, 1924

6 / A.W. Schmidt, 'The Foundation School Program – Its Purpose and Definition,' *Financing Education in the Public Schools*, Princeton, Tax Institute, 1956, p. 108

7 / Cameron, *The Financing of Education in Ontario*, p. 162

8 / Ibid., p. 166

9 / Ibid., p. 167

10 / Ontario, Committee of Enquiry into the Cost of Education in the Province of Ontario, *Report*, Toronto, King's Printer, 1938, p. 40

11 / Hope Report, pp. 724–30

12 / See pp. 60–2

13 / For a more detailed exploration of this argument, see D.M. Cameron and

J.F. Graham, 'Minimum Provisions in a Foundation Plan of Education Finance,'
Canadian Tax Journal, XVI, 1, Jan.-Feb. 1968

14 / Cited in 'Ontario Conference on Education,' *Canadian School Journal*, XL,
2, March 1962

15 / Ibid.

16 / Canadian Conference on Education, Montreal, 1962, *The Second Canadian
Conference on Education: A Report*, Toronto, University of Toronto Press, 1962

17 / Co-operative Commonwealth Federation, 'Looking to the Future,' programme adopted at the 1954 convention

18 / New Democratic Party of Ontario, 'Report of the Committee on Financing
Education in Ontario,' 1961, mimeographed

19 / See, for example, *Debates*, 25 March 1963, pp. 2125–7

20 / Ontario Separate School Trustees' Association and L'Association des
commissions des écoles bilingues d'Ontario, *Brief Presented to the Prime Minister,
to the Minister of Education, and to the Members of the Legislative Assembly of
Ontario*, December 1962, pp. 6–7

21 / Based on conversations with E.B. Rideout

22 / John P. Robarts, statement in the Legislative Assembly, *Debates*, 21 Feb.
1963, pp. 912–23

23 / William G. Davis, statement in the Legislative Assembly, *Debates*, 27 Jan.
1964, pp. 217–20

24 / The Alberta programme provided an annual capital expenditure level of
$47 per pupil.

25 / R.W.B. Jackson, memoranda to the author, 21 April and 8 May 1967

26 / Cameron, *The Financing of Education in Ontario*, pp. 34–5

27 / Minister's Report, 1963

28 / John P. Robarts, statement in the Legislative Assembly, *Debates*, 1 May
1964, p. 2705

29 / Based on data taken from school board financial statements

30 / Using the model foundation plan equation, the first option would be to set
the tax rate so as to yield $80 in the ablest district. Thus, $80 = 210 - (\text{FTR}) \ (28,000)$,
$\text{FTR} = 210 - 80/28,000, = .0046, = 4.6$ mills. The second option would be to set
the foundation level of expenditure so that the yield of eleven mills in the ablest
district would fall short of this amount by $80. Thus, $80 = \text{FLE} - (.011) \ (28,000)$,
$\text{FLE} = 80 + (.011) \ (28,000), = 80 + 308, = \$388$.

31 / Prior to the consolidation of public school districts into township school
areas in 1965, the grant applied to a considerable number of public school sections
as well as separate school zones. Whenever two or more public school sections had
jurisdiction within the same township, those with relative deficiencies were allocated their 'fair share' of corporate assessment. Only small amounts of grant were
paid to public school boards, however.

32 / Municipalities were required to levy two rates of taxation, one on residential
and farm assessment and the other, 10 per cent higher, on commercial and industrial assessment. The latter was used in calculating the corporation tax adjustment
grant.

33 / The federal government paid 50 per cent of the approved cost of night
school classes in English and citizenship for recent immigrants to Canada.

34 / This was designed to cover the initial cost of purchasing a stock of books
in 1964. The grant was intended to be reduced to $6 per pupil after the first year.

35 / This grant is particularly interesting in that it involved the use of provincial
resources to strengthen a voluntary association, one of the major purposes of which
was to pressure the provincial government. The grant was first instituted in 1951
and represented an attempt to counter the growing strength of the teachers'
federations.

36 / Smith Report, I, 389

37 / *Toronto Daily Star*, 4 Feb. 1964

CHAPTER 9

1 / Information regarding the positions of these committee members is taken from the Minister's Report, supplemented by personal discussions.

2 / The official title of this position was changed in 1965 from 'chief, grants office' to 'supervisor, grants sections.'

3 / Based on discussions with members of the committee

4 / The Ontario Separate School Trustees' Association and L'Association des commissions des écoles bilingues d'Ontario, *Brief Presented to the Prime Minister and the Minister of Education of the Province of Ontario*, October 1966

5 / Representations were made by the Burlington Board of Education in October 1964 and January 1966.

6 / Ontario Regulation 139/66

7 / The minimum requirement of a thirty-pupil increase was intended to avoid payment of the grant to boards whose increased attendance would not require the employment of additional teaching staff (an increase from twenty to thirty pupils would represent an increase of 50 per cent but would not entail an appreciable increase in expenditure, since only one teacher would continue to be required). The five per cent minimum increase was an arbitrary figure, and was substantially in excess of the provincial average increase. From 1963 to 1964 the actual province-wide increase in elementary ADA had been 3.7 per cent. From 1964 to 1965 the increase had been only 3.4 per cent.

8 / The 10 per cent was similarly arbitrary and in excess of the provincial average. From 1963 to 1964 the total increase in secondary ADA was 8.5 per cent and from 1964 to 1965 it was 5.9 per cent.

9 / Actually, the Treasury Board did not reject this particular proposal as such. Rather, it reduced the total estimate for the grant programme and this item was accorded the least priority by the department.

10 / *Debates*, 1 April 1966, p. 2160

11 / Ontario Regulation 351/66

12 / The foundation tax rate was three mills in 1966. If one-half mill were added for the local share of extraordinary expenditures, then the rate would have been exactly one-half that prescribed for the non-operating northern boards.

13 / Recruitment was undertaken by a committee of the supervision section of the Department of Education.

14 / The province was divided into three zones. Zone one consisted of all of southern Ontario including the southern portion of Nipissing District. Zone two contained the districts of Algoma, Cochrane, Sudbury, Timiskaming, and the northern portion of Nipissing. Zone three contained the districts of Kenora, Rainy River, and Thunder Bay.

15 / *Debates*, 20 Feb. 1967, p. 666

16 / Minister's Report, 1967, p. 22

17 / These were grants following municipal amalgamation or annexation, grants for evening courses of study (although additional courses were made subject to grant), for larger units of administration, for free milk, for membership in the Ontario School Trustees' Council, and for the salaries of locally-employed inspectors.

18 / These were the grants for home economics and industrial arts classes for students of other boards and the grant on school sites.

19 / Such happened in a number of communities when the province authorized secondary school boards to operate schools and classes in French.

20 / The preceding year is used here because the grant was paid on behalf of the preceding year's pupils and expenditures.

21 / The classroom is used as the unit for measuring expenditure rather than the pupil to avoid the distortions the latter would cause for very small school districts.

22 / The calculated tax rate does not indicate the rate actually levied. The rate was determined by subtracting the grant from the total expenditure and dividing the remainder by the equalized assessment.

23 / Equations for the four regressions lines are as follows:

a Elementary expenditure $= 5302 + (.003928) \ (x)$

b Elementary tax rate $= 8.04 - (.000000065) \ (x)$

c Secondary expenditure $= 9633 + (.00405) \ (x)$

d Secondary tax rate $= 8.61 - (.000000345) \ (x)$

Where $x =$ Equalized assessment per classroom.

CHAPTER 10

1 / Figures taken from Minister's Report, 1960 and 1967

2 / Earlier agreements were authorized under the Vocational Training Co-ordination Act of 1942 (6 Geo. vi, c. 34 sc).

3 / 14 & 15 Eliz. ii, c. 25 sc

4 / Canada, Department of Labour, Information Branch, *Education, Training and Employment*, Ottawa, Queen's Printer, 1961, p. 12

5 / Ibid., p. 41

6 / Cited in ibid., p. 25

7 / Ontario, Department of Economics and Development, Office of the Chief Economist, *Ontario Statistical Review, 1966*, Toronto, 1967, p. 15

8 / Canada, Parliament, House of Commons, *Debates and Proceedings*, 25 Nov. 1960, p. 231–2. Hereinafter referred to as *Hansard*

9 / Ibid., p. 234

10 / 9 Eliz. ii, c. 6, sc

11 / *Hansard*, 9 Dec. 1960, p. 672

12 / Ibid., p. 677

13 / Ibid., p. 681

14 / *Hansard*, 21 Sept. 1961, pp. 8681–2

15 / Canada, Department of Labour, *Annual Report of the Department of Labour, 1961–62*, Ottawa, Queen's Printer, 1963

16 / Ibid.

17 / *Hansard*, 9 Dec. 1960, p. 684

18 / *Debates*, 12 Dec. 1960, p. 401

19 / Ibid., 20 Feb. 1961, p. 1310

20 / Ibid., 28 March 1961, p. 2669

21 / Ontario, Department of Education, 'Technical and Vocational Training Agreement,' office consolidation copy, mimeographed, p. 3

22 / Ibid., p. 3

23 / Ibid., p. 7

24 / Ibid., p. 8

25 / L.M. Johnston, interview, 27 Nov. 1968

26 / Ibid.

27 / Cited in Minister's Report, 1962, p. xii

28 / *Debates*, 10 April 1962, pp. 2179–80

29 / Ibid., 28 March 1961, p. 2669

30 / The cost of the school site and its improvement was not eligible for federal grant

31 / The description of administrative procedures in this regard was obtained from R.H. Beach, in charge of the special section of the Department of Education responsible for federal-provincial agreements, 15 Nov. 1968.

32 / P.H. Cunningham, interview, 14 Nov. 1968, and R.H. Beach, interview, 15 Nov. 1968

33 / A detailed account of the reorganization of the Department of Education is contained in Chapter 13.

34 / A formula was developed for treating capital expenditures on vocational wings of composite schools. Facilities used exclusively for vocational instruction were approved in full, while those used jointly by academic and vocational pupils were approved in the same proportion that vocational pupils were of the total enrolment.

35 / Figures taken from Canada, Department of Labour, *Annual Report*, 1961–2

36 / Ibid.

37 / Ontario, *Public Accounts of Ontario*, 1961–2 and 1962–3

38 / *Debates*, 7 June 1966, p. 4402

39 / *Hansard*, 2 Oct. 1963, p. 3136

40 / 12 Eliz. II, c. 22, SC

41 / *Hansard*, 2 Oct. 1963, p. 3136

42 / Canada, Department of Labour, *Annual Report*, 1962–3

43 / The date upon which this quota was reached cannot be determined precisely. By 31 March 1965 Ontario had spent $269,545,000, just $10 millions below the quota. A year later the figure had reached $330,189,000. Therefore, the quota must have been reached shortly after 31 March 1965. (Figures taken from Ontario, *Public Accounts*, 1964–5 and 1965–6.)

44 / P.H. Cunningham, interview, 14 Nov. 1968

45 / Ibid.

46 / *Debates*, 2 June 1965, p. 3574

47 / In place of these agreements, the federal government proposed to assume full fiscal responsibility for adult occupational training and to provide unconditional grants to the provinces for all phases of post-secondary education.

48 / Ontario, *Public Accounts*, 1961–2 to 1966–7

49 / R.H. Beach, interview, 15 Nov. 1968

50 / *Debates*, 9 Feb. 1967, p. 339

51 / Ibid., 9 March 1967, p. 1214

52 / Minister's Report, 1967, p. 9

53 / Ibid., 1960, 1964, and 1967

54 / Canada, Department of Labour, *Annual Report*, 1961–2 to 1965–6

55 / Minister's Report, 1967, p. 121

56 / Ibid.

57 / See, for example, Donald V. Smiley, *Conditional Grants and Canadian Federalism*, Toronto, Canadian Tax Foundation, Tax Paper No 32, Feb. 1963

58 / Smith Report, II, 403

59 / The federal government did pay a grant in respect of operating expenditures, but only to a maximum of $841,000 per year for Ontario. In 1966 that amount represented a mere 0.6 per cent of the cost of operating the vocational programmes of the secondary schools.

CHAPTER 11

1 / Old-age pensions are a concurrent responsibility of the federal and provincial governments under the British North America Act. In cases of conflict, the provincial law prevails.

2 / 13 & 14 Eliz. II, c. 51, SC

3 / James Allen, treasurer of Ontario, budget speech. Cited in *Debates*, 9 Feb. 1966, p. 348

4 / The funds were extended to cover capital expenditures of library boards and retarded children's authorities in 1967 (15 & 16 Eliz. II, c. 63, SO).

5 / The Smith Committee noted that Alberta intended using the funds to support municipal undertakings generally, while Manitoba intended to support both school finance and industrial development projects. Smith Report, II, 464

6 / 12 & 13 Eliz. II, c. 85, SO

7 / 14 & 15 Eliz. II, c. 101, SO

8 / J. Allen. Cited in *Debates*, 9 Feb. 1966, pp. 348–9

9 / W.D. McKeough, minister of municipal affairs, *Memorandum to Municipal Treasurers and Treasurers of School Boards Authorized to Issue Debentures*, Toronto, Department of Municipal Affairs, 25 July 1968

10 / Ontario, *Public Accounts*, 1966–7, 1967–8, and 1968–9

11 / 13 & 14 Eliz. II, c. 51, sc

12 / J.S. Brown, interview, 15 Oct. 1968

13 / Smith Report, II, 491

14 / Ibid., p. 395

15 / R.W.B. Jackson, interview, 20 Sept. 1968

16 / Smith Report, II, 394–5

CHAPTER 12

1 / Opinions similar to this were expressed by a number of highly placed officials of the Department of Education and supported by academic observers of Dunlop's tenure as minister

2 / *Debates*, 21 Feb. 1963, p. 919

3 / Cameron, *The Financing of Education in Ontario*

4 / R.W.B. Jackson, interview, 20 Sept. 1968

5 / 12 & 13 Eliz. II, c. 95, so

6 / The only exception was the provision that townships with populations in excess of 10,000 could be divided into two school districts

7 / Ontario, Department of Education, *The Township School Area in Ontario*, Circular Elementary 15, 1950, p. 9

8 / Minister's Report, 1964, p. 3

9 / Ivor Kirtland, 'Larger Units of Administration,' unpublished paper, 1966

10 / 12 & 13 Eliz. II, c. 95, so, s. 3, 13(1)

11 / 13 & 14 Eliz. II, c. 109, so

12 / Ibid., s. 5(2)

13 / The formation of a district consultative committee was, however, related to high school district boundaries.

14 / Ontario, Department of Education, *Memorandum to Public School Consultative Committees Re Larger Units of Administration*, Toronto, 28 Dec. 1964, p. 2

15 / Based on conversations with the inspectors, school board members, and members of the consultative committees.

16 / Ontario Teachers' Federation, *A Comparative Survey of School Districts in Ontario*, Toronto, the federation, 1967, p. 2

17 / *Memorandum to Public School Consultative Committees Re Larger Units of Administration*, pp. 2–3

CHAPTER 13

1 / Ryerson replaced another clergyman, the Rev. Robert Murray, who had been appointed in 1841 when the position was created.

2 / See Harris, *Quiet Revolution*, p. 109

3 / The government of Ontario from 1919 to 1923 was comprised of members of an *ad hoc* party which grew out of the United Farmers of Ontario.

4 / See Harris, *Quiet Revolution*, p. 110

5 / Minister's Report, 1946, p. 98

6 / W.G. Fleming, 'Ontario's Educative Society,' draft manuscript

7 / Ibid.

8 / Ibid.

9 / Letter from William G. Davis to J.N. Allen, provincial treasurer, 21 May, 1963. Cited in ibid.

10 / *Debates*, 7 Jan. 1965, p. 3574

11 / Ibid., 4 June 1968, pp. 3881–2

12 / 13 & 14 Eliz. II, c. 86, so

13 / The institute also conducts an extensive programme in graduate education. In this regard it functions as a department within the School of Graduate Studies of the University of Toronto. In its research and development activities it is governed by its own board of governors.

14 / Throne speech, cited in *Debates*, 19 Nov. 1968, p. 4

15 / J. Ross, interview, 28 Nov. 1968

16 / *Debates*, 4 June 1968, p. 3882

CHAPTER 14

1 / John P. Robarts, 'Address by the Honourable John Robarts, Prime Minister of Ontario, at the Dedication of an Addition to Southwood Secondary School,' Galt, Ontario, 14 Nov. 1967, mimeographed, p. 3

2 / S. Thorson, 'Attitudes Towards School District Reorganization,' unpublished paper, Ontario Institute for Studies in Education, 1968

3 / Ibid., pp. 33–4

4 / *Debates*, 6 April 1966, p. 2316

5 / G.W. Waldrum, interview, 3 March 1970

6 / Ibid., and J.R. Thomson, interview, 27 Jan. 1969

7 / It was not possible to verify the authorship of the speech but several senior officials in the Department of Education suggested it was written, in fact, by the Deputy Minister.

8 / This lack of foreknowledge was admitted by several members of the committee.

9 / Ontario, Department of Education, *The Re-organization of School Jurisdictions in the Province of Ontario: A Guide for Southern Ontario*, Toronto, January 1968. The second paper was simply subtitled 'A Guide for Northern Ontario.'

10 / Bill 44, 'An Act to Amend the Secondary Schools and Boards of Education Act'

11 / Bill 112, 'An Act to Establish the Regional Municipality of Ottawa–Carleton'

12 / Ontario, Department of Education, *Index of School Boards of the Province of Ontario on and after January 1, 1969*, Toronto, October 1968, pp. vii–1 to vii–3

13 / Bill 120, 'An Act to Amend the Secondary Schools and Boards of Education Act'

14 / G.W. Waldrum, interview, 3 March 1970 and J.R. Thomson, interview, 27 Jan. 1969

15 / *Debates*, 21 Feb. 1963, p. 916

16 / Ibid., p. 919

17 / 30 & 31 Vic., c. 3, SUK

18 / *Debates*, 21 Feb. 1963, p. 916

19 / *Ottawa Separate School Trustees* v *City of Ottawa* and *Ottawa Separate School Trustees* v *Quebec Bank*, Supreme Court of Ontario (1915), 34 OLR 624. Cited in Carter, *Judicial Decisions on Denominational Schools*, p. 62

20 / John P. Robarts, 'Address by the Honourable John Robarts,' 14 Nov. 1967

21 / Ontario Separate School Trustees' Association, 'A Statement on the Reorganization of School Zones as Applied to the Separate Schools of Ontario,' March 1968

22 / In the case of Metropolitan Toronto, the two separate school districts which had retained their independence were to be merged into the Metropolitan Toronto Separate School Board, giving the latter jurisdiction over all separate schools within the federated municipality.

23 / Bill 168, 'An Act to Amend the Separate Schools Act'

24 / G.W. Waldrum, interview, 3 March 1970
25 / Ontario Separate School Trustees' Association, 'A Statement on the Re-organization of School Zones,' p. 6
26 / Bill 44, s. 98, and Bill 168, s. 87
27 / Ibid.
28 / G.W. Waldrum, interview, 3 March 1970

CHAPTER 15

1 / Bill 44 (17 Eliz. II, c. 122, so) and Bill 168 (17 Eliz. II, c. 125, so) authorized the lieutenant-governor-in-council to alter the boundaries of any school district, public or separate, by regulation.
2 / Figures taken from Minister's Report
3 / Ibid.
4 / The rate of increase dropped somewhat erratically from 5.3 per cent in 1960 to 3.8 per cent in 1967 (figures taken from Minister's Report).
5 / Annual expenditure increases were as follows:

1960	12.3 per cent	1964	15.5 per cent
1961	10.4 per cent	1965	12.5 per cent
1962	12.1 per cent	1966	15.2 per cent
1963	9.6 per cent	1968	19.3 per cent

(figures taken from Minister's Report)

CHAPTER 16

1 / Ontario Regulation 82/69, 12 March 1969
2 / 17 Eliz. II, c. 122, so, s. 87
3 / Ontario Regulation 297/69, 16 July 1969
4 / Ontario, Department of Treasury and Economics, Taxation and Fiscal Policy Branch, *1970 Budget*, Toronto 1970, p. 13
5 / Ibid., p. 16. This committment had been announced in the previous year's budget as well, but to take effect in 1970–1.
6 / Ontario Regulation 58/70
7 / Ontario Regulation 57/70
8 / Ontario Regulation 92/70
9 / Ontario, Department of Treasury and Economics, Taxation and Fiscal Policy Branch, *1969 Budget*, Toronto 1969, pp. 61–2
10 / Bill 228, 'An Act to Amend the Department of Education Act,' introduced 20 Nov. 1969
11 / W.G. Davis, interview, 4 March 1970

CHAPTER 17

1 / Eric Hardy, 'Provincial-Municipal Relations: With Emphasis on the Financial Relationships Between Provinces and Local Governments,' *Canadian Public Administration*, III, 1, March 1960
2 / Ibid., p. 17
3 / Harris, *Quiet Evolution*, p. 131
4 / Dupré, *Intergovernmental Finance in Ontario*, p. 5
5 / The Department of Municipal Affairs sponsored a number of reviews of local government in specific areas. One of these culminated in the creation of the two-tiered system of regional government for Ottawa and Carleton County, referred to earlier.

APPENDIX

Supporting tables

TABLE 41
Distribution of elementary school boards in Ontario
by number of boards and ADA* in classes
of equalized assessment per classroom, 1964

Assessment per classroom	All Boards		Public		Separate	
	No of boards	ADA	No of boards	ADA	No of boards	ADA
Under 50,000	241	19,792	79	2249	162	17,543
50,000–99,999	569	68,589	280	17,663	289	50,926
100,000–149,999	628	99,405	460	54,410	168	44,995
150,000–199,999	615	133,791	534	76,844	81	56,947
200,000–249,999	487	151,772	459	95,659	28	58,113
250,000–299,999	286	106,301	265	74,442	21	31,859
300,000–349,999	149	141,768	137	119,373	12	22,395
350,000–399,999	69	99,204	65	75,721	4	23,483
400,000–449,999	48	102,879	47	102,447	1	432
450,000–499,999	29	48,971	25	48,433	4	538
500,000–549,999	17	51,211	16	44,941	1	6270
550,000–599,999	23	4775	23	4775		
600,000–649,999	10	27,189	10	27,189		
650,000–699,999	7	1566	5	1545	2	21
700,000–749,999	5	1103	5	1103		
750,000–799,999	4	189	4	189		
800,000–849,999	4	998	4	998		
850,000–899,999	2	62,614	2	62,614		
900,000–949,999	1	267	1	267		
950,000–999,999	1	219	1	219		
Over 999,999	15	3190	15	3190		

*/Average daily attendance
SOURCE: Annual Financial and Attendance Reports, 1964

TABLE 42
Distribution of secondary school boards in Ontario by
number of boards and ADA in classes of
equalized assessment per classroom, 1964

Assessment per classroom	Number of boards	ADA
Under 100,000		
100,000–199,999	3	451
200,000–299,999	30	8197
300,000–399,999	43	18,151
400,000–499,999	83	59,982
500,000–599,999	63	45,127
600,000–699,999	27	34,479
700,000–799,999	17	51,805
800,000–899,999	11	45,038
900,000–999,999	6	39,876
1,000,000–1,099,999	4	7521
1,100,000–1,199,999		
1,200,000–1,299,999	3	3411
1,300,000–1,399,999		
1,400,000–1,499,999		
1,500,000–1,599,999	1	1116
1,600,000–1,699,999		
1,700,000–1,799,999	1	23,681

*/Average daily attendance
SOURCE: Annual Financial and Attendance Reports, 1964

TABLE 43

Numbers and indexes of enrolment in public and
separate elementary schools in Ontario, 1945/6–63

Year	Public school enrolment	Index	Separate school enrolment	Index	Total elementary enrolment	Separate as per cent of total
1945/6	436,709	100.0	108,298	100.0	545,007	19.9
1946/7	441,333	101.1	108,877	100.5	550,210	19.8
1947/8	453,116	103.8	111,413	102.9	564,529	19.7
1948/9	469,517	107.5	115,507	106.7	585,024	19.7
1949/50	493,532	113.0	122,687	113.3	616,219	19.9
1950/1	508,364	116.4	127,253	117.5	635,617	20.0
1951/2	544,483	124.7	134,117	123.8	678,600	19.8
1952/3	588,344	134.7	146,668	135.4	735,012	20.0
1953/4	620,446	142.1	162,738	150.3	783,184	20.8
1955	676,246	154.9	187,368	173.0	863,614	21.7
1956	706,319	161.7	205,577	189.8	911,896	22.5
1957	747,236	171.1	223,881	206.7	971,117	23.1
1958	784,167	179.6	243,431	224.8	1,027,598	23.7
1959	817,880	187.3	263,769	243.6	1,081,649	24.4
1960	843,737	193.2	282,651	261.0	1,126,388	25.1
1961	861,715	197.3	301,338	278.2	1,163,053	25.9
1962	880,198	201.6	316,831	292.6	1,197,029	26.5
1963	901,830	206.5	331,334	305.9	1,233,164	26.9

SOURCE: Minister's Reports

TABLE 44
Numbers and indexes of enrolment in public and separate elementary schools in Ontario by type of municipality, 1955–63

	Public or separate	Enrolment										
		Cities		Towns & Villages		Urban Townships		Rural		Crown land		Total
Year		Number	Index	Number	Index	Number	Index	Number	Index	Number	Index	
1955	Public	227,755	100.0	127,410	100.0	112,711	100.0	200,376	100.0	7,994	100.0	676,246
	Separate	87,607	100.0	43,458	100.0	17,454	100.0	38,849	100.0			187,368
1956	Public	232,606	102.1	135,280	106.2	121,686	108.0	207,592	103.6	9,155	114.5	706,319
	Separate	95,893	109.5	47,247	108.7	20,475	117.3	41,962	108.0			205,577
1957	Public	246,528	108.2	142,107	111.5	132,665	117.7	216,432	108.0	9,504	118.9	747,236
	Separate	107,096	122.2	51,515	118.5	23,527	134.8	41,743	107.4			223,881
1958	Public	253,684	111.4	155,085	121.7	143,883	127.7	221,240	110.4	10,275	128.5	784,167
	Separate	113,641	129.7	57,165	131.5	26,565	152.2	46,060	118.6			243,431
1959	Public	264,842	116.3	158,736	124.6	156,581	138.9	226,448	113.0	11,273	141.0	817,880
	Separate	122,873	140.3	60,856	140.0	30,894	177.0	49,146	126.5			263,769
1960	Public	274,691	120.6	163,489	128.3	161,539	143.3	232,319	115.9	11,699	146.3	843,737
	Separate	134,400	153.4	64,902	149.3	31,186	178.7	52,163	134.3			282,651
1961	Public	299,634	131.6	165,681	130.0	159,464	141.5	225,376	112.5	11,560	144.6	861,715
	Separate	144,887	165.4	68,430	157.5	32,969	188.9	55,052	141.7			301,338
1962	Public	305,564	134.2	173,280	136.0	169,080	150.0	220,033	109.8	12,241	153.1	880,198
	Separate	150,356	171.6	72,051	165.8	37,322	213.8	57,102	147.0			316,831
1963	Public	317,153	139.3	177,632	139.4	172,698	153.2	221,549	110.6	12,798	160.1	901,830
	Separate	160,925	183.7	71,714	165.0	38,898	222.9	59,797	153.9			331,334

SOURCE: Minister's Reports

TABLE 45

Numbers and indexes of enrolment for academic
and vocational pupils in secondary schools
of Ontario, 1945/6–63

Year	Academic		Vocational		Total secondary enrolment	Vocational as a percent of the total
	Number	Index	Number	Index		
1945/6	89,521	100.0	31,756	100.0	121,277	26.2
1946/7	94,343	105.4	33,504	105.5	127,847	26.2
1947/8	93,967	105.0	32,085	101.0	126,052	25.5
1948/9	95,670	106.9	31,718	99.9	127,755	24.8
1949/50	97,281	108.7	31,776	100.1	129,057	24.6
1950/1	100,871	112.7	31,819	100.2	132,690	24.0
1951/2	103,394	115.5	32,093	101.1	135,487	23.7
1952/3	109,272	122.1	33,919	106.8	143,191	23.7
1953/4	115,399	123.9	34,521	108.7	149,920	23.0
1955	131,236	146.6	43,326	136.4	174,562	24.8
1956	140,975	157.5	44,630	140.5	185,605	24.0
1957	155,641	173.9	47,884	150.8	203,525	23.5
1958	170,263	190.2	51,812	163.2	222,075	23.3
1959	181,337	202.6	56,239	177.1	237,576	23.7
1960	200,368	223.8	62,407	196.5	262,775	23.7
1961	227,018	253.6	72,159	227.2	299,177	24.1
1962	230,516	257.5	101,062	318.2	331,578	30.5
1963	226,537	253.1	137,673	433.5	364,210	37.8

SOURCE: Minister's Reports

TABLE 46

Net current and capital account expenditures of Ontario provincial and local governments: total and education, 1945–63

Year[a]	Provincial			Local			Total		
	Total net expenditure $millions	Net expenditure on education $millions	Education as % of total	Total net expenditure $millions	Net expenditure on education $millions	Education as % of total	Total net expenditure $millions	Net expenditure on education $millions	Education as % of total
1945	120.7	21.5	17.8	135.9	38.7	28.4	256.6	60.2	23.5
1946	132.3	27.8	21.0	154.2	41.8	27.1	286.5	69.6	24.3
1947	163.9	27.8	17.0	184.5	55.3	30.0	348.4	83.1	23.9
1948	201.1	35.0	17.4	229.1	73.7	32.2	430.2	108.7	25.3
1949	253.1	39.5	15.6	245.1	87.6	35.7	498.2	127.1	25.5
1950	282.8	45.2	16.0	274.4	99.5	36.2	557.2	144.7	26.0
1951	305.4	50.6	16.6	317.4	125.6	39.6	622.8	176.2	28.3
1952	372.3	57.5	15.4	364.7	152.4	41.8	737.0	209.9	28.5
1953	404.6	64.9	16.0	397.5	161.3	40.6	802.1	226.2	28.2
1954	419.7	69.2	16.5	512.7	180.2	35.1	932.4	249.4	26.7
1955	441.3	76.3	17.3	556.3	203.9	36.7	997.6	280.2	28.1
1956	522.3	82.9	15.9	616.8	230.5	37.4	1139.1	313.4	27.5
1957	592.3	94.5	16.0	693.5	259.9	37.5	1285.8	354.4	27.6
1958	671.3	118.1	17.6	729.7	261.9	35.9	1401.0	380.9	27.1
1959	750.1	151.7	20.2	826.9	308.2	37.3	1577.0	459.0	29.2
1960	842.3	174.5	20.7	942.9	367.1	38.9	1785.2	541.6	30.3
1961	871.6	191.2	21.9	974.6	363.1	37.3	1846.2	554.3	30.0
1962	977.5	218.5	22.4	1094.5	405.0	37.0	2072.0	623.5	30.1
1963	1106.5	296.2	26.8	1186.5	432.7	36.5	2293.0	728.9	31.8

[a] /Provincial fiscal year ending 31 March; local fiscal year ending 31 December.

[c] /Excludes expenditures on post-secondary institutions

SOURCES: Ontario Committee on Taxation, *Report*, I, 122, 128; Ontario, *Public Accounts of Ontario*

TABLE 47

Per-pupil expenditures in five categories for public
elementary schools in Ontario, 1947–63

Year	Instructional salaries		Administration*		Transportation		Debt charges		Capital from current funds	
	Amount	Index	Amount	Index	Amount	Index	Amount	Index	Amount	Index
1947	65.36	100.0	25.97	100.0	2.34	100.0	7.33	100.0	3.44	100.0
1948	70.62	108.0	30.93	119.1	2.70	115.4	7.27	99.2	5.26	152.9
1949	76.36	116.8	31.21	120.2	2.88	123.1	8.44	115.1	4.53	131.7
1950	81.42	124.6	34.43	132.6	3.33	142.3	8.48	115.7	5.26	152.9
1951	91.74	140.4	39.72	152.9	3.34	142.7	12.55	171.2	6.62	192.4
1952	102.02	156.1	39.89	153.6	3.86	165.0	13.37	182.4	7.49	217.7
1953	102.68	157.1	42.22	162.6	3.69	157.7	15.25	208.0	7.54	219.2
1954	106.37	162.7	44.16	170.0	3.83	163.7	17.19	234.5	6.90	200.6
1955	115.80	177.2	50.46	194.3	4.63	197.9	15.63	213.2	7.08	205.8
1956	124.90	191.1	53.85	207.4	4.46	190.6	16.89	230.4	7.41	215.4
1957	132.07	202.1	57.54	221.6	4.60	196.6	18.17	247.9	7.84	227.9
1958	141.05	215.8	60.89	234.5	4.76	203.4	20.68	281.1	9.21	267.7
1959	164.55	251.8	53.94	207.7	5.38	229.9	22.91	312.6	13.39	397.6
1960	163.90	250.8	67.97	261.7	6.16	263.2	26.20	357.4	12.96	376.7
1961	170.98	261.6	71.24	274.3	6.91	295.3	29.93	408.3	12.90	375.0
1962	176.53	270.1	74.66	287.5	7.58	323.9	32.31	440.8	12.43	361.1
1963	181.53	277.7	78.20	301.1	8.49	362.8	33.68	459.5	13.18	383.1

*/Includes administration, maintenance, supplies, and miscellaneous expenditures
SOURCE: Minister's Reports

TABLE 48

Per-pupil expenditures in five categories for separate elementary schools in Ontario, 1947–63

Year	Instructional salaries		Administration*		Transportation		Debt charges		Capital from current funds	
	Amount	Index	Amount	Index	Amount	Index	Amount	Index	Amount	Index
1947	35.57	100.0	16.65	100.0	.53	100.0	7.16	100.0	2.58	100.0
1948	39.53	111.1	17.89	107.4	.86	162.3	7.25	101.3	3.32	128.7
1949	40.49	113.8	22.05	132.4	1.14	215.1	7.89	110.2	2.39	92.6
1950	47.57	133.7	26.27	157.8	1.12	211.3	9.94	138.8	5.26	203.9
1951	54.02	151.9	28.77	172.8	1.60	301.0	13.27	185.3	8.05	312.0
1952	55.21	155.2	30.54	183.4	2.02	381.1	14.05	196.2	6.36	246.5
1953	57.23	160.9	25.32	152.1	2.55	481.1	16.55	231.1	6.05	234.5
1954	58.84	165.4	28.68	172.3	2.77	522.6	21.40	298.0	6.03	233.7
1955	62.91	176.9	30.07	180.6	3.16	596.2	20.75	289.8	5.82	225.6
1956	66.90	188.1	31.14	187.0	3.62	683.0	22.23	310.5	5.47	212.0
1957	72.01	202.4	34.71	208.5	3.77	711.3	24.58	343.3	6.23	241.5
1958	79.68	224.0	39.46	237.0	4.19	790.6	26.03	363.5	8.30	321.7
1959	95.20	267.6	36.58	219.7	4.85	915.1	29.04	405.6	8.40	325.6
1960	96.77	272.1	43.83	263.2	5.51	1039.6	32.83	458.5	7.60	294.6
1961	104.09	292.6	44.17	265.3	6.22	1173.6	36.15	504.9	6.42	248.8
1962	114.01	320.5	45.56	273.6	7.34	1384.9	35.11	490.4	13.77	533.7
1963	122.34	343.9	47.77	286.9	8.57	1617.0	41.56	580.4	12.28	476.0

*/Includes administration, maintenance, supplies, and miscellaneous expenditures

SOURCE: Minister's Reports

TABLE 49

Per-pupil expenditures in five categories for secondary schools in Ontario, 1947–63

Year	Instructional salaries Amount	Index	Administration* Amount	Index	Transportation Amount	Index	Debt charges Amount	Index	Capital from current funds Amount	Index
1947	118.14	100.0	49.00	100.0	4.53	100.0	20.60	100.0	7.02	100.0
1948	129.86	109.9	59.10	120.6	8.23	181.7	19.78	96.0	7.35	104.7
1949	144.59	122.4	58.21	118.8	11.94	263.6	27.75	134.7	8.47	120.7
1950	143.83	121.7	73.36	149.7	15.17	334.9	30.68	148.9	8.23	117.2
1951	179.29	151.8	73.05	149.1	19.84	438.0	30.65	148.8	12.39	176.4
1952	196.28	166.1	80.79	164.9	21.86	482.6	38.79	188.3	15.11	215.2
1953	198.83	168.3	83.59	170.6	22.01	485.9	38.17	185.3	13.27	189.0
1954	201.06	170.2	85.85	175.2	22.68	500.7	41.63	202.1	15.51	220.9
1955	210.21	177.9	100.95	206.0	23.24	513.0	42.26	205.1	14.32	204.0
1956	225.83	191.1	111.30	227.1	23.67	522.5	42.63	206.9	12.10	172.4
1957	239.57	202.8	109.52	223.5	23.93	528.3	43.45	210.9	16.87	240.3
1958	261.17	221.1	116.34	237.4	24.41	538.9	49.68	241.2	15.87	226.1
1959	309.27	261.8	108.65	221.7	25.03	552.5	53.64	260.4	26.48	377.2
1960	309.63	251.9	123.44	546.8	24.77	308.9	63.64	343.7	24.13	273.8
1961	308.94	261.5	126.77	258.7	24.03	530.5	64.83	314.7	23.21	330.6
1962	318.93	270.0	162.54	331.7	24.05	530.9	62.99	305.8	24.73	352.3
1963	341.50	289.1	154.16	314.6	23.67	522.5	64.34	312.3	25.78	367.2

*/Includes administration, maintenance, supplies, and miscellaneous expenditures
SOURCE: Minister's Reports

TABLE 50
Total school board expenditure in five categories showing each as a proportion of the total, 1947–63

Year	Instructional salaries		Administration*		Transportation		Debt charges		Capital from current funds	
	Amount	%	Amount	%	Amount	%	Amount	%	Amount	%
	($000)		($000)		($000)		($000)		($000)	
1947	48,081	61.03	19,642	24.93	1677	2.13	6675	8.47	2709	3.44
1948	53,390	59.21	23,947	26.56	2381	2.64	6724	7.46	3726	4.13
1949	59,924	59.88	25,033	25.01	3044	3.04	8537	8.53	3542	3.54
1950	65,361	57.83	30,041	26.58	3782	3.35	9479	8.39	4357	3.86
1951	78,976	57.89	34,282	25.13	4609	3.38	12,387	9.08	6166	4.52
1952	92,217	58.52	37,864	24.03	5477	3.48	14,841	9.42	7190	4.56
1953	99,495	58.04	41,455	24.18	5818	3.39	17,272	10.08	7394	4.31
1954	110,440	57.17	46,947	24.30	6559	3.40	21,310	11.03	7929	4.10
1955	126,795	57.07	57,380	25.83	7782	3.50	21,834	9.83	8378	3.77
1956	143,887	57.49	65,091	26.01	8287	3.31	24,414	9.75	8601	3.44
1957	163,543	57.51	73,055	25.69	9152	3.22	27,924	9.82	10,688	3.76
1958	188,002	57.37	83,193	25.38	10,177	3.11	33,586	10.25	12,769	3.90
1959	233,170	60.89	79,575	20.78	11,624	3.04	39,135	10.22	19,450	5.08
1960	247,006	57.45	102,178	23.76	13,268	3.09	48,105	11.19	19,425	4.52
1961	271,136	57.10	112,626	23.72	15,014	3.16	56,081	11.81	19,999	4.21
1962	297,251	55.85	134,048	25.19	16,970	3.19	60,446	11.36	23,502	4.42
1963	328,626	56.35	142,502	24.44	19,118	3.28	67,573	11.59	25,342	4.35

*/Includes administration, maintenance, supplies, and miscellaneous expenditures
SOURCE: Minister's Reports

TABLE 51

Average yields of samples of Canadian provincial and
municipal bonds: January and July 1948–68

Year	Month	Provincial	Municipal
1948	January	3.07%	3.25%
	July	3.15	3.47
1949	January	3.18	3.54
	July	3.21	3.59
1950	January	3.05	3.51
	July	3.14	3.46
1951	January	3.28	3.57
	July	3.78	4.33
1952	January	4.10	4.71
	July	4.13	4.64
1953	January	4.16	4.60
	July	4.18	4.70
1954	January	4.05	4.49
	July	3.38	3.79
1955	January	3.36	3.75
	July	3.30	3.65
1956	January	3.74	4.02
	July	4.12	4.59
1957	January	5.03	5.41
	July	5.15	5.62
1958	January	4.60	5.04
	July	4.72	5.17
1959	January	5.18	5.41
	July	5.61	5.86
1960	January	6.19	6.60
	July	5.51	5.84
1961	January	5.70	5.94
	July	5.39	5.62
1962	January	5.43	5.65
	July	5.87	6.17
1963	January	5.36	5.54
	July	5.44	5.59
1964	January	5.58	5.72
	July	5.59	5.71
1965	January	5.34	5.52
	July	5.68	5.81
1966	January	5.87	6.00
	July	6.27	6.48
1967	January	6.25	6.51
	July	6.70	6.98
1968	January	7.27	7.58
	July	7.48	7.71

SOURCE: *McLeod, Young, Weir Bond Averages*

TABLE 52

Per-pupil yield of foundation tax rate, basic grant, equalization grant, and minimum equalization grant: public elementary boards in classes of equalized assessment per classroom, 1965

Equalized assessment per classroom	No of pupils	% of total pupils	Yield of 11 mills	Basic grant	Equalization grant	Minimum equalization grant	Total revenue
Under 50,000	2249	.3	9	80	121		210
50,000–99,999	17,664	2.2	27	80	103		210
100,000–149,999	54,410	6.7	46	80	74		210
150,000–199,999	76,844	9.5	64	80	66		210
200,000–249,999	93,659	11.5	82	80	48		210
250,000–299,999	74,442	9.2	101	80		33	214
300,000–349,999	119,373	14.7	119	80		26	225
350,000–399,999	75,721	9.3	137	80		22	239
400,000–449,999	102,446	12.6	156	80		18	254
450,000–499,999	48,433	6.0	174	80		14	268
500,000–549,999	44,942	5.5	192	80		10	282
550,000–599,999	4745	.6	211	80		10	301
600,000–649,999	27,189	3.3	229	80		10	319
650,000–699,999	1545	.2	247	80		10	337
700,000–749,999	1103	.1	266	80		10	356
750,000–799,999	189	.02	284	80		10	374
800,000–849,999	998	.1	302	80		10	392
850,000–899,999	62,614	7.7	321	80		10	411
900,000–949,999	267	.03	339	80		10	429
950,000–999,999	219	.03	357	80		10	447
Over 999,999	3190	.4	520*	80		10	610

*/Based on median assessment of boards in this class

TABLE 53
Per-pupil yield of foundation tax rate, basic grant, equalization grant, and minimum equalization grant: separate elementary boards in classes of equalized assessment per classroom, 1965

Equalized assessment per classroom	No of pupils	% of total pupils	Yield of 11 mills	Basic grant	Equalization grant	Minimum equalization grant	Total revenue
Under 50,000	17,544	5.6	9	80	121		210
50,000–99,999	50,926	16.2	27	80	103		210
100,000–149,999	44,995	14.4	46	80	74		210
150,000–199,999	56,946	18.2	64	80	66		210
200,000–249,999	58,113	18.5	82	80	48		210
250,000–299,999	31,850	10.2	101	80		33	214
300,000–349,999	22,395	7.1	119	80		26	225
350,000–399,999	23,483	7.5	137	80		22	239
400,000–449,999	432	.1	156	80		18	254
450,000–499,999	538	.2	174	80		14	268
500,000–549,999	6270	2.0	192	80		10	282
Over 549,999	21	.01	246*	80		10	336

*/Based on median assessment of boards in this class

TABLE 54

Per-pupil yield of foundation tax rate, basic grant, and
equalization grant: academic pupils of secondary boards
in classes of equalized assessment per classroom, 1965

Equalized assessment per classroom	No of academic pupils	% of total pupils	Yield of 7 mills	Basic grant	Equalization grant	Total revenue
Under $100,000						
100,000–199,999	365	.2	48	175	197	420
200,000–299,999	5662	2.7	80	175	165	420
300,000–399,999	11,712	5.5	111	175	134	420
400,000–499,999	39,562	18.6	143	175	102	420
500,000–599,999	29,713	14.0	175	175	70	420
600,000–699,999	21,370	10.0	207	175	38	420
700,000–799,999	29,551	13.9	239	175	6	420
800,000–899,999	27,457	12.9	270	175		445
900,000–999,999	28,135	13.2	302	175		477
1,000,000–1,099,999	3710	1.7	337	175		509
1,100,000–1,199,999						
1,200,000–1,299,999	2471	1.2	398	175		573
1,300,000–1,399,999						
1,400,000–1,499,999						
1,500,000–1,599,999	939	.4	493	175		668
1,600,000–1,699,999						
1,700,000–1,799,999	12,037	5.7	557	175		732

TABLE 55

Per-pupil yield of foundation tax rate, basic grant, and
equalization grant: vocational pupils of secondary boards
in classes of equalized assessment per classroom, 1965

Assessment per classroom	No of voc. pupils	% of total pupils	Yield of 7 mills	Basic grant	Equalization grant	Total revenue
Under $100,000						
100,000–199,999	86	.1	48	250	252	550
200,000–299,999	2536	2.0	80	250	220	550
300,000–399,999	6438	5.1	111	250	189	550
400,000–499,999	20,420	16.2	143	250	157	550
500,000–599,999	15,413	12.2	175	250	125	550
600,000–699,999	13,109	10.4	207	250	93	550
700,000–799,999	22,253	17.6	239	250	61	550
800,000–899,999	17,582	13.9	270	250	30	550
900,000–999,999	11,741	9.3	302	250		552
1,000,000–1,099,999	3811	3.0	334	250		584
1,100,000–1,199,999						
1,200,000–1,299,999	940	.7	398	250		648
1,300,000–1,399,999						
1,400,000–1,499,999						
1,500,000–1,599,999	177	.1	493	250		743
1,600,000–1,699,999						
1,700,000–1,799,999	11,644	9.2	557	250		807

TABLE 56

Calculation of local tax rate after payment of grants
on recognized extraordinary expenditure to three
hypothetical secondary school boards: 1966 grant formula

		A ETA per classroom = $1,000,000			
REE	Local burden	Growth-need %	Growth-need grant	Local burden	Tax rate (mills)
$1000	$162	0	0	$162	.162
1500	243	2	30	213	.213
2000	324	4	80	244	.244
2500	405	6	150	255	.255
3000	486	8	240	246	.246
3500	567	10	350	217	.217
4000	648	11.2	448	200	.200
4500	729	11.2	504	225	.225
5000	810	11.2	560	250	.250
5500	891	11.2	616	275	.275
6000	972	11.2	672	300	.300
		B ETA per classroom = $2,000,000			
$1000	305	0	0	305	.1525
1500	457	2	30	427	.2135
2000	610	4	80	530	.2650
2500	762	6	150	612	.3060
3000	915	8	240	675	.3375
3500	1067	10	350	717	.3585
4000	1220	12	480	740	.3700
4500	1372	14	630	742	.3710
5000	1525	16	800	725	.3625
5500	1677	18	990	687	.3435
6000	1830	20	1200	630	.3150
		C ETA per classroom = $4,000,000			
$1000	591	0	0	591	.148
1500	886	2	30	856	.214
2000	1182	4	80	1102	.276
2500	1477	6	150	1327	.332
3000	1773	8	240	1533	.383
3500	2068	10	350	1718	.430
4000	2364	12	480	1884	.471
4500	2659	14	630	2029	.507
5000	2955	16	800	2155	.539
5500	3250	18	990	2260	.565
6000	3546	20	1200	2346	.587

TABLE 57

Mean current expenditures and current calculated mill rates for elementary boards in classes of equalized assessment per classroom, 1964

Equalized assessment per classroom	Mean current expenditures	Mean current mills
Under $25,000	5745	21.31
25,000–49,999	5453	7.7
50,000–74,999	5663	5.8
75,000–99,999	5891	7.2
100,000–124,999	5569	6.5
125,000–149,999	5576	6.5
150,000–174,999	5587	6.4
175,000–199,999	6181	6.9
200,000–224,999	6107	7.7
225,000–249,999	6224	7.8
250,000–274,999	6390	8.9
275,000–299,999	6298	9.0
300,000–324,999	6673	8.7
325,000–349,999	7156	8.7
350,000–374,999	6740	9.1
375,000–399,999	6973	8.3
400,000–424,999	6752	7.6
425,000–449,999	8185	9.8
450,000–474,999	8091	8.8
475,000–499,999	6845	8.4
500,000–524,999	8491	10.6
525,000–549,999	7347	8.3
550,000–574,999	8588	9.9
575,000–599,999	5775	5.6
600,000–624,999	7260	7.5
625,000–649,999	6838	6.1
650,000–674,999	7410	4.9
675,000–699,999	6764	6.2
700,000–724,999	6124	5.3
725,000–749,999	11,437	10.6
750,000–774,999	8259	7.5
775,000–799,999	6767	8.7
800,000–824,999	8221	6.9
825,000–849,999	11,932	11.0
850,000–874,999	9087	8.1
875,000–899,999		
900,000–924,999		
925,000–949,999	8250	5.8
950,000–974,999	7187	2.8
975,000–999,999		
Over 999,999	10,131	5.3

SOURCE: Calculated data from provincial grants

TABLE 58

Mean current expenditures and current calculated mill rates
for secondary boards in classes of equalized assessment per classroom,
1964

Equalized assessment per classroom	Mean current expenditure	Mean current mills
Under $100,000		
100,000–199,999	11,503	14.0
200,000–299,999	10,349	7.7
300,000–399,999	10,969	8.0
400,000–499,999	11,384	8.2
500,000–599,999	11,481	8.2
600,000–699,999	12,166	9.1
700,000–799,999	12,765	9.5
800,000–899,999	12,019	8.3
900,000–999,999	13,462	9.2
1,000,000–1,099,999	14,159	8.8
1,100,000–1,199,999		
1,200,000–1,299,999	14,784	8.1
1,300,000–1,399,999		
1,400,000–1,499,999		
1,500,000–1,599,999	15,167	7.1
1,600,000–1,699,999		
1,700,000–1,799,999	17,773	2.1

SOURCE: Calculated data from provincial grants

Selected Bibliography

BOOKS AND MONOGRAPHS

Benson, C.S. *The Cheerful Prospect*. Boston, Houghton-Mifflin, 1965
— *The Economics of Public Education*. Boston, Houghton-Mifflin, 1968
— *The School and the Economic System*. Chicago, Science Research Associates, 1966
— *State and Local Fiscal Relationships in Public Education in California*. Sacramento, California State Department of Education, 1965
Brown, A.F. *Changing School Districts in Canada*. Toronto, Ontario Institute for Studies in Education, 1968
Brown, W.J. *New Federal-Provincial Tax-Sharing Arrangements and their Significance*. Ottawa, Canadian Teachers' Federation, 1967
Burkhead, J. *Public School Finance: Economics and Politics*. Syracuse, Syracuse University Press, 1964
Cameron, M.A. *The Financing of Education in Ontario*. Toronto, University of Toronto, Department of Educational Research, 1936
The Canadian School Trustees' Association, School Finance Research Committee. *School Finance in Canada*. Edmonton, Hamly, 1955
The Canadian Tax Foundation. *The National Finances*. Toronto, Canadian Tax Foundation, annual
— *The Provincial Finances*. Toronto, Canadian Tax Foundation, bi-annual
The Canadian Teachers' Federation. *Financing Education in Canada*. Ottawa, Canadian Teachers' Federation, 1965
— *Financing Education in Canada*. Ottawa, Canadian Teachers' Federation, 1967
Carr, William. *School Finance*. Stanford University Press, 1933

Coleman, J.S. *The Struggle for Control of Education.* Baltimore, Johns Hopkins University Press, 1966

Conant, J.B. *Shaping Educational Policy.* Toronto, McGraw-Hill, 1964

Crawford, K.G. *Canadian Municipal Government.* Toronto, University of Toronto Press, 1954

— *Provincial Grants to Canadian Schools: 1941 to 1961.* Toronto, Canadian Tax Foundation, 1962

Cubberley, E.P. *School Funds and Their Apportionment.* New York, Bureau of Publication, Teachers' College, Columbia University, 1905

Dupré, J.S. *Intergovernmental Finance in Ontario: A Provincial-Local Perspective.* Toronto, Queen's Printer, 1968

Durrah, J.R. *Roman Catholic Separate School Support.* Municipal World, 1963

Finnis, F.H. *Property Assessment in Canada.* Toronto, Canadian Tax Foundation, 1970

Gauerke, W.E. and J.R. Childress, eds. *The Theory and Practice of School Finance.* Chicago, Rand McNally, 1967

Graham, J.F. *Fiscal Adjustment and Economic Development.* Toronto, University of Toronto Press, 1963

Greeley, A.M. and P.H. Rossi. *The Education of Catholic Americans.* Garden City, NY, Anchor Books, 1968

Guillet, H.C. *In the Cause of Education.* Toronto, University of Toronto Press, 1960

Halsey, A.H., J. Floud, and C.A. Anderson. *Education, Economy and Society.* New York, Free Press of Glencoe, 1961

Hanson, E.J. *Local Government in Alberta.* McClelland & Stewart, 1956

Harris, R.S. *Quiet Evolution.* Toronto, University of Toronto Press, 1967

Iannaccone, L. *Politics in Education.* New York, Center for Applied Research in Education, 1967

Johns, R.L., and E.L. Morphet. *Financing the Public Schools.* Englewood Cliffs, NJ, Prentice-Hall, 1960

Kaplan, Harold. *Urban Political Systems.* New York and London, Columbia University Press, 1967

Kimbrough, R.B. *Political Power and Educational Decision-Making.* Chicago, Rand McNally, 1964

La Forest, G.V. *The Allocation of Taxing Power Under the Canadian Constitution.* Toronto, Canadian Tax Foundation, 1967

Maass, A., ed. *Area and Power.* Glencoe, Ill., Free Press, 1959

MacKinnon, Frank. *The Politics of Education.* Toronto, University of Toronto Press, 1960

McEvoy, J.M. *The Ontario Township*. Toronto, University of Toronto Press, 1889

McLure, W.P. and V. Millar, eds. *Government of Public Education for Adequate Policy Making*. Urbana, Ill., University of Illinois Press, 1960

Maxwell, J.A. *Financing State and Local Governments*. Washington, DC, The Brookings Institute, 1965

Millar, J. *The Educational System of the Province of Ontario*. Toronto, Ontario Department of Education, 1893

Moehlman, A.B. *Public School Finance*. Chicago and New York, Rand McNally, 1927

Moffatt, H.P. *Educational Finance in Canada*. Toronto, Gage, 1958

Moore, A.M., and J.H. Perry. *The Financing of Canadian Federation*. Toronto, Canadian Tax Foundation, 1966

Mort, P.R. *The Measuring of Educational Need*. New York, Bureau of Publications, Teachers' College, Columbia University, 1924

Mort, P.R., W.C. Reusser, and J.W. Polley. *Public School Finance*. New York, McGraw-Hill, 1960

Netzer, Dick. *Economics of the Property Tax*. Washington, DC, The Brookings Institute, 1966

Norton, J.K., ed. *Dimensions in School Finance*. National Education Association, Committee on Educational Finance, 1966

Phillips, C.E. *The Development of Education in Canada*. Toronto, University of Toronto Press, 1957

Rosenstengel, W.E. and J.N. Eastmond. *School Finance*. New York, Ronald Press, 1957

Ross, R.K. *Local Government in Ontario*. Toronto, Canada Law Book Company, 1962

Sissons, C.B. *Church and State in Canadian Education*. Toronto, Ryerson Press, 1959

Smiley, D.V. *Conditional Grants and Canadian Federalism*. Toronto, Canadian Tax Foundation, 1963

Smith, W.O.L. *Government of Education*. Harmondsworth, Penguin, 1965

Strayer, G.D. and R.M. Haig. *The Financing of Education in The State of New York*. New York, Macmillan, 1923

Tax Institute, Symposium. *Financing Education in the Public Schools*. Princeton, Tax Institute, 1956

Thomas, J.A. *Educational Opportunity and School Finance in Michigan*. Lansing, Michigan Department of Education, 1968

Vaizey, J. *The Economics of Education*. London, Faber & Faber, 1962

Vieg, J.A. *The Government of Education in Metropolitan Chicago*. Chicago, University of Chicago Press, 1939

Walker, F.A. *Catholic Education and Politics in Upper Canada.* Toronto and
   Vancouver, J.M. Dent, 1955
— *Catholic Education and Politics in Ontario.* Toronto, Thomas Nelson,
   1964

ARTICLES

Alway, R.M.H. 'Mitchell Hepburn, Separate School Taxation, and the Ontario
   Election of 1937.' *Ontario Journal of Educational Research,* x, 1,
   autumn 1967
Beach, D.I. 'New School Grants for Ontario.' *Canadian Tax Journal,* xii, 3,
   May–June 1964
Bowland, J.G. 'Planning a Municipal Capital Budget.' *Canadian Public
   Administration,* vi, 4, Dec. 1963
Callard, Keith. 'The Present System of Local Government in Canada.'
   Canadian Journal of Economics and Political Science, xvii, 2, May 1951
Cameron, D.M. and J.F. Graham. 'Minimum Provisions in a Foundation
   Plan of Education Finance.' *Canadian Tax Journal,* xvi, 1, Jan.–Feb.
   1968
Clayton, F.A. 'Revenue Productivity of the Real Property Tax.' *Queen's
   University Papers in Taxation and Public Finance.* Toronto, Canadian
   Tax Foundation, 1966
Crawford, K.G. 'Some Problems of Assessment.' *Canadian Public Administra-
   tion,* vii, 3, Oct. 1964
Graham, J.F. 'The Application of the Fiscal Equity Principle to Provincial-
   Municipal Relations.' *Canadian Public Administration,* iii, 1, March
   1960
— 'New Municipal Services Program in Nova Scotia: An Evaluation.'
   Canadian Tax Journal, xv, 5, Sept.–Oct. 1967
Greenfield, T.B. and R. Baird. 'The Politics of Education: Controversy and
   Control.' *Canadian Administrator,* i, 8, May 1962
— 'The Politics of Education: Practice and Theory.' *Canadian Adminis-
   trator,* i, 7, April 1962
Groves, H.M. 'Decentralization in Decision-Making and Finance.' *University
   of Illinois Bulletin,* lviii, 75, June 1961
Hardy, Eric. 'Provincial-Municipal Relations: With Emphasis on the
   Financial Relationships Between Provinces and Local Governments.'
   Canadian Public Administration, iii, 1, March 1960
— 'The Serious Problems of Municipal Finance.' *Canadian Public Ad-
   ministration,* iv, 2, June 1961
Henderson, F.I. 'Ontario's School Grant Plan and Some of the Ideas Behind

It.' *Canadian School Journal*, XLIV, 6, Sept. 1966

Johnson, A.W. 'A Provincial-Local Government Budget.' *Canadian Public Administration*, IV, 1, March 1961

Lamontagne, Maurice. 'The Influence of the Politician.' *Canadian Public Administration*, XI, 3, fall 1968

McCordic, W.J. 'Metro's Dilemma in Public Education.' *Canadian Public Administration*, VII, 4, Dec. 1964

O'Connell, M.P. 'Municipal Borrowing: Problems and Prospects.' *Canadian Public Administration*, VI, 1, March 1963

Oliver, J. 'Municipal Revenue Other than Government Grants.' *Canadian Public Administration*, VI, 1, March 1963

'Ontario Conference on Education.' *Canadian School Journal*, XL, 2, March 1962

Powell, C.W. 'Provincial-Municipal Financing.' *Canadian Public Administration*, VI, 1, March 1963

Rideout, E.B. 'A New Dimension in the Measurement of Educational Need and Ability to Pay.' *Ontario Journal of Educational Research*, I, 2, 1958–9

Robertson, Ronald. 'Financing Education.' *Canadian Tax Journal*, XI, 6, Nov.–Dec. 1963

DOCUMENTS AND REPORTS

The Association of Ontario Counties. *A Blueprint for Local Government Re-organization*. Toronto, The Association of Ontario Counties, 1967

California, Senate, Senate Fact Finding Committee on Revenue and Taxation. *State and Local Fiscal Relationships in Public Education in California*. Eureka 1965

Canada, Department of Labour, Information Branch. *Education, Training and Employment*. Ottawa, Queen's Printer, 1961

Canada, Department of Labour. *Annual Report*. Ottawa, Queen's Printer, 1960–6

Canada, Parliament, House of Commons. *House of Commons Debates*. Ottawa, Queen's Printer, various issues

Carter, F.G., ed. *Judicial Decisions on Denominational Schools*. Toronto, Ontario Separate School Trustees' Association, 1962

Co-operative Commonwealth Federation, 'Looking to the Future.' Programme adopted at the 1954 Convention, mimeographed

Hodgins, J.G., ed. *Documentary History of Education in Upper Canada*. Toronto, Warwick Bros. & Rutter, 28 volumes, 1894–1910

— *Historical and Other Papers and Documents Illustrative of the Educational System of Ontario, 1792–1871.* Toronto, King's Printer, 1911–12
— *Legislation and History of Separate Schools in Upper Canada.* Toronto, William Briggs, 1897
Metropolitan Toronto School Board. *Meeting the Cost of Elementary and Secondary Schooling Throughout Metropolitan Toronto.* Toronto, Metropolitan School Board, 1961
— *The Case for Equalization of Educational Opportunity in Metro Toronto.* Toronto, Metropolitan School Board, 1962
— *Public Education in Metropolitan Toronto.* Toronto, Metropolitan School Board, 1963
New Brunswick, Royal Commission on Finance and Municipal Taxation. *Report.* Fredericton 1963
New York, Joint Legislative Committee on School Financing. *Final Report.* Albany 1963
Nova Scotia, Royal Commission on Public School Finance. *Report.* Halifax, Queen's Printer, 1954
Ontario, Committee of Enquiry into the Cost of Education in the Province of Ontario. *Report.* Toronto, King's Printer, 1938
Ontario, Committee on the Organization of Government in Ontario. *Report.* Toronto 1959
Ontario, Department of Economics and Development, Office of the Chief Economist. *Ontario Economic Review.* Monthly, various issues
— *Ontario Statistical Review, 1966.* Toronto 1967
Ontario, Department of Education. *County High School Districts in Ontario.* Toronto, Department of Education, 1946
— 'A History of Professional Certificates.' Toronto, Department of Education, 1935, mimeographed
— *Index of School Boards of the Province of Ontario on and after January 1, 1969.* Toronto 1968
— *A Letter from the Hon. G.H. Ferguson, Minister of Education, to those interested in Rural Education.* Toronto, King's Printer, 1925
— *Memorandum to Public School Consultative Committees Re Larger Units of Administration.* Toronto 1964
— *Report of the Minister.* Annual
— *Schools and Teachers in the Province of Ontario.* Annual
— *The Township School Area in Ontario.* Toronto, Department of Education, 1950
Ontario, Department of Municipal Affairs. *Annual Report of Municipal Statistics.* Toronto, Queen's Printer
— *Municipal Directory.* Toronto, Queen's Printer, annual

Ontario, Legislative Assembly. *Debates and Proceedings*. Toronto, Queen's Printer, various issues

Ontario New Democratic Party. 'Report of the Committee on Financing Education in Ontario.' Toronto, 1961, mimeographed

Ontario New Democratic Party Caucus, Research Department. 'A Foundation Tax Plan for General Municipal Purposes.' Toronto, 1968, mimeographed

Ontario, Ontario Committee on Taxation. *Report*. Toronto, Queen's Printer, 1967, 3 vols.

Ontario Teachers' Federation, Optimum Size Committee. *A Comparative Survey of School Districts in Ontario*. Toronto, Ontario Teachers' Federation, 1967

Ontario Teacher's Federation. *A Survey of the Consolidation of Ontario School Districts*. Toronto, Ontario Teachers' Federation, 1965

Ontario, Treasury Department. *A Conspectus of the Province of Ontario*. Toronto, King's Printer, 1950

— *Public Accounts of the Province of Ontario*. Toronto, Queen's Printer, annual

Ontario, Royal Commission on Education in Ontario. *Report*. Toronto, King's Printer, 1950

Ontario, Royal Commission on Metropolitan Toronto. *Report*. Toronto, Queen's Printer, 1965

Prince Edward Island, Commission on Educational Finance and Related Problems in Administration. *Report*. Charlottetown, 1960

United Kingdom, Royal Commission on Local Government in Greater London. *Report*. London, HM Stationery Office, 1960

United Kingdom, Scottish Education Department. *Public Education in Scotland*. Edinburgh, HM Stationery Office, 1963

University of the State of New York and State Department of Education. *A Guide to Programs of State Aid for Elementary and Secondary Education in New York State*. Albany 1967

BRIEFS

The English Catholic Education Association of Ontario. 'Brief Presented to the Prime Minister of Ontario and to the Members of the Legislative Assembly by the Catholic Bishops of Ontario.' Toronto 1962

Gray, A.J.B. 'Assessments and their Relation to School Grants.' Brief Submitted to the Ontario Royal Commission on Education, Brief no 15

Loyal Orange Association of British America. 'Ontario Segregation is Wrong.' Brief presented to the Premier and Members of the Legislature, 1963

Ontario Catholic Education Council. 'Brief Submitted to the Hall Committee on Aims and Objectives in Education.' Jan. 1966

Ontario Property Owners' Association and Property Owners' Association of Toronto. 'Provincial Grants to Education.' Brief Submitted to the Ontario Royal Commission on Education, Brief no 5

Ontario School Inspectors' Association, Committee on School Costs. 'School Costs.' Brief Submitted to the Ontario Royal Commission on Education, Brief no 85

Ontario Separate School Trustees' Association. 'A Statement on the Reorganization of School Zones as Applied to the Separate Schools of Ontario.' March 1968

Ontario Separate School Trustees' Association and L'Association des Commissions des Ecoles Bilingues d'Ontario. Brief Presented to the Prime Minister, to the Minister of Education, and to the Members of the Legislative Assembly of Ontario. Dec. 1962

—   'Brief Presented to the Prime Minister and The Minister of Education of the Province of Ontario.' Oct. 1966

Scarborough Township Council. 'Legislative Grants for Educational Purposes.' Brief Submitted to the Ontario Royal Commission on Education, Brief no 78

Ontario Trustees' Council. 'Resolutions presented for the consideration of the Honourable William G. Davis, Minister of Education.' Oct. 1966

Toronto City and Toronto Board of Education. 'Brief in Support of Amalgamation.' Brief Submitted to the Royal Commission on Metropolitan Toronto, 1964

CONFERENCE PAPERS

Canadian Conference on Education, Ottawa 1958. *Canadian Conference on Education: Addresses and Proceedings.* Ottawa, Mutual Press, 1958

Canadian Conference on Education, Montreal 1962. *The Second Canadian Conference on Education: A Report.* Toronto, University of Toronto Press, 1962

—   *Conference Studies.* Ottawa, Canadian Conference on Education, 1961

Canadian Teachers' Federation. 'Paying for Schooling.' Papers delivered at the 1965 CTF Conference on Education Finance, Toronto 1965

—   'The Piper and the Tune.' Papers delivered at the 1967 Conference on Education Finance, Winnipeg 1967

Rideout, E.B. 'The Financial Support of Education.' Paper presented to the Invitational Conference on Emerging Trends in Education, Saskatoon 1968

UNPUBLISHED PAPERS AND THESES

Baird, N.B. 'Educational Finance and Administration for Ontario.'
    Unpublished D PAED thesis, University of Toronto, 1946
Graham, J.F. 'Provincial-Municipal Fiscal Relations in a Low-income
    Province: Nova Scotia.' Unpublished PH D thesis, Columbia University,
    1959
Kirtland, Ivor. 'Larger Units of Administration.' Unpublished paper, 1966
Orlikow, Lionel. 'Dominion-Provincial Partnership in Education with Special
    Emphasis Upon the Technical and Vocational Training Assistance Act,
    1960–67.' Unpublished PH D thesis, University of Chicago, 1969
Semple, S.W. 'Matters Relevant to the Establishment of Public School
    Consultative Committees in Ontario.' Unpublished paper, Ontario
    Institute for Studies in Education, 1967
Thorson, S.J. 'Attitudes Towards School District Reorganization.'
    Unpublished paper, Ontario Institute for Studies in Education, 1968

Index